EDUCATION TECHNOLOGY

By

Dr. REKHA YADAV

M.A., B.Ed., M.Phil, Ph.D.

Lecturer

SGPG College

Meerut, Uttar Pradesh

UNIVERSITY SCIENCE PRESS

(An Imprint of Laxmi Publications Pvt. Ltd.)

BANGALORE • CHENNAI • COCHIN • GUWAHATI • HYDERABAD
JALANDHAR • KOLKATA • LUCKNOW • MUMBAI • RANCHI
NEW DELHI

Published by :
UNIVERSITY SCIENCE PRESS
(An Imprint of Laxmi Publications Pvt. Ltd.)
113, Golden House, Daryaganj,
New Delhi-110002
Phone : 011-43 53 25 00
Fax : 011-43 53 25 28
www.laxmipublications.com
info@laxmipublications.com

Price : **Rs. 295.00** *Only.* *First Edition* : 20

OFFICES

© **Bangalore**	080-26 61 15 61	© **Chennai**	044-24 34 47 26
© **Cochin**	0484-237 70 04, 405 13 03	© **Guwahati**	0361-254 36 69, 251 38 81
© **Hyderabad**	040-24 65 23 33	© **Jalandhar**	0181-222 12 72
© **Kolkata**	033-22 27 43 84	© **Lucknow**	0522-220 95 78
© **Mumbai**	022-24 91 54 15, 24 92 78 69	© **Ranchi**	0651-221 47 64

UET-9538-295-EDUCATION TECHNOLOGY-YAD **C. 1736 /010/0**
Typeset at : Kalyani Computer Services, New Delhi. *Printed at* : Sanjeev Offset Press, Del

CONTENTS

SYLLABUS

EDM-109
EDUCATIONL TECHNOLOGY

Maximum Marks :100

Time Allowed :3 Hrs.

Note: 'There will be nine questions in the question paper. Students are required to attempt five questions in all. All questions shall carry equal marks.
Question no.1 shall be compulsory which will comprise of eight short answer type questions/parts and students are expected to answer any five parts.
There will be eight other questions comprising of two questions from each of the four units. Students are expected to attempt one question from each unit.

Course Contents:

UNIT-1

- Meaning and scope of Educational Technology: System approach to education and its characteristics, Component of Educational Technology-Hardware and Software.
- Multimedia approach in Educational Technology.

UNIT-2

- Modalities of teaching: Teaching as different from indoctrination; instruction conditioning and training.
- Stages of teaching: Pre-active, Interactive and Post active.
- Teaching at different levels: memory, understanding and reflective levels of organizing teaching and learning.
- Programmed instruction: Origin Principles and Characteristics.
- Types: Linear. Branching and Mathetics.
- Development of programme: Preparation, Writing, Try out and Evaluation.

UNIT-3

- Modification of teaching behaviour: Micro teaching, Flanders interaction analysis, simulation. Communication process: Concept of communication, Principles, Modes and Barriers to communication, Classroom communication (interaction, verbal and Non verbal)
- Models of teaching: Concept, Different families of Teaching Models.

UNIT-4

- Designing instructional system: Formulation of instructional objective, Task analysis, Designing of instructional strategies: Lecture, Team teaching, Discussion. Seminars, Tutorials and Brainstorming session.
- Development of Evaluation tools: Norm referenced tests and Criterion referenced tests. Application of Educational Technology in Distance Education: Concept of Distance Education: Distance and Open learning system, Student supports service, Evaluation strategies In Distance Education; Counseling in Distance Education.

UNIT-1

LEARNING OBJECTIVE

Meaning and scope of educational technology: System approach to education and its characteristics, Component of Educational Technology-Hardware and Software. Multimedia approach in Educational Technology.

EDUCATIONAL TECHNOLOGY: AN INTRODUCTION

Origin and Development

Technology of instruction was probably the first phase of development in the field of educational technology. Of course, testing if considered technology had also developed independently in the first decade of the 20the Century. Later on application of technology extended itself to the field of administration, organization, and curriculum also, but the greatest impact was made in the area of teaching or instruction. The origin and development of the concept and practice of educational technology may be traced back to 1873 when an exhibit .from an American school with maps, charts, text books and other equipment won admiration at the International Exhibition in Vienna-in 1873.American school display at Paris in 1878 was even more outstanding (Oliver, 1956). But, during the period of Industrial Revolution education, particularly instruction was not much affected by the revolutionary changes that were taking place in the field of industry. Instructional technology throughout this period remained at the per-industrial level. Although during the period from 1900 to 1950 as a result of the two world wars lots of developments had taken place in American technology transforming American society, it "only washed lightly upon the shores of instruction". High-speed printing techniques, radio, sound motion pictures, television and other pieces of communication technology had been developed. But, their application in American education was, missing. It was approximately in 1955 that the Ford Foundation experts Dr. Alvin C. Enrich and Dr. Alexander J. Stoddard gave the instructional process of American education a sharp push into mass production technology. First the television, both closed circuit and broadcast, was chosen as the prime hardware. The Ford impetus made provision, for.the first time, for a technology system in education to go along with the hardware. The Ford group made use of technology in creating the impetus in the first place. The

National Educational Television and Radio Center was set-up, National Association of Educational Broad-casters and Educational Facilities Laboratories were revitalized. Thus, a trend towards mass instructional technology began which machines and systems suitable for that purpose governed. Foremost of all was the television of which there were three instructional types. 1) Broadcast on a commercial channel, 2) Closed- circuit TV in which live instructors were used either to supplement instruction or to provide direct instruction exclusive of classroom teachers, and 3) The TV in which filmed lectures were distributed via the closed-circuit medium as replacement for classroom teacher. In all cases the objective was to reach more students with fewer teachers or to obtain "quality instruction". Another form of mass instructional technology included "massed film systems" like that of EBF series in physics and chemistry amounting to over 300 half-hour motion pictures intended to be used where there were no science teachers or where teachers there were but they were not considered qualified. Still another example of mass instructional technology was the use of overhead transparency projectors. Side by side a trend may also be seen during the same period towards growing technology for individual instruction which resulted into the development of teaching machines, systems and instruments of various types, such as 1) individual's reading papers and similar devices. (2) Individual viewing and listening equipment for existing slides, filmstrips, motion pictures, and recordings, (3) Language laboratories of all types, (4) specifically programmed printed materials such as scrambled text books and the Lumsdaine note book and (5) True teaching machines of the Skinner or Pressy type containing carefully worked out verbal or pictorial programs. Thus, both the mass instruction systems and the technology of individual instruction got terrific momentum leading to total educational automation having a possibility of eliminating not only the teachers but the school system also. A very important' development took place after that with the Airborne TV experiment of the Ford Foundation over a city in Indiana under' which circling overhead one or more air planes 'carrying multiple -

television transmitters could -broadcast signals over much greater distance. However, it is very difficult to say when exactly the concept of educational technology was born. Its birth-date is not definite. But, most writers agree that its christening took place in the early sixties.

MEANING OF EDUCATIONAL TECHNOLOGY

In one sense, educational technology or technology of education means technology applied to education. This emphasizes, particularly, the use of products of technology such as television, radio, tape-recorder, computer, etc., in education with a view to strengthen the process and organization of educational activity. In fact, this mode was the first phase of the development of educational technology as discussed in the foregoing paragraphs. This meaning of educational technology was largely confined to teaching or instruction.

Another meaning of educational technology implies application of scientific principles or principles drawn from any branch of knowledge to the development of some technique, method, device, model or design which improves the quality 0f any existing practice in education. It may not be confined only to teaching or instruction. It may happen in any branch of education such as administration, testing, curriculum development, teacher training, and so on. This is the same as science to technology. Just as technology is an applied science, educational technology may also be considered as an applied science which means any principle discovered in any branch of knowledge used for developing some more effective technique of educational practice.

Lumsdain (1964) holds that educational or instructional technology is understood in. two ways, although it is difficult to distinguish between these two meanings of instructional technology. One meaning implies application of principles of learning psychology to practical problems of teaching. According to Francis Mechner (1965) the educational technologist believes that by applying a few principles of psychology of learning he can design a more effective method or technique of imparting knowledge or changing the student behaviour. To Melton (1959) educational technology is based on the assumption that all forms of students' behavioral changes can be managed by applying principles of psychology. The second meaning of educational technology refers to the application of engineering principles in the development of electromechanical equipment used for instructional purposes (De Cecco and Crawford, 1977) such as motion pictures, tape-recorders, teaching machines, and computers.

The difference between science and technology is that the science discovers a principle or constructs a theory on the basis of experimentation while technology uses that theory or the principle for upgrading the existing practices and facilities. For example, producing television, which may be used for enriching the life's experiences, is technology, but the discovery of principles of electronics in the laboratory by the scientist is science. Educational technology used in this parlance means borrowing a principle or theory from any field of discipline and using that for developing procedures and techniques in the field of education, which can improve the existing practices in the field. Educational Technology has been regarded as the application of systematic knowledge about learning and instruction to teaching and training with the aim of improving their quality and efficiency. It includes a wide range of presentation, control and feedback devices such as teaching machines. simulators and computers. In the past educational technology has drawn heavily on disciplines like psychology, sociology, management, physics, mathematics and engineering or developing its techniques and methods. Depending upon these contributions of other fields to educational practice,- educational technology has been classified into three types-educational technology-I, educational technology-II, and educational technology-III.

Educational technology-I, also known as hardware approach to teaching; learning is a technology of machines applied to teaching This is based on the application of principles of physical sciences to education and teaching system. It stresses the importance of teaching aids the whole field being known a few decades back as audio-visual aids to teaching. The aim of this segment of educational technology has been to increase the impact of teaching.

Educational Technology-II also known as software approach to teaching refers to the application of principles of learning, particularly the principles of Skinnerian psychology to teaching. It particularly, concerns itself with the control of the student behaviour, direct and deliberate shaping of the behavioural being the focus of the efforts made. Its origin lies in the application of principles of behavioral sciences to the problems of teaching, learning and motivation. It is characterized by task-analysis, writing precise objectives, selecting appropriate learning strategies, reinforcing correct responses and continuous evaluation.

Educational technology-III takes the whole view of the learning system to determine how each of the many constituent parts fit's- with each other. In fact it utilizes management approaches to teaching-learning. It combines both hardware and software approaches to reaching. It sees teachers as manners of learning resources, charged with the roles of choosing or deciding between alternatives of learning and regards teaching as an independent variable, the condition to be manipulated. Consequently, there is beginning to emerge an associated general theory of teaching. Bruner characterized such a theory of teaching as one that sets forth rules concerning the most efficient way of achieving knowledge, skills and attitudes. Systems approach to teaching, cybernetic approach to teaching, training psychology approach, most of the teaching theories and models of teaching fall within this segment.

DEFINITIONS OF EDUCATIONAL TECHNOLOGY

Like any other term, educational technology has been defined variously. Following definitions of educational technology throw adequate light on its various facets, in the field of education.

1. B. C. Mathis: Educational technology refers to the development of a set of systematic methods, practical knowledge for designing, operating and testing in schools.

2. De Ceoco (1971): Educational technology is in the form of detailed application of the psychology of learning to practical teaching problems.

3. Department of Education and Science (DES)-U.K.: Educational technology is the development, application and evaluation of systems, techniques and aids in the field of human learning.

4. Derek Rowntree (1973): Educational tech11010gy is a rational problem solving approach to education, a way of thinking skeptically and systematically about learning and teaching.

5. Dieuziede, Director General of UNESCO's Division of Methods, Materials and Techniques: Educational technology implies all the intellectual and operational efforts made during recent years to re-group, re-arrange and systematisc the application of scientific methods to the organisation of new sets of equipment and material.

6. D. Unwin (1969): Educational technology is concerned with the application of modern skills and techniques to requirements of education and training. This includes the facilitation of learning .by manipulation of media and methods, and the control of environment in so far as this reflects on learning.

7. E.H. Hadden : Educational technology is that branch of educational theory and practice., which is concerned primarily with the design, and use of messages. which control the learning process.

8. G.O.M. Leith (1967): Educational technology is application of scientific knowledge about learning, and the conditions of learning to improve the effectiveness and efficiency of teaching and learning.

9. LK. Davis (1971): Educational technology is concerned with the problems off education and training and is characterised by a disciplined and systematic approach- to the organization of resources for learning.

10. J. Bloomer (1973): Educational technology is the application of scientific knowledge about learning to practical learning situations.

11. J.B. Gases: Educational technology has to be seen as part of a persistent and complex endeavour of bringing pupils, teachers and technical means together in an effective way.

12. Maximum Nickson (1971): Educational technology deals with the application of many fields of science to the educational needs of the individual as well as of society.

13. Michael J. Apter: The term educational technology can be interpreted in a rather narrow way to mean little more than the use of sophisticated hardware (like TV, Projectors etc.) in teaching or in a broad but trivial way to mean the use of any new educational technique.

14. Michell (1973): Educational technology could be helpful in educational innovation by considering new systems and materials along with inventing instruments and finding procedures and then thinking proper solutions for educational challenges.

15. National Council of Educational Technology U.K. (1967): Educational technology is the development, application and evaluation of systems, techniques and aids to improve the process of human learning.

16. National Academy of Engineering's Instructional Committee on Education- U.S.A.: Educational technology is the body of knowledge resulting of from the application of the science of teaching and learning to the real world of the classroom, together with the tools and methodologies developed to assist in these applications.

17. Robert A. Cox (1970): The application of scientific process to man's learning conditions to what has come recently to be called educational or instructional technology.

18. Robert M. Gagne: Educational technology can be understood as meaning the development of a set of systematic techniques and accompanying practical knowledge for desiring testing and operating schools as educational systems.

19. Scottish Council of Educational Technology: Educational **technology is a systematic approach to designing and evaluating teaming and teaching methods and methodologies and to the application and exploitation of media and the current knowledge of communication techniques in education, both formal and informal.**

20. Shiv K. Mitra (1968): Educational technology can be conceived as a science of techniques and methods by which educational goals could be realized.

21. S.S. Kulkarni (1968): Educational technology may be defined as the application of the laws as well as recent discoveries of science and technology to the process of education.

22. Takashi Sakanato (1971): Educational technology is an applied or practical study which aims at maximizing educational effects by 'controlling' such relevant facts as educational purposes, educational content, teaching materials. educational methods, educational environment, conduct of students, behaviour of instructors and interrelations between students and instructors.

23. U.S. President Commission of Enquiry (1979): Educational technology may be defined as a systematic way of designing, carrying out and evaluating a total process of teaching and learning in terms of specific objectives based on findings from research on human learning and communications.

24. W. Kenneth Richmond (1979): Educational technology is concerned with providing appropriately designed learning situations which holding in view the objectives of teaching or training, bring to bear the best means of instruction.

NATURE AND CHARACTERISTICS OF EDUCATIONAL TECHNOLOGY

A review of the above-mentioned definitions of educational technology points out the following characteristics of educational technology.

1. Educational technology is the application of scientific principles to education.

2. Educational technology lays stress on the development of methods and techniques for effective teaching learning.

3. Educational technology stresses the organisation of learning situations for the effective realisation of the goals of education.

4. Educational technology emphasizes the designing and measuring instruments for testing learning outcomes.

5. Educational technology facilitates learning by controlling environment, media and methods.

6. Educational technology involves input, output and process aspect of education.

7. Educational technology is not confined to the use of electronic media in education. It includes systems approach also.

8. Educational technology is an important medium of communication.

9. Educational technology is not to be taken as a synonym to audio visual aids in education.

10. Educational technology is a very comprehensive term and is not to be viewed in terms of its parts or processes. It includes instructional technology, teaching technology, programmed learning, microteaching and system analysis etc.

SCOPE OF EDUCATIONAL TECHNOLOGY

Scope of educational technology is a wide as education itself. Its scope ranges from the concrete educational process to the most abstract and subtle ones. It includes the sue of hardware and software and systems analysis in various educational operations. The possibility of using educational technology in almost all areas of education has been and is being explored. These are three major areas in education in which its scope is very wide.

These are :

1. Technology related to general educational administration and management. 2. 2. Technology related to general educational testing.
3. Technology related to the instructional process.

Rowntra (1973) has stated the following as the province of educational technologies:

1. Identifying aims and objectives of learning.
2. Planning the learning environment.
3. Exploring and structuring the subject matter.
4. Selecting appropriate teaching strategies and learning media.
5. Evaluating the effectiveness of the learning system.
6. Using the insights gained from evaluation to improve their effectiveness for the suture.

Important areas which should comprise educational technology are as under:

1. Concept and various facets of educational technology.
2. Teaching- learning process.
3. Individualized instructional technology.
4. Programmed learning.
5. Teaching models

6. Learning theories
7. Multimedia approach to teaching
8. Mathetics
9. Cybernetics
10. Task analysis
11. Modules
12. Systems approach

FUNCTIONS OF EDUCATIONAL TECHNOLQGY

Important functions of educational technology may be listed as under:

1. Identification of the educational goals and objectives of the community.
2. Developing appropriate curriculum for the achievement of the stipulated goals.
3. Analysing the process of teaching and learning.
4. Developing suitable teaching-learning material.
5. Selecting and developing proper teaching-learning strategies for obtaining optimum results.
6. Developing and selecting appropriate audio-visual aids.
7. Utilizing effectively the hardware and software media.
8. Providing essential feedback and control through evaluation.
9. Preparing teachers in the use of new technology of teaching.

SYSTEM APPROACH

The dualism between hardware and software domains of educational technology gradually began to disappear when the theory and principles of systems development marched into the orbit of educational activities. A feeling in America that there was "an excess of equipment over its planned uses" motivated this march. Something of the same kind occurred in Britain also (Unwin, p.l0). The dissatisfaction caused by this overemphasis on equipment and hardware was expressed by some in the words that "It was education plus technology, not education) technology" (Unwin, 1977). It was emphasized, then, that educational technology proper must be based on the behavioral sciences and it ought to be contered on the study of instructional methods and systems, not on equipment", The point emphasized was that the objective of teaching-learning should be identified in behavioural terms requiring an analysis and objective description. It was also emphasized that while educational technology focuses on the methods of. instruction, there is the need to take into consideration the characteristics of the whole system of instruction or the whole system in which instruction has to take place. The movement of systematic improvement of education which had its beginning in U.S.A in the 1950's as a result of feeling of defeat and frustration on the front of education against U.S.S.R. who had succeeded in launching the Sputnik in the atmosphere got an impetus during the 60's with the result that systems analysis and systems; development approaches borrowed from the field of management were very much welcomed in. the arena of instruction for improving its quality. This resulted into a large number of designs of improved instruction and a well accepted approach to innovations in the field of education. In course of time it carved for itself the third: domain of educational technology, and was known as educational technology-III. It tended to be, associated with the production, implementation and maintenance of systems and sub- systems. A realization grew up those educational, processes such as instruction, administration, counseling, scheduling, curriculum design, etc. should be viewed as systems, as assemblages of compounds, each having its own objectives. The trend emphasized, that educational systems ranging from the university or college or department to the individual student can be known by analysis and described in objective terms. That all the educational processes can be identified and measured, that all the essential internal components called as sub-systems, functions, programmes, etc, can be described in clear terms and resources needed for achieving the objectives can be specifically known. Systems analysis is a process of breaking down a system into its products or objectives, its functions and its inputs or resources. In fact, the discipline of systems analysis and design seems to have, arisen from the operational research ideas developed during the Second World War.

Basing on this approach a large number of new approaches to instruction, models and designs were developed All these constitute the domain of instructional technology-Ill. To mention a few of these there are progreammes like team teaching, microteaching, interaction-analysis, flexible scheduling, extended school year, voucher system, performance contracting, behavioural objectives. planning-programming-budgeting system, models of teaching, training psychology, instructional design, etc. All these. are innovations backed by the spirit of educational technology-III.

When scope of educational technology is described from the point of view of the areas of education to which it is applied, there are said to be following branches or types of educational technology.

1. Teaching Technology or Instructional Technology
2. Training Technology
3. Organizational Technology
4. Curriculum Technology
5. Evaluation Technology.

EDUCATIONAL TECHNOLOGY AS SYSTEMS APPROACH TO INSTRUCTION

Before going to discuss systems approach to education and examine educational technology as systems approach, it seems unavoidable to explain what systems approach means, what a system is and how this theory came into origin.

General and Social Systems Theories

A system is defined by Flagle and, his associates (p. 58) as "an integrated assembly of integrating elements designed to carry out cooperatively a predetermined function". Several authors have offered a classification of systems. Boulding 0956) classified them into static, clockworks (simple dynamic systems), theml0stat (control systems), cell (open and self-maintaining), plant, animal, humans, social, and transcendental (ultimate and absolutes) systems. Miller (1965) wrote of "conceptual", "concrete" and "abstracted" systems. Systems can be either closed or open, living or non-living. All living systems are open systems. Ludwig von Bertalanffy is said to be the father of general systems theory who said in 1952 "The principles of wholeness, of organization and of the dynamic conception of reality, become apparent in all fields of science". The primary focus of system's theory or approach is on organizational systems, social systems that are concrete, open and living consisting of plurality of individual actors interacting with each other. Schools are viewed globally as social systems. Instruction or teaching is considered a sub-system within the social system of the school alongwith a number of other subsystems such as classroom, faculty, student groups, informal groups etc. Education is considered a complex organization of technical, managerial and institutional systems. The technical system is involved in actual task performance within the organization, e.g. teaching or instruction consisting of, largely, the teachers and their support personnel. All schools, are open systems as they have certain exchanges with their environment e.g. receiving' and processing pupils, responding to so many diverse demands from conflicting interests in the environment. Open systems-, receive a variety of inputs, processes these inputs and provide outputs. Hence, from this point of view schools too are input-output systems. A given school organization includes a wide variety of input-output systems such as decision-making subsystems, supervisory subsystems, instructional subsystem, personnel subsystem, record-keeping subsystem and so on.

Any person who approaches his job from a system's viewpoint thinks in conceptual as opposed to concrete terms, focuses on both wholes and parts, recognizes the dynamic interrelationships among various aspects of a situation and is goal-oriented. Conceptual thinking means the examination of general propositions to determine their relevance for the specific problem. Systematic thought is both analytic and holistic. Having developed a concept of the whole, the system theorist can proceed to deal with the parts of the problem; He stresses the relationships. among the parts of a system and open systems, the relationships between a system and its environment. He realizes that parts of a situation and their properties are in some manner related so that a change in one part will be reflected in changes in another.

Systems Approach to Instruction: As described earlier' a system is a set or arrangement of things so related or connected as to form a unity or organic whole, a regular, orderly way of doing things. Order, method, regularity are emphasized. So when we look at instruction as a system it emerges that its parts interrelate and interconnect so as to form a total entity that is more than a sum of its parts and is a complete, composite structure. Within this system there are three interrelated parts the instructor, the learner and the goals of instruction. The instructor is the person responsible for the system and for guiding and shaping the process through which goals of instruction are achieved. He is the decision maker and has certain choices and alternatives for plans 0f action, which must be taken in an orderly, and rational way because the whole system of instruction is an organized whole committed to achieve predetermined goals. He himself is a system consisting of several sub-systems such as his value system, his mental set, his nervous system etc which interact with other subsystems of the instructional system, the learners, the goals to be achieved and the environment in which instruction has to take place.

The learner is another subsystem of the instructional system. He comes with his own psychological and sociological background; and each learner in the class significantly differs, from another. All these learner systems with all their unique qualities and characteristics interact with one another and also with the instructor and his characteristics; the instructor has to keep in mind these unique learner-systems and adjust his instruction to their peculiarities. Even the slightest maladjustments and misfits in these interactions may affect instruction adversely. Though it is very difficult, it has to be attempted with all seriousness.

Another subsystem of the instructional system is the immediate learning task, which consists of cognitive, affective and psychomotor transformations of the learners. In order to achieve this objective the instructor has to construct and manipulate another subsystem of the processes which most appropriately can achieve the goals of instruction. Taking all these component subsystems into consideration the instructional system can be represented as an input-output system. Instruction As Input-Output System': This may be described, diagrammatically as follows:

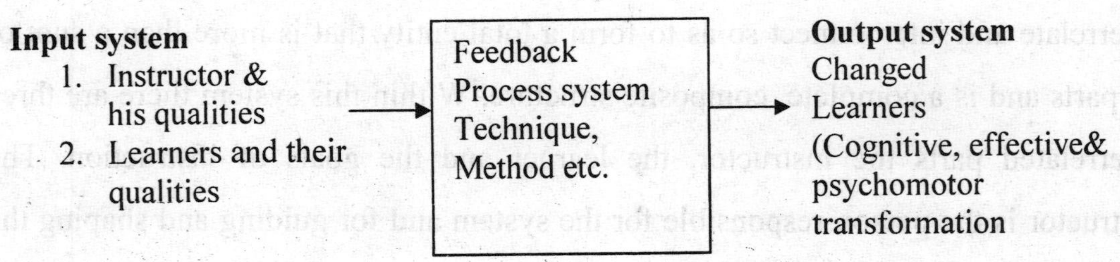

To understand this input-output system briefly, it may be noted that the immediate learning task in the system' is the achievement of the goals of instruction" which are in the form of cognitive, affective and psychomotor transformation of the learners and constitute the output system of the instruction. In order to achieve this objective the process system consisting of various components such CIS ordering of knowledge, choosing appropriate instructional strategies, media, feedback and environment, has to be manipulated in the most effective manner by the instructor by connecting it to the. power-input system. Without linking it to the power input the system will remain static and will not produce defined outcomes. The process system cannot work without this power input system. Before wheels can turn there must be power. This power flows from the instructor and the learners. The instructional system may, thus, be considered to have an intellectual and an emotional power component in the form of knowledge, abilities and motivation. All these put together constitute the input system of the instruction. The system works only with this power input. The function of the system of instruction is to provide a coherent structure, which coincides with the structure of the output system.

To sum up, the systems approach to education emphasizes following actions:

1. Identifying and stating the goals to be achieved.

2. Identifying the processes, methods, techniques and strategies that may be most relevant to achieving the predetenl1ined goals.

3. Building up theoretical foundation justifying the relevance of these processes to achieving the goals.

4. Determining specific interactions visualized existing among various other components of inputs.

5. Specifying the various kinds of controls needed in the total system at

different points.

6. Keeping the whole in mind all the time while preparing the model or the system.

This way of looking at education and its specific activities and components is outcome of the insight which emerges from educational technology

COMPONENT AND SOURCES OF EDUCATIONAL TECHNOLOGY

Following are the five divisions of educational technology:

Educational Technology (I). Here direct use of psychological principles is recommended. It. deals with diagnostic assessments of pupils,' educational objectives in bchavioural terms, deciding for methods, devices for classroom instruction, and stimulus-control for self-instructional strategy.

Educational Technology (II). Here instructional materials and communication means are produced after designing and examining them carefully. Emphasis is towards selection, processing and collections used for communication purposes.

Educational Technology (III). Here the management aspects are considered here as planning, programming budgeting, decision making operations, research, system analysis and organization of models for problem solving, computers and information system, and organization of a man-machine systems.

Educational Technology (IV). IT covers educational systems engineering, i.e., the planning, designs, construction and evaluation of instructional systems administrative systems operating systems (course, resource center, curricular development work).

Educational Technology (V). Educational planning is considered here just like the manifestation of educational systems engineering. The economic aspects and finances are the main bases here.

THE HARDWARE APPROACH

This was, perhaps, the first phase of educational technology, the first application of technology to instruction. This appeared in the form of straightforward use of audio-visual aids in teaching learning. The most innovative contribution was made by Sidney Pressey whoworking at Ohio State University produced a teaching machine in the 1920s, which was designed to automate testing procedure but evolved into a teaching machine. Lumsdaine and Glascr (1960) have given an account of attempts made to mechanize teaching during the thirties and forties. Since then an assorted collection of media and mechanisms has moved under the umbrella of educational technology. Television and videotapes also moved into the classroom in course of time. In the U.S.A. and Great Britain C.C.T. V provided a coordinated communication service in most academic institutions. Centers and Units have been set up for photographic or repro graphic services, for closed circuit television, for audio-visual aids with gradual excursion into every aspect of educational technology. Language laboratories are another example of technological installations in education, which were being used for multiple purposes and, hence, were properly called learning laboratories. These laboratories were not confined to language teaching only. Their use was extended to the teaching of other subjects also. The past half-century in the U.S.A. has brought about phenomenal growth in multimedia materials and equipment, particularly electronic devices. In education the multimedia center has torn" down the walls of the traditional classroom. The diversity of the materials, there increased accessibility and their growing appeal have revolutionized teaching methods. Well-equipped learning centers motivate children and individualize instruction. Their printed materials, real objects and representatives of objects which can be read, seen, heard, felt and manipulated provide increasingly richer opportunities for learning, although criticisms are" made that the computer and other sophisticated devices may destroy the humanizing value of education. Some of the critics also feel that much of the feeling and personal interaction of the real world is lost in the representations of the multimedia centers.

In India the hardware approach has not made any significant dent in the classroom teaching at any level. The Government of-India has established center for Educational Technology (CET) at New Delhi. It has developed some teaching-learning material and its programmes are sometimes broadcast on TV. The U.G.C. has also made a meager beginning in the direction of using television for educational broadcasting. But inside the school and the classroom nowhere the teachers are found using the hardware equipment. The equipment like tape-recorder, overhead projectors and transparencies, educational films and film projectors has been supplied to some departments in the universities. But, they are just lying there and not used.

SOFFWARE APPROACH

Software refer to programs which are produced in the form of printed material and are different form the machines. These materials are prepared in a scientific manner based on the application of psychology of learning to practical teaching problems. Software and programs may be considered essential characteristics of educational technology, a really big milestone in the development-of educational technology. This truly emerged in the middle fifties with the work of B.F. Skinner (1954,1958) who achieved great success in controlling and changing the behaviour of animals and then, applied this experience to the education of human beings. Thus was born what came -to be known as programmed learning. In fact, the emphasis on educational technology which emerged after sometime was a direct outcome of the Skinnerian Movement. The processes commonly adopted by programmers such a, task analysis, behavioral objectives, active responding feedback, Validation, etc. constitute the foundation stones of most media and methods that were developed later on. In the 1960s the term educational technology came to be applied largely to programmed learning and teaching machines, both being founded on sound principles of the psychology of learning and both being most promising techniques of individualizing instruction. B.F. Skinner's small teaching machine, which he developed in the 1950's, involved the learners in active response as they moved through successive frames of very small steps proceeding from the known to the unknown in a straight line sequence. This was the case of linear or extrinsic programming. Soon it was followed by the branching programs of Norman Crowder, which provided for alternative paths through a course. If the student responded incorrectly he was shown his error and was directed to return to the original or alternate frame to correct his answer. In course of time programmed texts incorporating the principles of the original machines replaced teaching machines. Slides, films, pictures, diagrams and tape recordings complemented the printed material of the scrambled texts, which provided the learner with alternative paths. Programmed texts have gained acceptance over teaching machines because of their financial economy and greater flexibility. They provide proper feedback to guide and motivate pupils allow learners to move at their own rate. The computer-assisted instruction a.1so utilizes the technique of programmed learning.

It may he noted that the two approaches, hardware and the software are merging together interacting in the design and use of equipment to provide control over the learning situation. In organizing instruction the application of the psychology of learning and electro-mechanical engineering both are combined together to produce the desired results. Software and hardware have become complimentary to each other.

MULTI-MEDIA APPROACH

There has been a terminological evolution in this field beginning from correspondence education' through' distance education' to 'open learning'. The openness refers to the dimensions of prior educational qualifications, place of learning, accessibility, choice of subjects, diversity in instructional designs, flexibility in ,delivery mechanism and in the pace of learning allowed to the learners. In operational terms the essence of open learning lies in its being imparted and received in a non institutional setting; making use of multimedia packages of distance education like print material, audio and video cassettes, radio and TV programmes, etc., and supplementing this packaged programme by contact programmes. In the case of vocational course requiring skill development, some training practice facilities in work place are to be made available for hand-on-experience.

Open Learning System and Non-Formal Education

Open Learning is common with non-formal education, emphasises flexibility and learner centredness. However, if non-formal education does not make use of distance education methods, it cannot be termed open learning.

Open Learning System and Distance Education

An open learning system makes use of distance education methods. However, all distance education is not necessarily open in the sense that the courses it offers are open to all types of applicants. Thus, professional programmes of continuing education, being limited to accredited members of a particular profession, are not categorized as open education.

Open Learning System and Correspondence Education

The correspondence education though a form of distance, can not be called as open learning system since it is entirely governed by rules and regulations covering institutional course, in such matter as curriculum, scheme of studies a admission criteria and soon. The open learning system is distinct from the rigidly formal institutional system, in respect of curriculum instructional packages and evaluation methods.

Limitations of Traditional System of Education

The traditional universities and educational institutes suffer from the following limitations

(1) The educational institutes are considered as appendages of the conventional universities. They do not have the freedom in designing their study courses.

(2) Their courses, rules, for admissions and other policy are in the hands of others. The courses are rigid and designed for regular students.

(3) In these educational institute, the method of instruction is through print media or correspondence education.

(4) The academics and administrators of traditional system treat the correspondence education system as a second-class system.

Policy Precursors of Open Learning System

(1) Policy recommendations bearing on 'Open Learning System' in NPE 1986 and in the documents relating to 8th plan are specified below.

(2) NPE-1986-the reference to Open and Distance Education and related aspects like Non-formal Education, Technology etc are interspersed throughout the NPE They are quoted below:

National System of Education

"Life-long education is a cherished goal of the educational process. This presupposes universal literacy. Opportunities will be provided to the youth, housewives, agricultural and industrial workers and professional to continue the education of their choice, at the pace suited to them. *The future thrust will he in the direction of open and distance learning.*

Adult Education "A vast programme of adult and continuing education will be implemented through various ways and channels, including" :

(a) Establishment of centres in rural areas for continuing education;

(b) Worker's education through the employers, trade unions and concerned agencies or government.

(c) Post-secondary education institutions;

(d) Wider promotion of books, libraries and reading rooms;

(e) Use or radio, TV and films, as mass and group learning media;

(f) Creation of learners' groups and organization;

(g) Programme of distance learning

(h) Organising assistance in self-learning; and

(i) Organising need and interest based vocational training programmes.

Non-Formal Education-Modern technological aids will be used to improve the learning environment of NFE centers. Talented and dedicated young men and women from the local community will be chosen to serve as instructors, and particular attention will he paid to their training. Steps will be taken to facilitate their entry into the formal system in deserving cases. All necessary measures will be taken to ensure that the quality of nonformal education is comparable with formal education.

Vocationalisation-Non-formal, flexible and need-based vocational programmes will also be made available to be literates, youth who have completed primary education, school dropouts, persons engages in work and unemployed 6r partially employed persons. Special attention in this regard will be given to women.

Open University and Distance Learning

(l) The Open University system has been imitated in order to augment opportunities for higher education and as an instrument of democratizing education.

(2) The Indira Gandhi National Open University, established in 1985 in fulfillment of these objectives, will be strengthened.

(3) This powerful instrument will have to developed with care and extended with caution.

Delinking Degrees from Jobs

(4) A beginning will he made in de-linking degrees from jobs in selected areas.

(5) The proposal cannot be applied to occupation-specific courses like Engineering, Medicine, Law, Teaching etc. Similarly, the services of specialists with academic qualifications to be required in various job positions.

(6) *De-linking will* be applied in services for which a university degree need not be a necessary qualification. Its implementation will lens to a refashioning of job-specific courses and afford greater justice to those candidates who, despite being equipped for a given job, are unable to get it because of an unnecessary preference for graduate candidates.

(7) Concomitant with de-linking, appropriate machinery, such as a National Testing Service, will be established, in appropriate phases, to conduct tests on a

voluntary basis to determine the suitability of candidates for specified jobs and to pave the gay for the emergence of norms of comparable competence across-the nation.

Technical and Management Education-In view of the present rigid entry requirements to formal courses restricting the access of a large segment of people to technical and managerial education, programmes through a distance-learning process, including use of the mass media, will be offered. Technical and management education programmes, including education in polytechnic will also he on a flexible modular pattern based on credits, with provision for multi-point entry. A strong guidance and counseling service will be provided.

Appropriate formal and non-formal programmes of technical education will be devised for the benefit of women, the economically and socially weaker sections, and the physically handicapped.

Media and Educational Technology-Modern communication technologies have the potential to bypass several stages and sequences in the process or development encountered in earliest decades. Both the constraints of time and distance at once become manageable. In order to avoid structural dualism, modern educational technology must reach out to the most distant areas and the most deprived sections of beneficiaries simultaneously with the areas of comparative affluence and ready availability.

Open Education in Universities-The conventional attraction for degrees and diplomas and the desire of many a secondary certificate holder to acquire further qualifications while in employment or working for employment led to the demand and provision of 'external' degree courses. Correspondence courses followed, as an improvement. The University Grants Commission formulated guidelines for correspondence courses in Indian Universities. A few Universities relaxed formal qualifications for entrants to correspondence courses. By 1989-90, correspondence courses' in various disciplines had been instituted by 38 Universities, at the under-graduate, postgraduate and diploma/certificate levels.

The first Open University in the country was established in Andhra Pradesh in 1982, followed by the establishment of the Indira Gandhi National Open University in 1985. More Open Universities got established thereafter, viz., Kota (1987). Nalanda (1987) and YC Maharashtra enrolled in open and Nashik (1989). Nearly five lakh students are at present enrolled in open and correspondence system. This constitutes 12% of a total enrolment of about 42 lakhs in higher education. Open Universities account for about one fourth of the non-institutional enrolment in higher education, the remaining being in traditional correspondence courses.

The Objectives of Open Education System

There is an urgent need of open education system in our country; it fulfils the social. economic and national needs of the country. It has the following main objectives :

(l) To facilitate by providing equal opportunities of education to citizen of the country.

(2) To provide education and training as well as orientation of various segments of the populations so as to achieve wage-employment/self-employment managerial skills.

(3) To build up the capabilities of educational functionaries for achieving universalisation of elementary education (UEE) and adult literacy, in terms of access, rctGntion and education achievement;

(4) To make provision for the substantial demand for secondary education

and beyond, resulting form UEE;

(5) To provide diversified academic and vocational education or good quality at the secondary level and beyond so as to meet the emerging needs for personal, social and economic growth; and

(6) To gear various levels and types of educational opportunities for enhancing the overall quality of life in the national contexts.

(7) To provide wider access to higher education to a large population and maintain high quality of education.

History of Open Education

Open or distance education programmes have been operational for over 250 years. mainly in Europe and North America, in the form of 'correspondence education for adults wishing to secure diplomas, degrees or just skills and information of their special interest. Early in the 20th century, universalization of primary education in remote geographical areas was carried out by Australia, Canada and New Zealand, through postal tuition.' Later, correspondence education began to cover secondary, higher and some branches of professional education. The use of radio and television for learning-support brought in the term 'distance education'. But the establishment of the United Kingdom Open University (UKOU) in 1969, gave a new direction to this field. Along with print-materials, it introduced audio and video materials and a system of personal guidance through contact audio and video materials and a system of personal guidance through contact centered for learners and their counsellors. The thrust of the Open University towards equality of educational opportunity for the forgotton mil1ions' such as workers and housewives received appreciation. Soon after, many a 'correspondence' course got converted firstly into 'distance education', and then into 'Open Education' using the new style of postal tuition supported by personal contact and multi-media packages of learning materials.

1. United Kingdom Open University (UKOU)

The UK0U came into being primarily to provide a second opportunity for those who could not go for higher education but are interested in continuing their higher education. In 1969, the political will in Britain, especially at Prime Ministerial level, played a major part in the establishment of the United Kingdom Open University.

The UKOU promoted the use of new communication technology for educational purposes from the very beginnings and one of its objectives was the advancement and dissemination of learning 'by teaching and research by a diversity of means such as broadcasting and technological devices appropriate to higher education, by correspondence tuition, residential courses and seminars and in other relevant ways'.

In spite of being called the 'University of the Air', broadcasting was never regarded by the UKOU's planners as being more than an element in a multi media approach. The report of its planning committee (1969:6, quoted by Rumble and Harry, p. 212) explained this attitude thus it is however neither practically possible nor pedagogically sound to rely on broadcasting as the principal or exclusive means of instruction in an operation designed to provide disciplined courses at University level. The only method of individual instruction capable of being made available everywhere and capable of indefinite expansion as new needs arise is correspondence tuition, which can readily incorporate these newer 'techniques'. Further the Report proposed that each course should 'make substantial use of correspondence course techniques' which would 'form the nucleus around which an integrated sequence of radio and television programmes could be built'

(a) Print as the Primary Medium-In the UKOU, the decision about media-use is taken at curricular level for all courses, Although the combination of media varies in each course, the main emphasis is on printed text. The printed text is normally produced for use over a period of at least four years. A course lasting 32 weeks has 32 'Texts'. Printed supplementary materials are also provided to the students. Supplementary materials generally consists of broadcast notes to accompany radio and television programmes, off prints, computer marked and tutor-marked assignments, lists of recommended reading, and such other information which needs to be revised regularly. Open University main texts are illustrated with diagrams and photographs and closely integrated with additional reading materials, with assignments and with radio and television programmes to form units of work which require one week of study. These texts also contain self-assessment questions to help the student assess his progress.

(b) Radio and Television-Approximately 65 percent of students' time is devoted to study the printed matter in UKOU course. Obviously, most of the UKOU courses have a radio and a television component. The approach to medic, adopted by the UKOU is an integrated approach-radio and television broadcasts are part of complete course. Instructions are provided in the main printed text to go for radio or TV broadcasts and related media and notes are supplemented. The University has the University's Broadcast sub-committee which decides about the needs for various courses and on the length and number of broadcasts necessary.'

Generally, foundation courses have a weekly radio and television programme. Second, third and fourth level under-graduate courses generally have fewer broadcasts of late the broadcasting authorities have reduced the amount of available transmission time progressively.

In 1980, the *BBC* used to produce about 250 twenty five minute television progranlmes and 300 twenty minute sound programme per year in partnership with the University. Lately, the amount of radio transmission and transmission of television programmes has decreased as a result of the increased use of audio and video cassettes.

It appears that the enthusiasm for educational broadcasting lessened due to three factors:

(i) The general public interest in a number of educational television and radio projects in the 1960s diminished gradually;

(ii) These. programmes were not appreciated by researchers and educators (as evidenced in various studies and books); and

(iii) The development of new technology, during the past decades, has prompted continuous monitoring of broadcasting and of other media.

(c) Other Media-Home kits are supplied to students to enable them to undertake scientific experiments at home. Field work in introduced to understand the practical application of theoretical principal.

Attendance at residential school is compulsory for students of some higher level courses. The residential schools are held mainly on conventional university campuses during the summer vacation. In these schools opportunities for learning through face-to-face lectures, seminars, field work, laboratory work and informal discussions are provided. Thus, it appears that the UKOU is using a quite healthy. combination of different media to produce effective courses of distance teaching.

(2) Central Radio and Television University (CRTVU) China

China's distance higher learning system has its own characteristics. The national, multi-media distance learning institution of China is called the Central

Radio and Television University (CRTVU). If we take into account the number of students and their geographic distribution, this university appears to be the largest distance teaching institution of the world. The chief aim of the University was to overcome the shortage of technical and management personnel and qualified teacher in the country.

The success of the institution points to the feasibility of using the media of Television and Radio to train more people for the modernisation of the country in a shorter time and on larger scale than conventional education system.

(a) Multi-media Approach- Television and radio are chosen as the master medium for communication by CRTVU. Yet the courses of CRTVU follow a multi-media approach. Most of these courses consist of radio and television broadcasts supplemented by printed teaching material. The input of these nonprint media varies according to the subject area. For example, the proportion of TV programmes for science and engineering courses is greater than that of the other media. For social science courses is greater than that of the other media or social science courses radio is the chief medium.

TV programmes arc transmitted by the Central China Television (CCTV) nationally through the micro-wave network. The transmission of radio programmes is the responsibility of provincial radio stations.

Likewise, courses offered by Provincial Television Universities are produced and transmitted jointly by them and Provincial Radio/TV stations.

These stations have authority to decide how much time they should use for these programmes. TV classes also organise courses taught by part time tutors who sometimes also use audio or videotapes produced by the CRTVU.

Printed textbooks are compiled and offered by CRTVU. These textbooks are not written or developed by CRTVU. They are selected from the available textbooks prepared mostly buy conventional universities. The CRTVU is engaged in preparing supplementary teaching material and distance teaching materials for radio and television presentation.

(3) Fern Universitat Hagen (Germany)

Primary Medium-The Fern Universitat, Hagen Germany exists in a country which is a world leader in communication technology. Yet in 1981 the FeU offered 1,200 courses and all of them were print based.' Forth used supplementary audio cassettes and fifteen had optinal use of video-tapes. It appears as though the goal of this University, viz., "The be engaged in reform of University teaching by the development of new methodologies and media", has remained restricted to 'new methodologies' and experimentations with new media have not taken place. The reason for the same is that academic tradition of Germany laces great importance on the professor's scholarly skills and the autonomy" of his teaching. This tradition in turn, leads to the choice of print based course materials by the FeU. The inherent superiority of print based material over the non-print media is generally accepted.

The FeU has been using computer systems for some of its administrative function. nut no course offered by it is computer based. Videotex, the latest technique, is also used to provide information about the programme in general rather than specific instruction. The University does not have radio or television broadcasts. Little use is made of telephone tuition.

(4) Univcrsitad Estatal Distancia (UNED) Costa Rica

The Universitad Estatal a Distancia of Costa Rica offers a wide range of material Is and media to help its learners pursue their educational objectives. The primary obi.ectives of the University were to provide higher education to a greater number of population and to grow a manpower for agriculture and industry. To achieve these aims the University uses a multi-media approach. The Unidades didactics' or text books are still cotl.sidered the basic source of instruction. There are two types of tutoring sessions provided by the University the regular face-to-face session held at weekends at the 19 academic centers located around the country, and the telephone tutoring sessions which are available to all students on week days from 6.00 to 9.00 p.m.

In addition, three basic types of audio-visual material media are made available to students

(1) The first type is television programmes that are broadcast at weekends for a total or three hours. These programmes are of the supportive type and are either 15 or 30 minutes long.

(2) The second type consists of book-cassettes or librocassettes which consist of a series of diagrams, graphs or other simplified written material that are group in a booklet form and a recorded cassette tape that guides the student through its content including exercise on the subject. Each book-cassette consists of a cassette with a topic on each side and a booklet divided into two pans. These materials are either sold to the students or made available on a loan basis.

(3) The third type comprises lecture cassettes, which proved students with short lectures and literature analysis that do not necessarily require a written accompallying text or other complementary materials.

(5) Indira Gandhi National Open University (IGNOU)

The National Policy on Education (1986) recognising the importance of distance education in India, emphasised on the establishment of a National Open University. It was posited, "The Open University system has been initiated in order to augment opportunities for higher education and as an instrument of democratizing education". Regarding the media use and communication technologies the Policy Document observed: "Modern communication technologies have the potential to bypass several stages and sequences in the process of development encountered in earlier decades. Both the constraints of time and distance at once become manageable. In order to avoid structural dualism, modern educational technology must reach out to the most distant areas and the most deprived sections of beneficiaries simultaneously with the areas of comparative afi1uence and ready availability."

Thus, the prime objective of Indira Gandhi National Open University (IGNOU) is to provide wider access to higher education to a large number of populations and at .the same time maintain high quality in instruction. The university has adopted the policy of using new technological devices to support the printed material: because it was contended that modern media use would expand educational opportunities and help in maintaining quality of instruction. Although there is a broad range of media available for educational purposes, the choice of IGNOU is limited to the technology available within the country.

The chief focus, at this early stage of growth is on supplying audio and video cassettes along with the printed texts. IGNOU has one Division of Communication to produce video and audio materials to support the texts. Each block of a course has some audio and video input. These cassettes can be sent at a later stage (not necessarily along with the texts) and provide additional, information-a different experience based on the same knowledge contents.

Indira Gandhi National Open University (IGNOU) was established in 1985. It offers a variety of courses but its most popular courses are Diploma in management, which has an enrollment of 15148 students and non-formal Bachelor's Degree course with 26392 students. IGNOU has its own audio-video production studio. It has produced 169 video and 249 audio programmes to supplement printed material. For student services, it has an impressive network of 13 regional centres and 131 study centres throughout the country. By the end of 8th plan. it proposes to establish a study centre in each district of the country. IGNOU is also exploring the possibility of establishing study centres sponsored by industry and voluntary agencies. Mobile Study Centres for reaching remote areas are also planned. IGNOU is expected to have an enrollment of2 lakh students at the end of the 8th plan. (Proposed enrollment in March 1992: 1.50 lakhs). Apart from expanding the present certificate, diploma and graduate programmes in management, distance education, creative writing, commerce and library science, IGNOU is planiling offer courses in rural development, higher education and basic sciences in the near future. During the 8th plan, IGNOU's thrust would be on introduction of non-traditional employment oriented courses, courses in counselling and guidance for primary teachers, nutrition and health education, early childhood care and education, construction management and wider resources management.

Yaswantrao Chavan Maharashtra Open University (YCMOU)

YCMOU, although formally established in 1989, had its antecedents in the Open Institution of the University of Poona under which a lot of preparatory work was done. The goal of the University is to become a 'mass varsity'. As much, it emphasizes vocational, technical and professional as well as general education programmes not only at the territory level but also at functional levels and outside the academic format related to development and increased individual incomes.

This open university has planned courses in agriculture and horticulture. Ten representative crops have been selected, viz., grapes, mangoes, cotton, groundnut, onion, 'toor' or 'arhar' (pigeon-pea), kardi (software oil seed), her, (jnjube), pomegranate and sugarcane. Working farmers study production processes with the help of specially written print materials audiovisual aids two-way communication between individual farmers and agriculture experts and contact sessions. For contact sessions, the university uses the concept of 'prayog parivaars' i.e., a sort of extended, the university uses the concept of 'prayog parivaars' i.e., a sort of extended' family' of 'experimenters' which enables producers/ learners to get together to exchange ideas and benefit from each other's experience.

Open University in Andhra Pradesh

The Government of Andhra Pradesh considered a proposal to start an open university in the state as early as 1978. However, the proposal was not given any practical shape. Meanwhile, the Osmania University initiated proposals to start an Open Education College to strengthen its distance education system. The college, though a part a part of the university, was to have full autonomy and the University was only to award degrees. At about the time the college was to be established. The new Chief Minister of Andhra Pradesh, Bhavanam Venkatram, perceived the idea of establishing an open university and appointed in 1982 a committee to examine the proposal. This committee recommended the establishment of an Open University in the State to provide access to higher education to the adult population of the State, for- upgrading their functional capacities and improving the quality of equalisation of educational opportunities and the emergence of a new concept of life-long education: Soon after, the wheels of administration moved very fast and the Andhra Pradesh Open University was inaugurated in August 1982.

UNIT -2

Learning objective

Modalities of teaching -Teaching as different from indoctrination, instruction conditioning and training Stages of teaching pre-active, interactive and post active. Teaching at different levels memory, understanding and reflective levels of organizing teaching and learning.

Programmed instruction: Origin Principles and Characteristics.

Types: Linear, Branching and mathetics.

Development of programme: Preparation, Writing, Try out and Evaluation

MODALITIES OF TEACHING

Modality is derived from 'mode', which means form or method of conducting some activity. Modalities of teaching, therefore, mean the ways of teaching. In other words the term refers to methodology of teaching, the various ways including all sorts of activities and experiences that assist in the realization of educational objectives. Teaching has been the most fundamental activity of education and has existed throughout the long evolution of education. During this long continuous evolution of the process of education teaching has utilized various methods procedures and techniques. Depending upon the philosophies of education and the predominant theories of learning during a particular period new modalities of teaching have been suggested, old modalities have been modified and redesigned. In fact it may not be far from truth to say that most of the modern modalities or methods of teaching are adaptations of teaching procedures that were used in the past. Several of these modalities of teaching have been used for many decades, rather centuries with relatively little alteration. Some of them still occupy a prominent and rightful place in the scheme of teaching at all levels. The Greeks considering education as a social institution used group discussions, field trips, debates forums, argumentation, etc. which are considered "progressive" methods even today. Socretes said. "Teaching is the direction of activities and so emphasized' questioning, analysing, reasoning, concluding and generalizing as the five steps involved in teaching. Plato recommended inductive method of teaching combined with objective. experimentation, scientific observation, rational thought and conduct. In ancient Rome Cicero advocated rhetorical method of teaching while Quintilian stressed a progressive methodology which entailed motivation through interest, leading rather than driving. During the middle ages the Greco-Roman tradition was preserved using predominantly the question and answer method. The renaissance period was marked by an emphasis on child's allround development and stress on seminar type teaching, Francis Bacon during the sixteenth and seventeenth centuries stressed the importance of inductive method or teaching and Johann Amos Commenius said teaching should be "true, full, clear and solid", emphasizing the importance of education of sense' perception and science, After seventeenth century Rousseau. Pestalozzi and Herbart suggested far reaching changes in the modalities of teaching. Herbart's five formal steps of teaching are popular with teachers all over the world even today. Many developments took place in the USA during the 19th and 20th century particularly in the second half of the 20th century when the Russians shot the Sputnik into the sky. Curricular changes along with innovative methods of teaching accompanied mass education movement in America. John Dewey, the great American educationist said, "The best education method is the reconstruction of experience" and advocated earning by doing through scientific method and problem solving. Originality, interest and initiative were incorporated as ii1 1portant elements in the teaching-learning process. The perspective on modalities of teaching presented in the foregoing discussion may serve as useful background for the following discussion of modern and newer thinking about teaching modalities.

TEACHING AND INDOCTRINATION

Indoctrination is inculcation of belief in religion or politics. In teaching, the forcing on the child of one point of view, to the exclusion of contrary ideas or values.

The term “teaching” implies to some extent ‘indoctrination’, prescribed or imposed learning. But, instruction is considered a process dependent upon inquiring mind of the instructor and the pupil. Indoctrination is outside the meaning and nature of instruction.

Difference between Teaching and Indoctrination

The process of indoctrination is the highest order of the teaching process. The maximum use of intelligence is expected to reach this highest level. In this process, the beliefs, ideas & assumptions etc. are impressed upon others. In teaching the indoctrination can be included but it is not sufficient. The teaching can be possible even without Indoctrination but Indoctrination is not possible without teaching.

TEACHING AND INSTRUCTION

Teaching is described by Means to be "the art and science of instructing, act of providing activities, materials, direction and guidance to facilitate learning in either formal or informal situations" the same author describes instruction as "practice of providing direction in the learning process emphasizing the imparting of information, knowledge or skill, sometimes used in a more limited sense that the term "teaching". These descriptions do not reflect that the two modalities, teaching and instruction are significantly different from one another. The purpose and the process involved in both are the same. A very slight difference that is pointed out is that instruction sometimes is used in a more limited sense that the term "teaching". Searles (p.22) also made a little distinction between the two terms. He said teaching is any imparting of information that leads to learning. Instructions is the imparting of ordered information. There is a pattern and structure to the information. Looking to the root of the word, instruction means to place in a structure. In this instance it means a structure of an idea or of a conditioning or a psychomotor skill. He further says that as the information increases this distinction will have to be made. Even today the distinction is made; the dictionaries make it in the same way. Now it has to penetrate into the schools, the social organization designed for instruction.

Gagne (1904) also holds the same view when he says that to explain and control the teaching act the requires a science and a technology in its own right. In one of his basic books he deals with the growing discipline of instruction and pleads for developing the science and technology the science and technology of instruction.

From the preceding account following specific conclusions may be drawn :

1. The differences between teaching and instruction are a matter of emphasis and specificity. They are not substantially different from one another. Teaching may be considered a traditional concept being used throughout the ages to point out to the efforts on the part of the teacher to impart knowledge and stimulate the growth of the learner. From time to time suggestions for improvement in the process and purposes of teaching have been made. The objectives of teaching, learner's characteristics, teacher's personality, processes and methods of teaching all have been analyzed and discussed thoroughly from time to time. Modifications and new ways of teaching have always been suggested. Also, teaching and instruction both the terms have been used in the past interchangeably. Even today they are used the same way. Current literature on teaching is replete with the use of the term 'teaching'. 'Objectives of teaching', 'methods of teaching', 'evaluation of teaching', 'models of teaching', 'principles of teaching', 'teaching technology', etc are some of the phrases, which are found in the recently written books. Hence, it is misnomer to say "differences between teaching and instruction." It only creates confusion in the minds of the students. There is no basic difference between the two. The connotations of the terms remain the same. Only the emphases shift. In' a way it may be said that the traditional concept of teaching has been more specifically defined as a result of technological impact, particularly the, application; of electromechanical devices such as television and the computer and this has made the. use of the term instruction more popular than-that-of the teaching. But, that should not be taken to mean that the nature of teaching has changed or that some fundamental difference

has occurred. The following points clarify how and where the focus or the emphasis has registered a change,

2. The term 'teaching' as traditionally understood was a more general and broader term in the sense that it would take into consideration many more things such as philosophies of education, theories or learning, general methods of classroom learning, etc, which were not specifically geared to classroom teaching. Instruction as understood today is used in a very narrow and limited sense confining to efforts made in the classroom only. Greater attention to classroom teaching renders it to he highly specific.

3. 'Teaching' as understood traditionally did not concentrate on the structure of knowledge very superficially. So knowledge remained a general concept under traditional teaching. The modern emphasis on ordered information, structured knowledge, planned and deliberate things to be taught is the life-blood and heart of instruction.

4. Teaching is a traditional concept, instruction may be considered a modern concept which has gained popularity only after 1950's as a results of Skinnerian revolution.

5. Teaching focuses on the process of learning, but instruction focuses on the 'product of learning'.

6. Teaching aims the beam at the student while instruction does so at the teacher as instruction emphasizes that it is the teacher who has to structure the learning situation and hence, he has to learn how to do this job.

7. Teaching considered all components of teaching separately and individually. Instruction is considered to be a 'system' an organic whole of the objectives, the learner, the processes and the instructor which interrelate and interconnect so as to form a total entity that is more than a sum of its parts with a definite structure. Teaching was never looked upon from this point of view.

Although, the emphasis and focus of teaching have changed yielding place to instruction, it should not be believed that the two terms are entirely different from one another. Keeping is mind the recent emphases as clarified' above, the two terms can he used interchangeably, and they are being so used even today.

TEACHING CONDITIONING AND TRAINING

Conditioning is the theory of learning, which explains how people can learn behaviors. It had it 'origin in the laboratory experiments of Pavlov and was known as classical conditioning. It was demonstrated by .him that simultaneous and repeated presentation of two stimuli, one the unconditioned (the real and natural cause of the response) and the other the conditioned one (neutral which was not the real cause but becomes the cause of the response) strengthens a new stimulus - response hondo Gagne (1970) refers to classical conditioning as signal learning as the conditioned stimulus anticipates (signals) the conditioned response. This theory was found to he having less possibility of its application in situations of human learning, A somewhat more complicated theory was propounded by B.E Skinner which is known as operant conditioning theory of learning or instrumental conditioning. In this case it is necessary that the organism must be able to make a particular response (operant). The objective of operant conditioning then is to increase the frequency of this operant behaviour by reinforcement, contiguity and practice. These are two basic learning theories. The differences between them lies in the reinforcement procedure. In classical conditioning the rein forcer (the unconditioned stimulus) occurs on every trial. In operant conditioning it occurs only when the organism makes a correct response, which means that, the)reinforcement is contingent upon the organism's making a correct response. Secondly, in classical conditioning the presentation of the reinforcement determines' the response while in operant conditioning-the response determines the presentation of the rein forcer. There are other psychologists also such as Thorndike, Hull, Guthrie, Tollman and Lewin who have prpounded stimulus - response approaches to learning, though in several respects they differ from one another. But the truth is that the conceptualization of learning as the reinforcement of :stimulus- response connections has been the most influential approach.

Verbal Learning and Skill Learning: - Both of these learning's can be explained and established on the basis of conditioned learning, particularly operant conditioning. At its most basic level verbal learning may be considered the process of forming verbal associations. For example, a child is shown the picture of a dog and is told that it is a dog, he learns the meaning of dog. The child observes the picture and next time he will say that it is the dog. This is just naming or attaching a name to an object, the labeling behaviour, According to Gagne verbal learning at its. most basic level is like skill learning in that it involves a chain of at least two links. The first link is the presentation of the picture (the stimulus) and seeing the picture (the response). In the second link seeing the picture results in certain internal stimuli which give rise to the verbal response, "dog". This immediately explains how verbal learning is related to basic S - R learning. Verbal learning resemble skill learning in that both involve the chaining of responses. Each link in the chain is an individual S - R association which acts as a stimulus for the next link. The difference between the verbal and skill chains lies in the type of response. Skill chains involve motor responses while verbal chains involve syllable and word responses.

Applications of Conditioning to Teaching Procedures: - Principles and procedures of conditioning can be and are being applied to teaching and training quite successfully. In fact, much of teaching and training is 'substitute learning' in which one small part of learning is substituted for slightly larger part and that larger part is substituted for a still larger part and so on. In planning teaching and training from conditioning point of view one should analyse the material and procedures in terms of unconditioned (what is known already) and conditioned (to be learned) stimuli. Programmed instruction is an example of this kind in which the programme frame is the stimulus, students response to the frame is the response and confirmation of the ,response is the reinforcement or .feedback. De-Cecco (p.236) suggests following steps to be followed in the application of conditioning theory of learning to instruction and training.

1. Describing what the instructor expects the student or the trainee to learn.
2. Examine the instructional task and materials for their meaningfulness.
3. Assess entering behaviour for the availability of meaningful responses and verbal mediators.
4. Provide appropriate practice conditions.
5. Provide knowledge of correct results.
6. Provide conditions which maximise retention.
7. Use suitable method of measurement.

TRAINING

The Department of Employment's Glossary of Training Terms (1971) defines training as "The systematic development of the attitude, knowledge, skill, behaviour' patterns required by an individual in order to perform adequately a given task or job". It refers to the development of an organized and co-ordinated pattern of mental or physical activity in relation to an object usually involving both receptor and effect or processes. It is built-up gradually as a result of repeated training experiences. It's serial in the sense that each part of the- skill involved is dependent on the preceding one and influences the next. Almost all trainings involve skills which are perceptual motor, manual, intellectual, social etc. depending upon the context. Training is essentially an area of applied psychology as it concerns people's learning which is the domain of psychology. But in the past decade electromechanical and psychological manipulations have resulted into what is known as "technology of training". Yet it can not be denied that basically training involves manipulation of principles of learning. Principles of learning by conditioning, particularly may be seen to be very relevant in this context. Training is largely a kind of skill development; and skill-acquisition is viewed as the integration of smaller units of behaviour into a hierarchically organized structure. This may be considered as an extenstion of the psychology of S-R connections, emphasizing the role of reinforcement as the basis of control of human behaviour.

Conditioning:- A close relationship between learning by conditioning and training may not be difficult to be observed. The Skinnerian principle of reinforcement may be considered important in this regard. Skinner considered reinforcement an important basis for controlling. behaviour. The important aspect of reinforcement, he said, is that S-R learning occurs' automatically after the occurrence of a desirable reinforcer contingent upon a correct response. In human learning the words "right" and "good" are reinforcers commonly used, Training can be analyzed and conceived of as the gradual strengthening of connections between a stimulus (S) and a response (R).

Training involves learning of a series of skills. Each skill has to be learnt separately: and finally all needed skills are organized into a coherent whole pattern. The learning of a skill involves a chain of motor responses. Motor responses may be viewed as individual S-R associations. A skill is thus, a series or chain of such movements. Each S-R link acts as a stimulus for the next lime These S-R chains of organized into larger response patterns may take the shape of a learnt complex skill. These S- R chains, which constitute larger response patterns, are also called subtasks or subroutines. One must learn all the subordinate chains before he can perform a particular skill. The skill is the total response pattern, Skills are hierarchical response patterns.

In building the S-R chains the principles and procedures which conditioning theory of learning evolved are helpful. These are known, in the context of training or skill-learning, as the basic conditions of learning. These are

1. Contiguity
2. Practice, and
3. Feedback (Knowledge of results)

Contiguity means simultaneous occurrence of the stimulus and the response. In case of skill learning which is an essential aspect of training the S-R units in the chains are at the basic level. At the higher level it constitutes simultaneous occurrences of the chains, which constitute the overall pattern of the complex skill. Proper sequencing of the S-R units and chains is important. The success of training procedure depends on this sequencing. Second important thing to be taken into account is the time succession of these S-R units and the chains in the overall response pattern. Delay in succession may defeat the purpose.

Practice means repetition of the response in the presence of the stimulus It is necessary for developing the skill to the autonomous stage of learning. Practice leads to perfect performance. Distributed practice method and massed practice method both are used for this purpose. The principle of contiguity was the cardinal principle of Skinner's operant conditioning.

The third basic condition for skill learning is said to be the feedback (reinforcement in Skinner's language). Some distinction is made between the term feedback and reinforcement. But here it is not important to discuss that Feedback may be in the form of the knowledge of result, consequence of behaviour, which is rewarding and satisfying. In fact feedback is the single most important variable governing the acquisition of skills involved in .any training pragramme. But the feedback has to be immediate. Following are the steps involved in the skill-development or training programme.

Steps of Training Programme:

1. Analysis of the skill, a kind of task analysis.
2. Assessment of trainee's entering behaviour.
3. Arrangement of abilities, skills and component units for training.
4. Describing or demonstrating the skill for the student.
5. Providing [or the three basic learning conditions, i.e contiguity, practice' and feedback.

Difference between Teaching and Training

The term 'Training' is used to shape the habits, while the term 'teaching' is used to form the habits. Both the terms are closely related, but these terms are not the same. The training is only an element of teaching. Actually the term 'training' is more nearer to the conditioning. The training includes the process of attaining various skills. But it is certain that the training cannot lead the human being to the higher levels of the education.

STAGES OR PHASES OF TEACHING

The most recent view on teaching is that it must concern itself with directing the growth of the pupil. The school, the libraries, the laboratories and the teacher all are there because the students are there for a particular purpose. If there are no students, there are no teachers, in fac1no schools. Dewey once said a teacher can no more teach without a learner than a seller can sell without a buyer. Obviously teaching is useful only to the extent that it facilitates learning. There is only one single purpose of the school being there, of the teachers being there, of the learners being there that the pupils should learn and grow: Hence, the most important thing that should go on in the classroom is learning amidst all activities including teaching. Psychology makes very clear the fact that the pupil must do his own learning; no one else can do it for him. This however should not mean that teachers cannot play their positive role and should abdicate from the throne. Rather it should mean that their task and responsibility have become several times more difficult now. It is easy to take the horse to the pond, but very difficult to make him drink. And that is what exactly the teacher of today is enjoined to do. He has to do all that makes the pupil learn. This new concept of teaching has made the work of the teacher considerably more challenging and more difficult. Instead of having to concern himself only with a few patterns of effective presentation of subject matter the modern teacher's responsibility is one of assuring himself that all that goes on in the classroom is of maximum benefits in promoting the all-round development of the child. According to the criterion of effective teaching which characterized education years ago, the teacher's knowledge of his subject and of methods of effective presentation were of fundamental importance. According to the modern concept of teaching these are still essential but learning now is considered a much more dynamic and continuous process involving all phases of pupil's growth and a development with the result that the complexity of his job of teaching has increased vastly and he now has to perform a lot of things in the class while teaching, before going to the class for teaching and also at the end of his teaching.

These tasks are discussed in the following sections. To facilitate the discussion of these tasks the whole job of teaching is divided into three phases.

Phases of Teaching : - Teaching does not mean only that which goes on in the classroom between the teacher and the students. In fact it extends far beyond that. For performing on a job adequately a lot of thinking, prior preparation, ensuring appropriate conditions etc. are required. Similarly, having completed the job one has got to know to what extent he has been able to do as he intended. 1t is true about teaching also. Looking from this point of view teaching has been considered as having three distinct phases. Sometimes these are also known as stages of teaching. They are:

A. Pre active phase

B. Interactive phase

C. Postactive phase

Thus, teaching is a three-stage integrated activity of the teacher.

PREACTIVE PHASE

Generally, it is believed that teaching means what the teacher does in the classroom. He is considered, to be active only in the classroom. Beyond the classroom boundaries he is not seen to be doing anything. This is a wrong notion. about teaching and teacher's sphere of operation. Teaching is a large continuous activity of complex nature which extends, at least, over three phases or stages. In other words the teacher is not active, i.e doing something only in the class, but he is active and doing lots of things even prior to his going to the class. Also having finished his main task of teaching he remains active and does many more things.

The preactive phase or stage of teaching, thus, refers to all that the teacher does pertaining to teaching but before entering into the class. It is the first and the beginning phase of his teaching. To put it in more simplified way preactive phase of teaching refers toe the preparation and planning aspect of teaching. Effective, teaching, depends on good preparation and meticulous planning: Every conscientious teacher makes a thorough preparation for teaching. He thinks a lot about it and visualizes mentally how he will organize his work and conduct activities in the class. Even very experienced teachers consider it important on their part to undertake planning for teaching. They feel it is useful and essential. It is not like' this that preactive phase operation and planning are necessary only for the beginning teachers. In fact, it is an imperative stage of teaching for every teacher and for every individual class. Sometimes, more time is spent on preactive phase as compared to actual active phase of teaching in the classroom. Some teachers need more time, some less to complete the task involved in the preactive phase. This depends on teacher's own abilities and competence. Some of the most important components of the task' the teacher is required to engage himself in prior to going to the class for teaching arc as follows.

1. Objective Analysis of the Knowledge, Skills and Attitudes to be Developed in the Students: - This is essential because effective presentation of the subject in the classroom is very much contingent upon this analysis. Whatever the topic the teacher has to teach in the class it has a definite structure of knowledge. This structure should be clearly analysed. The structure analysis should identify the most important facts which the students are expected to learn and remember, essential concepts that need to be explained and understood by the students, important relationships between the facts and concepts, principles, major understandings and generalizations which in order to be functional the students must know and understand.

Every single topic that is taught in the class contains some important facts, concepts, generalizations, principles and understandings. They constitute the structure of knowledge contained in the topic. They should be clearly identified so that while teaching in the class they may not miss the focus. This is also known as the mapping of the knowledge or the subject matter to be treated in the class. This has to be done before entering into the class during the preactive phase of teaching.

Knowledge alone is not the concern of teaching. There are certain skills also inherent in each subject and they need to be developed in the students. A lesson in language teaching, for example, requires the students to pronounce the words correctly, to speak fluently, to write neatly and clearly,' to 'have a good handwriting and so on. Similarly, a lesson in arithmetic, may require the students to develop the skill of speedy calculations. During the preactive phase the teacher is required to make this kind of skill-analysis of the topic to be taught. He should identify important skills involved in the topic and need to be developed.

Similarly" the teacher should engage himself in sorting out if certain essential attitudes can be developed in students through the teaching of that topic. Brief notes may be prepared of all these specifications or they may simply be kept in mind. It is necessary that a very clear outline of these should remain in the mind of the teacher throughout his teaching. But unless prior analysis is done it is not possible to take care of these while working in, the class. All this work is to be essentially done during the preactive phase. This requires a lot of thinking. imagination and use of creative process. Perhaps the teacher for this purpose has to be more active during this phase and, hence, labeling this phase as pre active, i.e before being active, is a misnomer from this point of view. But since "active" is used specifically for actual classroom teaching the phrase "pre active phase" may be retained as it is.

2. Objective Analysis of Cognitive Abilities to Be Developed: Imparting knowledge of the subject is not the sole concern of teaching. Development of pupil's intellect and the ability to use his mental processes is also considered equally important and for that teaching of tae knowledge is just the vehicle. So, the teacher is required to identify and pinpoint these; abilities to be developed through the classroom work. Abilities of analysis, application, synthesis, reflection etc. may be crucial in the teaching of certain subjects. The teacher should note down which of them should be in focus while teaching in the class.

Thus, a two-dimensional grid of knowledge and abilities should be prepared. This work requires a lot of time and can be done only during the preactive phase of teaching in the form of a long or short lesson plan which maybe written or unwritten.

3. Identification of Intervention Strategies: - Just mapping out of the most critical points where the shafts have to be sunk is not enough for effective teaching. The teacher has to find out most relevant and powerful ways and means of sinking these shafts, i.e achieving the said purposes. The point relates to identifying the most useful methods; techniques and strategies through which earlier mentioned objectives can be achieved. He has to jot down in relation to each knowledge and ability item the strategy that may be most relevant and. useful. There are numerous such techniques and strategies such as the lecture, the demonstration, experimentation, discussion, discovery, outdoor excursion, seminars, brain-storming, role-playing, assignment and so on. The teacher has to think which of them may be more effective for achieving which purpose. It is to be remembered that there can not be just one way of achieving the specific purpose as there can not be Just one way of earning money. So taking into consideration his own competence and abilities, students characteristics and the characteristics of the situation in which teaching is to take place, the teacher has to decide which strategy or method he can most gainfully use. Use of a strategy may imply the availability of certain apparatus or equipment. The teacher should ensure how this can be made available, what efforts he is required to make in this regard, etc. Also he must plan for emergencies and alternatives if things go wrong or these are not available. All these decisions have to be taken prior to going for teaching. At the nick of time if something fails or is not available the whole session of teaching may prove to be a waste of time and energy. The pre active phase of teaching provides ample opportunity to teachers, to think, to plan, to decide so as to escape frustration and disappointment.

4. Preparation of Auxiliary Material: - Successful teaching calls for the use of various kinds of supporting material. This has to he prepared by the teacher himself or to be processed from other sources. How it can be done is another problem for the teacher, which has to be solved before going into the class. He must prepare diagrams, charts, graphs etc if they are needed for teaching. If he needs the overhead projector, he should prepare the transparencies and must ensure the availability of .he overhead project or, must test whether it is in working order or not. If he is going to show some film he must make a rehearsal prior to taking it to the class.

5. Preparation of Evaluation Toots: - An essential aspect of teaching is evaluation of the teaching done. This part of the drama comes at the end of teaching. But the tools to he used for this purpose have to be prepared beforehand during the pre active phase of teaching. The questions that the teacher will like to put to the students in the class for testing whether they have understood or not should be prepared beforehand. At least the crucial questions should be necessarily listed down. If the teacher is going to administer some short objective type test, he must prepare it, get it cyclostyled or photocopied in enough numbers. But this whole job requires a serious thinking and has to be done during the pre active phase of teaching.

Thus during the preactive phase of teaching the teacher has to engage himself in a vigorous decision-making process pertaining to what ought to be taught, when it should be taught, what kinds of learning experiences are desirable, how these experiences should be carried out and so on. Besides, he has to ensure how facilities for teaching will be arranged.

B. INTERACTIVE PHASE

Teaching is sometimes defined as an interaction of the teacher with a group of students in a contrived setting. The school in the form of a classroom or a laboratory provides the setting. In ordinary language this is know as classroom teaching. This actual teaching in the classroom is the interactive phase of teaching or second phase of teaching, the first phase being the pre active phase as discussed earlier. During the preactive phase the teacher plans for the job and during the interactive phase he executes it. The execution in a way means achieving the predetermined goals, the learning and the development of the pupils in the class. It is the job like that of a craftsman who is given some material and is asked to give it a particular shape and for executing the desirable shape in the most appropriate manner. There are several requisite-, for achieving this. They are discussed in the following sections.

Motivating or Leading the Students :- This is the most important requisite of effective interaction. Interaction implies active involvement of the pupils and the teacher both. Student motivation provides power inputs to the system of instruction, which turns the wheels, and the system works. Without this power input the system cannot work. The teacher is the person who puts into the system this power input. Interaction can be effective when pupils are willing to interact Creating this willingness in the pupils is fundamental during this phase. Motivation is the key to this as motives energize the organism, direct the behavior towards a goal, select and emphasize the correct responses. It is a well-known fact that learning cannot take place without students being motivated. It is also a psychological fact that effectiveness of learning is in direct proportion to the motivation of the students. It is evident therefore that the real problem of the teacher during this phase is to establish strong motives in order to make student participate in learning experiences willingly and make classroom interaction lively and fruitful.

Modern psychology of learning emphasizes that a stimulus is effective for motivating students only in relation to the environment of which- it is a part including the learner and his past experience. A reward, for example, may be an excellent stimulus to some students while for others it may be quite meaningless. This is, generally, due to varying experiential background and acquired attitudes, interests, apperception of the learners this means that the teachers do not provide all sources of motives. Students come to the school with motives already at work. Hence, the teacher should try to discover what motives students already have which can be exploited for teaching a particular topic. It requires knowledge of student's background especially their interests, attitudes values and purposes. Brink (p. 67) defines motivation as the development within pupils of a genuine interest in and a favourable attitude towards the activities, which are to result in effective learning.

Motives have also been defined as basic drives, attitudes, values appreciations, needs, interests and habits. The teacher can capitalize on all of these for motivating the students to participate in learning experiences resulting from the classroom interactions. For this the teacher can profitably utilize following techniques and steps. But, it should be remembered that there can not be a set and standardized way of motivating the students. Some suggestions to this effect may be as follows:

1. Securing spontaneous attention of the pupils: This is the first step to be followed during interactive phase of teaching. Efforts on this should be made in the very beginning at the stage where students are prepared mentally and emotionally for participating in learning experiences of the classroom. This may be done in several ways such as establishing some kind of common purpose. A few questions may serve this purpose. Questions may challenge the students and may focus students attention on what is going to happen further. This may help students in organizing ideas around the questions and may better prepare them mentally and stimulate them emotionally. Besides something interesting in forceful and appealing language may be told to the students like a salesman who begins by presenting something interesting related to what he has to sell. Some interesting activity may be introduced with an attempt on capitalizing on the interesting activity may be introduced with an attempt on capitalizing on the basic drives of the pupils. Attractive pictures, specimens, slides, motion pictures, experiments, stories and the like may be utilized for arousing curiosity and provoking discussion. Sometimes it may work well to make a direct attack on the objectives ofteachil1g learning, try to establish a desire or purpose related to the work at hand. Some students already have a desire to attain the objectives. Students, thus prepared, will have completed half job of the interacting phase. But this is just the beginning of the interacting phase. A lot yet remains to be done.

2. Meaning the interest Throughout: The interest of the students has to be maintained throughout the period of classroom interaction. Although it pays to relate the interacting experiences to the motives, interests and to purposes of the pupils, it is not possible to do so in case of every learning need or objective.

Hence, new purposes, new motives and new interests have to be deliberately fostered in the pupils. All teaching material cannot be made interesting. There are things worth teaching but not of immediate interest to students. In such situations "persuasive talking and suggestion" like the forceful salesman bringing out the value and importance of the activity or the topic of teaching may help the teacher to a great extent. Discussion of their importance may create a desire in the students to learn about them. An appeal to the present ideals, appeal to the desire for social approval on the basis of good performance, use of intrinsic and extrinsic incentives, rewards and punishment (unless unavoidable), success and failure, praise and reproof, competition may all be utilized wherever found workable. Social reinforcement may also be effective in case of some pupils. Particular Attention should be paid to promoting a high morale in the class and orienting students towards worthwhile objectives.

3. Presentation of the Subject-Matter: - Interactive phase of teaching centers around the achievement of the goals of teaching. One of its determinants, motivating the students has already been discussed. Another important determinant of the same is the way the learning tasks and the subject matter arc presented in the class. Meaningfulness and sequential presentation encourage student's participation in the classroom interaction. Meaningful material is learned more quickly and is retained longer. Understanding the logic and principles underlying facts and concepts aid both learning and retention. For this purpose the material has to be organized and reorganized. Understanding should be emphasized and rote learning avoided as far as possible. New learning should be presented in a familiar context in relation to what the students know already. It should be related to the apperceptive mass of the students. The material should be presented in well- structured and orderly form. Each item of information should follow the previous one in a logical sequence. Using Asubel's Advance Organizers for weaving the knowledge and information into a compact structure may be useful and more meaningful. The best unit for learning is the most compact, structured and well integrated one. A few other points of significance may be (1) facts should be presented in varied contexts as this results into superior learning, (2) the material should be presented in small steps, (3) the language used should be simple and precise, (4) the teacher should proceed further only when it is ensured that the previous point or material has been understood.

4. Use of Appropriate Strategies: - Interactive phase is basically concerned with helping and enabling the students to learn. Just delivering a plain, straight lecture is not a sufficient guarantee that learning will take place. During this phase of teaching the fundamental task of the teacher is to make each and every student understand and learn desired things through all possible means techniques and strategies. Since there are varied kinds of objectives of teaching and all of them can not be achieved through one single strategy the teacher has to select and use the one which is most, relevant for achieving the particular objective. For teaching concepts, for teaching creative thinking and aesthetic appreciation, for teaching skills in dealing with people and for teaching values of life no one single method of teaching will serve the purpose. Similarly this is also not the correct viewpoint that for achieving one particular goal there has to be just one and only one particular strategy. A more reasonab1c viewpoint is that an objective can be achieved through several techniques and methods.

It is the insight and the wisdom of the teacher, which helps the teacher in identifying and using the most relevant and effective strategy.

There are various kinds of strategies developed and popularized such as the lecture. lecture-cum-discussion, seminar, discovery approach addition to a large number of instructional designs and models of teaching. The teacher may select and use the one, which in the given situation is the most relevant.

5. Use of Appropriate instructional Material: - Proper selection and use of instructional material goes a long way in motivating the students and making information and knowledge more meaningful. There are finds of them ranging from chalkboard to T.V. broadcasts; but a numerous preoccupation with the media- material is nit desirable. The attitude that "something must essentially be used" is not a correct way of looking at instructional material. What is essentially desirable is their selective and planned use.

6. Effective Communication: - Students do not expect teachers to be orators or actors. But they have a right to expect clear and effective communication. Effective communication depends very much on clarity of objectives that the teacher has in mind. Expression and language too contribute to it. A good background and understanding of the concepts involved is also needed. An urge within the teacher to help students really understand things always adds to the effectiveness of communication.

7. Managing the Feedback: - The term feedback has more than one connotation. It means sometimes knowledge of results, sometimes information feedback and sometimes reinforcement. The teacher can see scope for each of the ways feedback is understood. All unanimously accepts the importance of feedback in teaching- learning. Feedback may be intrinsic or extrinsic. While the teacher and the students are engaged in teaching learning experiences both intrinsic and extrinsic feedback may be used. If the student performance is up to the mark as desired this information must be immediately provided to him. Delayed feedback has no meaning to the student. Students who are attentive disciplined, active participants, alert and enthusiastic must be rewarded verbally or in other ways so that they may continue to be so. Feedback serves as a regulatory device of functions in performance and learning. Feedback is necessary for the teacher also.

He also needs to know how he is performing. This information he receives in the form of student's actions and answers. For that he has to make use of various types of questions at different stages. The answer given by the students may reveal whether his communication is clear or not, whether he has been able to explain clearly whether the students have understood the concept, whether the students are taking interest, whether they are feeling that they are benefited by teacher's work and son on. The teacher to identify the directions in which he is required to improve, to fill up the gaps, to remove the distortions, to devise new strategies if needed, may use this information. In fact effectiveness of teaching -learning is essentially a function of feedback control or feedback manipulation by the teacher.

C. POST ACTIVE PHASE

This is the last and the final phase of teaching. It is more formal stage involving tests, measurement and evaluation. The teacher judges the students on the adequacy of his ability to have done the job satisfactorily. Evaluation is an essential component of teaching learning. This answers the questions like (1) have the objectives of teaching been achieved (2) have the students acquired specified and desirable knowledge and skills, (3) has the teacher been successful and soon.

The teacher for this purpose, has to prepare evaluative devices. These devices differ depending upon the time and the purpose. If evaluation has to be done, in the class immediately after having finished teaching, evaluation may be done orally through a few key questions based on the most crucial aspects of the classroom teaching. It may be done by using a short objective type test too which should have been prepared during preactive phase. It may be done through some well thought -out assignments also. However, if evaluation is done after having completed full unit of the subject matter spread over several lectures of teaching sessions, the device of evaluation has to be a well prepared written short-answer or objective type test. Its reliability and validity must be considered important.

This should be remembered that evaluation has a definite purpose. It must inform the students and the teacher both about their performance. That is, it must tell the students how well they have learnt. It must also tell the teacher how efficiently he has performed his responsibility. Hence, it is essential that the results of the evaluation be made known to the students immediately after the testing is over. Delay in communication of this information will defeat the purpose.

Another important thing is that the results of evaluation should be used without fail for corrective action if need be. The test is not just for knowing who has done how well. A more important purpose of evaluation is to use the information for guidance of the students and removing the distortions and the deficiencies. If some students are found lagging behind they should be helped by resorting to essential remedial measures, Remedial teaching or remedial guidance can not be treated superfluous, unessential or not the part of the mainstream of teaching. It should be considered inseparably an unavoidable component of teaching.

Thus, teaching is a long continuous chain of activities to be performed by the teacher beginning with planning and preparation (pre active phase), mediated by motivation of students and meaningful presentation of learning material (interactive phase), terminating with the purposeful testing and evaluation for taking corrective and remedial actions (post interactive phase).

LEVELS OF TEACHING

What happens as a result of teacher's interaction with a group of students is difficult to list down. But, two outcomes are very well known (i) growth of knowledge and (ii) development of intellectual power of the students. The subject matter taught serves as the vehicle of child's mental development. The child acquires knowledge and simultaneously develops certain mental abilities. But, this kind of learning does not occur uniformly at the same level in case of all teachers teaching in the school. Depending upon the way the students are taught, learning takes place at different levels. This simply emphasizes the point, that there is an essential correspondence between the levels of learning and levels of teaching. Looking from this point of view there have been identified three levels of teaching resulting into three levels of learning. Interpreted in terms of cognitive functioning of the pupil teaching- learning situations as described by Bigge' (p. 315) may have a wide range varying from being "thoughtless" to "thoughtful" meaning thereby that in some cases teaching may be so factual that it does not evoke even the least thinking in the students while in. others it may be such as it stimulates the students to vigorous thinking. Development of thinking ability i.e., sharpening the intellect of the pupils is one of the imperative need of the individual student as well as that of the society. This is the function that education is enjoined to perform. Stuffing the student only with loads of knowledge is purposeless. Our schools by and large feel that their tasks have been completed if they by various means have enabled the students to amass knowledge of the subjects taught to them. But, if one considers development of all potentialities of child's personality, particularly his intellectual power of thinking and problem solving, this is only the very preliminary and insignificant aspect of teaching- learning. The process of learning thus broadly interpreted implies something more than the acquisition of facts and knowledge through mechanized procedures of drill and repetition. More important is development of such abilities as thinking, reasoning, problem- solving and creativity. But their development calls for more dynamic and imaginative method of teaching. The method of teaching greatly influences the kind of learning of the pupil. If subject matter is presented in a plan less fashion and students are required to memorize facts and to acquire knowledge without understanding things there will be little use of that for the individual and the society. Hence, if teaching has to be of any use pupils have to be afforded opportunity for broad interpretation and application leading to thinking and reasoning i.e. increased power of the mind. Teaching is and should be done at three levels. These levels are (1) memory level, (2) understanding level and (3) reflective level.

The activity called teaching learning is hierarchical in nature, the lowest level being the memory level and the highest being the reflective level. Most of the teaching-learning in our school begins and ends at the memory level only with the result that the students fail to develop their higher abilities of the mind, particularly understanding and problem-solving is presented as follows:

1. MEMORY LEVEL TEACHING-LEARNING

Bigge (p.316) describes this level of learning as "committing factual materials 10 memory". Teaching which emphasizes only this aspect of student learning is. therefore, termed memory level teaching. In other words .emphasis on rote learning characterizes memory level teaching. It is just acquision and retention of the learning material through mechanical procedures such as analysis, synthesis etc. anything can be learned in this way with practice' Even nonsense syllables can be learned in this way with practice. Rote learning is just forming the neural bonds or associations between the stimulus and response with no purpose or thought involved though this view is not accepted by the cognitive-field psychologists as they assume presence of some insight in all kinds of learning. Factual information is, by and large, acquired by way of memory level teaching learning. . Factual information includes facts, events, actual state of affairs, association of the names or level with the object or the event for which it stands. Concepts etc. as learning and memorization of these does not involve much of higher abilities or the mind. Even principles, generalizations and major understandings can be learned at this level. For example, just learning that for testing a research hypothesis (Hi) it has to be changed into null-hypothesis (Ho)" without realizing why it is so what relationship null-hypothesis has with the statistical theory of probability, how it relates to research hypothesis, etc is memory level learning. A teacher who only asks the students to learn and remember this much does only memory level teaching. This, memory-level teaching-l earning remains devoid of much of its meaning.

Memory level learning cannot be considered entirely useless or even of a degraded nature. Every school subject contains a lot of material which calls for memory level learning. It contributes to intelligent behavior also. Problem-solving and creative production involves a lot of memory of things and material acquired through rote memory. Even a thoughtless memory of many concepts helps in convergent and divergent thinking. This is also true that many students have wonderful capacity to memorize and they, generally, make good marks in the examinations,' although in situations requiring imagination and reflective thinking they may fail miserably. This has also been found that some very genius persons have very poor memory. This goes to prove that memory level learning and higher levels of learning are not exactly the same. They may be related in some ways but are riot identical.

Most teachers teach at this level only. Very few rise to the understanding level, which is a higher level of teaching learning. And hardly anyone reaches the reflective level. This is because memory level teaching is easiest while understanding level teaching requires the teacher to, himself have a good understanding of things to be taught. It requires' explaining things, relationships and understanding of principles which only those teachers can do who-themselves know all these. Since very few teachers are of that kind, it is only memory 1evel teac1 1ing learning, which by and large, goes on in our schools. From this it should not be gathered that memory-level teaching- learning should be totally avoided. Rather, it means that more useful and important are understanding and reflective level teaching while not many useful and durable results can be expected from memory- level teaching.

2. UNDERSTANDING LEVEL TEACIDNG-LEARNING

Bigge (p,315) holds that Memory level teaching-learning is most "thoughtless" and reflection-level most "thoughtful" He further says that teaching at understanding and reflective levels both results into the development of understandings or insights. He uses understanding and insight interchangeably. But reflective level teaching is a little more than that. Teaching at reflective level results into increased ability of the learner to achieve further understandings or insight independently in addition to understanding which is gained through teacher's efforts; It is necessary, in the first instance to examine what understanding level teaching means.

Meaning of Understanding Level Teaching: It has already been stated that if anything is committed to memory verbatim, it, by and large, involves meaningless material or meaningful material learned as meaningless. Just opposite to this understanding level teaching-learning is meaningful learning. Bigge (p.318-321) proposes three basic criteria of understanding level learning-(1) seeing relationships, (2) usability of learned material, and (3) seeing both relationships and tool use of the material learned.

Seeing relationships implies that the learner has come to know where the' learned material belongs, how it is related to other things, ideas and principles, what its cause or effect may be, etc. If he can explain the occurrence of an event or phenomenon in terms of the factors responsible for it bringing out its dynamic relationships to those factors, it may be said that he understands it. For example, if a student has learned a formula for computing the mean as AM + ∑fd I N x i and can explain what AM means and why it is added to the value of ∑fd IN, what ∑fd I N means, why' f is multiplied by 'd', what'd' means and why ∑fd is multiplied by i that is, the rationale underlying each of these components, it may be said that he understands the formula. If he has crammed the formula and can reproduce the same when asked and can also, solve a numerical problem by applying the formula without knowing the above rationale of each component, it is just memory level learning, not understanding. Thus, understanding means meaningful comprehension, a thorough grasp something with its "why" and "how" familiarity. One who understands something can explain, illustrate it, give examples, relate it to other things, describe its context, bring out its implications, and so on. Understanding results into generalization based on observation and experiences and generalizations can also be split into its individual elements if there is a clear understanding of the phenomenon. Seeing solitary facts in relation to a general principle is the essence of understanding" says Bigge (p.320),

Another criterion of understanding level learning as laid down by Bigge is the use of the learned material. He feels that if a person understands something he may be in a position to see what use that material can be put to or how that can be used for achieving a certain purpose, To him "purpose" is always involved in understanding meaning thereby that one wants to understand something for achieving some objective. This may not be a satisfactory criterion as even the use of learned material, in many cases, may be acquired through rote without an understanding of the same. A student can successfully use the meaninglessly learned formulae of mean or standard deviation to solve the numerical question based on them. Even the camera (the example given by Bigge) can be efficiently used for photography without understanding the functions of its various components. Of course, in certain situations use of learned material is possible only after a thorough understanding of the functions or relations of component units. For example, a watch repair cannot use his knowledge of watch repairing unless he understands the specific functions of every component part of the watch and their interrelationship. However, this is acceptable that understanding is more than just knowing what is what.

Understanding involves analysis, application, and synthesis of the various units of information or knowledge of things learned. It is deeper level grasp of things learned. Understanding is the prerequisite for solving problems a.-td creative expressions. Progress in all walks of life is largely dependent on understanding. Knowledge is incomplete without understanding.

3. REFLECTIVE LEVEL TEACHING-LEARNING

As defined by Bigge (p.324) "reflective level learning is careful, critical examination of an idea or supposed article of knowledge" and arriving at a new conclusion. This operation of human mind rests on a sound foundation of understanding of the said idea or piece of knowledge. Without a sound understanding "careful" and "critical examination is not possible. Thus, reflective level learning may be seen as an extension of understanding, a higher level of understanding. But, as seen by Bigge also in case of reflective level learning "search for understanding is pursued in a different fashion". Reflective- level teaching learning rises above and centers around. some problem, some felt difficulty, which stimulates the learner to explore the solution by tapping the whole of his accumulated knowledge. It is a high level thinking in new directions largely controlled by the learner's own appreciative mass or to use cognitive field theory construct, the life space of the learner. It must he noted that reflective level learning is related to understanding which provides a base for this and at the same time it is different from that in' this that reflective level learning calls for a " more active participation, more criticism of conventional thinking and more imagination and creativeness (Bigge, p.325). To use Guilford's language it may be seen as discovery or rediscovery or recognition" (Klausmeier and Goodwin,p.259). Reflective thinking seems to be very close to guilford is divergent thinking in which case new information is generated from known or remembered information and the learner thinks in different directions, sometimes searching, sometimes seeking variety. His convergent thinking may be equated to understanding level thinking. But divergent thinking definitely involves reflective level thinking, which by all psychologists, is considered as the apex of the hierarchy of learning. Reflective level learning, according to Helmholtz (Skinner, p.239), involves "penetration into the deeper relations and meanings of human experience." To Spearman (p.83), " it is a" creative act.

Teaching at reflective level requires to structure the learning situation in an entirely a different manner. To subject the students to the "tyranny of marks" and focus on teaching the prescribed curriculum and school examination only defeats stupefaction the intellectual vitality. In order to reflective thinking in the students the teacher has to structure the teaching-learning situation in such a way that students act of reflection, scrutiny, analysis, reasoning and imagination all can have a free play in that. Students should be provided opportunities to evaluate and critically examine the given experiences. Instead of preparing them to get high marks in the examinations, they should be provided with an opportunity to experience the thrill of being in the class. They should be made to think for themselves. Even if their responses and reactions are far removed from the reality they may he tolerated to be unique, different from the common ones. Dewey defines reflective thinking as "active, persistent and careful consideration of any belief or supposed form of knowledge in the light of the grounds that support it and further conclusions to which it trends". The student should be deliberately made to do this "careful consideration" in a planned manner. Discussion groups may serve to provide for this by evoking insight, inspiration and illumination in the students. To achieve vigorous mental growth it is necessary to experience deeply. Recall vividly and express candidly and clearly. The teaching-learning situation should be contrived close to achieving these objectives.

Model and. Strategies for Developing Reflective Thinking Several strategies and techniques of teaching may be helpful in developing reflective thinking in the students. Enquiry Model of Teaching, Group Discussions, Brain Storming, Synectic Model of Teaching, are specialized methods of teaching, which may be gainfully used, for achieving this purpose. Apart from these there are many important suggestions made by experts, which may be used. Klausmeier (p.278-288) has made following suggestions.

1. Present a problem before the students in a way that it generates thinking.
2. Make the students recoganize and focus on the problem to the
3. Assist students in finding information, which may solution of the problem.
4. Help students process information as solving a problem requires the application, analysis, stating and testing the hypotheses.
5. Encourage the students to state and test the hypotheses.
6. Encourage independent discovery and evaluation.
7. Encourage creativity in many media such as figural, symbolic, and semantic.
8. Foster divergent production such as fluency, originality, flexibility, etc.
9. Foster a creative personality, as creative persons tend to be emotionally sensitive, unconventional, independent and self-confident.
10. Encourage continuing creative expression, as creative abilities require a nurturing environment over a period of time.
11. Encourage productivity as creativity is manifested in objects Ideas,

compositions, and methods that are novel to the individual.

A few more suggestions may be as follows.

1. Establish responsive environment in which the pupils and the teachers are free to interact, in which pupils ask their own questions, seek answers they need in order to fill their conceptual gaps or deficiencies, in which pupils strive to understand father than arrive at the correct answer. In this setting pupils are not motivated by the examination marks and divisions; rather they are stimulated by the thrill of the experience and intrinsic satisfaction emerges from the active pursuit of real learning.

2. The lecture which is delivered should be followed by a series of provocative questions.

3. Present open-ended demonstration followed by pupil observation, explanations, theorization and testing of theories.

4. Use multi method approach involving a combination of a variety of methods and multisensory materials followed by better pupil adaptation of individual learning styles to process data.

Klausmeier discusses all these points in detail in the context of development of problem-solving ability and creativity, which involve reflective thinking. Dewey (p.6) considers reflective thinking as a conscious adjustment to a practical situation involving a felt need felt need of course, appears in the form of a problem. Skinner (p. 234) considers reflective thinking and creative thinking as "natural complements" He further holds that though there may be slight difference between "reflective thinking or problem-solving, and creative thinking' "it should not be imagined that one, is superior to, opposed to, or can be substituted for the other." These are perhaps, all related and reciprocal mental processes. To Johnson a spell of reflective thought has a definite beginning in the realization of the problem and the focusing of effort on that problem but once the wheels beginning to grind anything can happen in any sequence.

Constraints on Understanding and Reflective Level Teaching

Why are understanding and reflective level teaching rare commodities in our schools? There arc several factors that stand in the way of teachers' rising to these levels while teaching in the classrooms. The most pervasive constraint is the evaluation philosophy and the prevailing examination system. Emphasis on marks and grades force the teachers and the students to cover the course and cram the material. The essay type questions asked in the examinations require the students to reproduce the book matter. They do not tap understanding of principles and generalizations. Another constraint is that the teachers are required to cover the syllabus prescribed. If they use discussion method and other strategies conducive to developing understanding' or reflective thought, which are time-consuming, they will not be able to finish course. For fear of this, they fall back heavily on the memory level teaching emphasizing memorization of facts and other information. A third constraint is poor understanding of most of the teachers. They themselves do not understand the concepts, principles, problems and generalizations contained in the discipline to be taught. Hence, they cannot explain and create a strategy required for making pupils understand. They find it easier and more convenient to dictate notes or deliver straight jacket lecture and reproduce knowledge in the class as found in the books. Still another constraint is teachers' alienation and low morale which make them cut off the teaching profession and be indifferent to teaching and to the learners. Inadequate preparation for teaching which is a complex and specialized activity is also to some extent, responsible for this said affair. In order to put like in classroom teaching and make it vital enough so as to achieve the real goals of education, the whole systems of education needs to be renewed. But, a lot of reflective thinking is required to arrive at some concrete solution to this problem.

Relative Importance of Three Levels of Teaching: All the three levels of teaching-learning arc hierarchical in nature. For teaching at understanding level memory level teaching learning constitutes the base Understanding cannot take place in the vacuum. The solid bricks, which used in raising the structure of understanding, are provided by memory level teaching learning. Understanding cannot develop in the absence of facts and pieces of information acquired through memorization. Memory of numbers, number tables, spellings, dates, rules of grammar, sequence of events in history, statistics, etc. is essential for arguments, generalizations, deriving principles and developing major understandings which are the products of understanding. All conceptual thinking is built upon factual information. This, however should not be taken to mean that memory level teaching is most important or important alone. The point is that memory-level teaching-learning can not he ignored while at tide same time it should not be considered the beginning and the' end of teaching. Understanding level and reflective level teachings are equally important which at the moment are largely ignored for various reasons: They are important both from the point of view of the self actualization of the pupil and the progress of the society. Ninety percent of the inventions and breakthroughs underlying industrial and technical growth, socio-cultural progress and services available IS the result of peoples high level thinking and understanding.

PROGRAMMED INSTRUCTION

Skinner (1958) , Crowder (1958) and Pressey (1950, 1926) are generally credited for having introduced the theory and practice of programmed instruction first through the teaching machines and then, through programmed or scrambled books. Skinner made an outstanding contribution in this field. Programming refers to the arrangement of the stimulus material in the order of presentation, which will maximize the rate of acquisition of the behaviors to be learned. Proper programming results into the gradual shaping of the learner's responses from low to high levels of approximation of the desired responses. Pressey paid little attention to careful and systematic programming as he was interested only in developing testing devices. Skinner and Crowder took it more seriously and grove it a sound scientific base. Crowder, however, developed a program which was different from that one which was developed by Skinner. His program is known as branching program or extrinsic program. This program with several different branches would permit the learners to retrace his steps through that portion of the program that his' errors would indicate that he did not adequately learn. Crowder called Skinner's program as intrinsic program. Programmed learning is the change in the response or the behavior brought about through the use of materials built into a carefully organized sequential system. It refers to, specifically, the utilization of teaching machines, programmed texts and computers. B. F Skinner's small, inexpensive teaching machine of the 1950 involving the learners in active response through successive frames of very small steps in a straight-line sequence is perhaps the most promising advance in this field. In the beginning it were the machines through which the program material was presented. In a few years after that programmed textbooks incorporating the principles of original machines virtually replaced the teaching machines. Slides, films, pictures, diagrams and tape recordings complement the printed material. Programmed texts have gained acceptance over teaching machines because of their financial economy and greater flexibility. It appears that much of the programmed learning in future will emanate front computer-assisted instruction.

Origin of programming: The origin of programmed instruction is linked with the psychology of learning. Most people give credit to Sidney L. Pressey a psychologist working, at Ohio State University for developing in the 1920s a machine which could teach as well as test. After Pressey B. F skinner and James

G. Hollond the Harward psychologists devised their auto- instructional techniques around 194 Skinner and his collegues used programming technique for teaching a pigeon to play a modified game of ping-pong and learn social behaviors such as 'Competition' and cooperation (Smith & Moore, p. 20-21). It is claimed that this modest beginning of shaping behavior in a laboratory experiment brought programmed instruction as a teaching-learning device in the field of education. In 1955 Norman, A Crowder suggested a modification in the use of Prĕssey type teaching machine. He termed it "automatic tutoring by intrinsic programming. Since these developments took place, the concept of programmed' learning or programmed instruction has been constantly gaining popularity and broadening its scope. Susan Markle (1967) gave a wider definition of programmed learning.

She said that it is a method of designing reproducible sequence of instructional events to produce a measurable and consistent effect on the behavior of each and every acceptable student" (p. 104).

'Types of Programs: There have been mainly three approaches to the preparation of programs: (i) Linear Programming and (ii) Branching Programming (iii) Adjunct Programming.

1. Linear Program

Linear programming is associated with B. E Skinner'. This is also known as Intrinsic Programming. Branching programming is associated with Crowder. This is also known as Extrinsic Programming These are also called, sometimes, scrambled programs or scrambled books. There are other variants of these basic types of programmes.

The linear program is one in which the student is allowed to cover one frame at a time, responding to each one by one, getting feedback and going on, in a straight-line fashion. Every learner goes through the same series of tasks. It is based on Skinner's operant conditioning theory of learning. It is an arrangement of "contingencies of reinforcement", which means the relations which prevail between behavior on the one hand and the consequences of that behavior on the other. In this kind of program the behavioral consequences called "reinforcements" are so arranged that they shape up the behavior of an organism almost as desired. Also, it enables to maintain behavior in desired states of strength for long periods of time. Principles of learning which underlie these programs have been summarized by Skinner (1954) and Gilbert (1958). These arc: (1) Learning takes place most rapidly if the student is actively engaged with the subject matter (2) learning is most effective if the student develops the skills and - knowledge in a fom1 which will readily generalize to the real 1ife. (3) Learning takes place most rapidly, if immediate knowledge of results is given for each response. (4) Learning takes place most rapidly if the subject matter is organized in a hierarchical form, and (5) Receiving frequent "knowledge of results" keeps students working at the assigned task.

2. Branching Program

Branching programs of Crowder have points at which the student is told to skip over certain tasks if he has already mastered them. If he has a difficulty he is asked to go through a few other tasks. This is a simple type of branching program. Other programs of this kind present a few sentences or a paragraph and then ask the student to answer a multiple-choice question.' After each possible choice there is a page number to which the student refers if he checks that number. Some of these pages, i.e., those referred to in a wrong answer may say something like "no you are wrong. Go back and make another selection." In this way the student goes through the program and completes it.

The branching program is different from linear program. Branching program assumes that errors are bound to occur during learning. Hence it is necessary for any program to clarify or remove these difficulties before the student moves further through the pr gram. The learner in this program, is presented with a multiple choice type question" The correct response allows him to move on through the program while an incorrect response directs him to appropriate material to clear up his misunderstanding or the error. He goes to a branch of the main programme, studies this additional material and having understood that returns to the original question where he was stuck up and then moves further. Thus, errorless learning (a principle of Skinner's linear program) is not at all considered relevant in branching program. The questions in branching program have a diagnostic function. Crowder has developed the scrambled text to implement this view. The student is directed to move to different pages of the book depending upon the response he chooses. Much information is presented without asking the student for a response. Branching program, no doubt, is different from the linear program in its format and presentation of the material; yet, there are several points common to both. But linear programs are much more popular than the branching programs the reason being that they are easier to construct.

3. Mathetics

The third type of program is the Adjunct Program of Pressey who is often credited with devising the first teaching machine in the 1920s Pressey is opposed to applying principles of animal- learning to human learning. He considers programming only of secondary importance to used as a supplementary device as an adjunct or facilitating material. "He proposes that material should be presented to the learner in the same way as it is done in the textbooks and then, multiple-choice items should follow along with answers. One important feature of Pressey's Adjunct Program is that it may be based on presentation of an advance organizer or a topical outline or some other classification with the result that the student is helped to see through the structure of knowledge by more readily perceiving the relationships among parts. It may be used for various purposes such as making the student relearn the material, review it, revise it and evaluate his knowledge and understanding. Structure or knowledge is preserved in this kind of a program which is not possible in case of linear program.

DEVELOPMENT OF PROGRAMS

Program' development involves three stages. These are.

1 Preparation of the Program

2. Actual Writing of the Program

3. Try-out and Revision of the Program.

1. Preparation of the Program

There arc five steps involved in the preparation of a program as follows.

1. Selecting a unit or topic which forms the basis of the program.

2. Preparing a content outline of the topic selected.

3. Define objectives in behavioral terms.

4. Constructing a test of entering behavior.

5. Construction, a test of terminal behavior.

1. Selecting a Unit or Topic: Lysaught and Williams (1963) have given five criteria for the selection of a topic of programmed instruction. These are:

1. Selecting the subject matter from one's own field of study, i.e., with which the program-writer is thoroughly familiar.

2. Length of the unit, i.e. restricting to a very small area of the subject matter.

3 Selecting a subject matter that is easy to program. e.g. it is easy to develop a program in mathematics than on a topic in psychology.

4. Logical order of material, i. e., the subject matter of the topic or the unit should have a logical order.

5. The exclusiveness of special needs of students

2. Preparing a Content Outline: This means specifying the subject matter that should be covered b the program to be developed. This outline is generally derived from a number or sources such as textbooks, reference sources, teachers teaching that subject, and so on. Consultation with the subject expert may also help.

3. Define the Objectives: The importance and ways of identifying and stating the objectives in behavioral terms have been discussed in a separate chapter. It is sufficient to point out here that this involves two operations: (a) task description, and (b) task analysis. Task description means description of the to terminal behaviour, and task analysis means component behaviors leading the learner to the terminal behavior. Most often these behaviors represent criterion behaviors.

4. Construction Entering Behaviour Test: This test is meant for knowing whether the students for whom the program is being constructed have the requisite behaviors without which they cannot answer the questions of the program. These behaviors form the basis of constructing the test of entering behaviors. This test reveals what the students already know and from where one must start in order to prepare the program. If the group of students for whom the program is being developed shows sufficient unifonl1ity and homogeneity in entering behaviors, the linear program may be quite suitable. But if a great .diversity is revealed, then it is the branching program, which may serve the purpose better.

5. Constructing Terminal Behavior Test: This is based on the objectives which: have' already been defined in behavioral terms. This is used for measuring the final performance of the students, i.e., outcome-of program learning. Care has to be taken that the test items cover all aspects of the material learnt. The items should be arranged in the test in an scrambled manner and should not follow the same, order in which entering behaviors are listed. The test-construction procedure follows the same procedure, which underlies the construction of objective test in general.

3. PROGRAM WRITING

Following five steps are involved in preparing the actual program:

1. Writing the frames.
2. Requiring Active Responding.
3. Providing for Confirmation or Correcting Responses
4. Using Prompts to Guide Students' Responses.
5. Providing Careful Sequencing of the Frames.

1. Writing the Frames: As defined by Taber and his associates (1965) A frame is a small segment of subject matter which calls forth particular student responses". The purpose is to elicit student responses which gradually lead to the terminal behavior. The frame is so constructed that it evokes a desired response.

The frame consists of four essential parts: (1) the stimulus and stimulus context, (2) the cues or prompts, (3) the response, and (4) enrichment material.

The stimulus and the stimulus context serve to elicit the desired response. It presents the information in response to which the learner makes a response. This includes the words or information with which the learner is familiar. They may be words that precede or follow the blank in the frame. The blank is the space left for the response of the learner. Also, they may, sometimes, be word-patterns, rhyming or synonyms, etc. which are already in the repertoire of the learner. Important, in this regard is that the context should be relevant meaning, thereby, that the context should be capable of evoking the desired response at sometimes in future.

Appropriate cuing is another important characteristic of a good frame. Effort is made to ensure that every student gets every response correct. Proper cuing helps in this matter. This cuing or prompting is used only to introduce the new stimulus material and is gradually withdrawn when the student behavior comes under the control of the new subject matter. A good frame is one which uses cues precisely containing only necessary words which can reliably produce the desired response. Neither "over cuing" nor "under cuing" is desirable. Hence, the programmer should not provide more cues than necessary.

The making of student's response to the prompts should be ensured while writing the frames. The student learns by doing, not by hearing or seeing. 'Active responding" by the learner is the first principle of programming. Overt, recorded responses are preferable as in that case enough data are made available which can be used for further revision of the program. De Cecco and Crawford (p. 373) hold that the stimulus material of the frame and the response, which the student makes to the stimulus material, constitute an S-R relationship.

Enrichment material of the frame is not the essential part of the frame. It is auxiliary or supplementary material, which makes the frame interesting, readable and understandable. If considered essential in a frame this part should be relevant precise and compact.

2. Requiring Active Responding: Response to be made by the learner is an essential part of the frame. While writing the frame the rule of "critical response" formulated by Margulies (1964) should be followed. It simply means that the frame should not contain unnecessary words or information. It should contain only the material to which the student has to respond correctly. By analyzing the terminal behavior in sufficient detail the programmer can clearly find out the critical responses the student should make. It is the important part of the subject matter such as understanding the key words, new illustrations, etc. which determine [he responses in the frames. The location of the response in the frame is also important in this connection. It should be as close to the end of the frame as possible. Overt responding is a practical necessity. At least in the initial development of the program.

3. Providing For Confirmation or Correction of Student Responses: This is done by providing the correct response with which the student compares his own response. If the student finds after comparison that his response is correct, he lets confirmation. When it is found to be incorrect, he receives correction: This should be done immediately as it is a source of feedback resulting into motivation to learn.

4. Using Prompts: Prompts are cues used to guide the student to the correct response. They themselves are not sufficient to produce the response; but help the learner in constructing or selecting the correct response. For example, study the following frames.

1. The capital of India is ____________
2. The capital of India is-----------New Delhi.
3. The capital of India is New....New Delhi.

The frame no. 1 is unprompted, frame no.2 and 3 are prompted frames. In frame no. 2 the number of dashes and in number 3 the word New serve as, prompts for eliciting the correct response. Prompts serve two purposes: (i) they guide the student to the correct response; and (ii) they prevent the student from making unnecessary errors. Copying frame is not considered a prompting frame although it may be used sometimes. But, they should not be overused. Margulies (1964) suggests ways and means of improving the copying frame. A careful use of such frames may help avoid its disadvantages. It is important that gradually the use of prompts should be withdrawn and the student should be able to achieve the terminal behaviour without the prompts. This is known as the process of vanishing or fading of the prompts or the cues.

5. Sequencing of the Frames: When all the frames have been written out they have to be assembled together to make an integrated whole. The most, important aspect of this is the way they are put together, i.e., their sequence in the program. Two factors determine this sequencing of the frames. (i) description and analysis of the behaviors to be learned, and (ii) learning conditions of various tasks.

Depending upon the type of the programs, there are two kinds of sequencing of frames- (i) Linear and, (ii) branching. Linear sequencing is associated with Skinner while Crowder introduced branching sequencing.

Linear Sequencing: In case of linear program the frames are arranged in a single line one after the other and each student has to read and respond to each of these frames in the same way starting from frame one to the last one moving in a straight line. The frames, by and large, use constructed responses. But, it is not essential. Constructed and multiple-choice responses both can be used. Use of shorter frames is a general principle. But, it is not essential. If necessary longer frames, even as long as a paragraph may be used. Even the rule of single path may be modified, and multi- path programs can be prepared. Still another variation of linear sequence is to include, sometimes, the criterion frames also.

Branching Sequencing: In this kind of a program there are several paths open to the students. After having responded to a frame, where the student will go depends on, what his response has been. If his-response is correct he goes to the next frame and moves on in a straight line as long as he gives correct responses. But, if his response is incorrect then he goes to study the group of frames (a branch of the program) indicated by his response.' As said by DeCecco and Crawford (p.387) "The errors branch him to supplementary material designed to give him remedial instruction". In "this kind of a program the frames are much-longer like paragraphs. Each frame -is followed' by three alternative multiple choice items or responses. 'I 'he student selects, one of these responses: which indicates a page number and the student, then, goes' to that page.

Pressey's Adjunct Auto-instruction: Pressey dose not support the idea that in order to teach the material should be broken into numerous small size pieces. He considered small-step frames 'arrangement a waste of time. He thinks that the conventional instructional material can be used for teaching more effectively if it is supplemented by an objective testing device. He suggests that the material to be taught should be well organized with concepts and understandings placed in a hierarchical order which can be read by the student in a shorter time. This must be, then followed by a. test having multiple-choice type questions. This procedure he called adjunct auto instruction These auto instructional items or questions may be placed at the end of the chapter of a book also 6 r there may be clusters of them inselied within the chapters at suitable places, where and when they are needed. This program is in a way an "integration of testing and teaching into one episode. It is a device, which at once informs the student about the correctness of his answer to a question. This, as Pressey claims, not only tests him but more than that "it also teaches him", He also claims that self-instructional objective test covers more ground of the subject matters than would be possible otherwise. Thus, instead of having small-size frames in the program Pressey prefers to have a "self instructional tests", which can be used systematically as an integral part of the teaching method resulting into an improved understanding of the topic or the material as a whole. Pressey (Smith & Moore p. l48) says "In short" human engineering" can aid educational and training programs by test teach- devices of various types".

3. TRYOUT AND EVALUATION

This is the third stage of program development It has three steps.

1. Preparing the preliminary or original draft.
2. Editing the draft.
3. Tryout and revision of the draft.

1. Original Draft: This is the write-up of all the frames put together in a desired sequence hand-written or mimeographed. This is, then, administered to 5 to 10 students to find out where the students face difficulties and how they can be removed. I\t this-stage the programmer works very closely with each student and revises the frames or- frame sequence if so revealed by student experience. Then, after making necessary changes, if required, whole program is rewritten or cydostyled This is the original draft.

2. Editing the Draft: The draft program or the original drift of the program is edited three times (Klaus, in Smith & Moore, p. 95). Another programmer does the first editing. The technical expert who reviews the frames to ensure their technical accuracy does the second. A third editing is done by someone skilled in writing who can make the draft and its frames more interesting and enjoyable with good and appealing language. Markle (1964) has prepared a checklist of points to be taken into consideration while editing the draft. In brief some of these points are reproduced by. DeCecco and Crawford (pp. 385, 86) as follows: 0) good

English, (2) correctness of content, (3) relevance of student's response to purpose" (4) feasibility of alternatives of multiple-choice questions, (5) sufficiency of frame context, (6) no more points in one frame than the studro can respond, (7) No irrelevant material (8) liberal use of thematic is prompts and sparing use of formal prompts, and so on.

3. Tryout and Revision: The edited program now, is ready for tryout on a larger sample. This thus- edited program is called by Peter Pipe 0966) as the fledgling (raw, incomplete) program. Hence, this is then, put to tryout and revision for final use. The program,' at this stage, is administered to about 15 to 40 or more students. Larger the number, still better. The students should work on the programme independently without any prompting, guiding or helping by the "programmer. The programmer should note down the difficulties faced by the students and also their reactions to the frames, errors committed by them, any question asked by them, etc. At the end the students. should be given the test of terminal behaviour. Any frame remaining un-attempted should also be noted. High rate of error on any frame or a section of the program should also be noted Students comments may also be invited. On the basis of information revealed in this way the program should be finally revised. Ten percent error rate is tolerable. Generally four types of analysis are done after field testing: (1) Finding error rate, i.e.. percentage of incorrect responses on a frame, or a set of frames or the whole program (Susan Markle, 1964, p. 301), (2) program density, i.e., the extent or degree to which the material is weighted or repeated in the forms which may be of independent or cumulative type, (3) sequence progression, and (4) 90/90 criterion, i.e., 90 percent student getting 90 percent of the material or score of 90 percent or better by 90 percent of the students on the final criterion test These standards should be ensured by the finally prepared program after tryout and revision.

PRINCIPLES OF PROGRAMMED INSTRUCTION

Following are the principles of the construction of programmes. These have already been explained in the foregoing sections. These are.

1. Principle of Small Steps.
2. Principle of Active Responding
3. Principle of Immediate Confirmation.
4. Principle of Self-pacing.
5. Principle of Student Testing
6. Principle of Proper Cuing
7. Principle of Appropriate Context.
8. Principle of Frequent Repetition.

These principle or rules have been explained by Klaus (pp. 99- 107) A few don'ts are also suggested by him (pp. 102- 106). These are:

1. Don't lecture, but teach, i.e., frames should be short, not the paragraphs.
2. A void i6-elevant responses
3. Do not provide more cues than necessary
4. Do not assume too much knowledge, i.e., do not have too many facts within a single frame.
5. Do not present two new facts in one frame.

All these rules and principles have been explained already in the foregoing sections.

Principle of small steps. It is shown by experiments that even the dullest students can learn as effectively as the brightest students if the subject matter is presented to them in suitable small steps. When we divide the task to be learnt into very small steps, and ask the students to learn only one step at a time, then probably, all the students will be able to learn one small step at a time and sequentially learn all the steps. It is a difficult task to climb a mountain but once steps are built even a child can climb the mountain very easily. This is known as the 'Principle of small steps'. Principle activity responding. The second psychological principle is that the students learn better and faster when the are actively participating in the teaching-learning process. In our classroom teaching the teachers do ask a few questions and the students respond. But it is not possible for the teachers to ask all the students to respond at each small step. A teaching machine text or a programmed text contains a large number of questions-one question at each small step and the students respond actively. The principle of active responding is used for the programmes. The teaching machines and programmes have proved to be superior because they provide opportunity to every learner to respond at every small step.

Principle of reinforcement. Every response even approximately correct must be reinforced immediately. Delayed reinforcement fails to work. This is possible only when a teacher has to teach only one student at a time. The most ideal situation is when the teacher can cater to the needs of his students individually. But in classroom teaching this is hardly possible. No teacher, however efficient and sincere he may be, can reinforce each correct. response of each of his students as soon as it is made in a classroom situation where he has to teach about 40/50 students. The teaching machines and the programmes do the job more efl iciently.

Principle of self-pacing. The programmed instruction is based on the basic assumption that learning take place effectively if the learner is allowed to learn at his own pace. Therefore, a good programme of the material always takes care of the principle of self-pacing. A learner moves from one frame to another according to his own speed of learning.

Principle of student-evaluation or student testing. Continuous evaluation of the student and the learning process leads to better teaching-learning. In the programmed instruction, the learner has to leave the record of his response because he is required to write a response for each frame on response sheet. This detailed record hc1ps in revising the programme.

Prof. Edward F.G. classifies principles of programmed instruction in two broad categories:

Mandatory And Optional Principles.

Mandatory Principles. These include:

1. Principle of objective specification
2. Principle of empirical testing

It includes: (a) Individual try-out (b) Small group try-out (c) Field try-out

3. Self-pacing

Optional Principles

1. Ovel1 responding
2. Immediate feedback
3. Small step size.

RULE VOR THE ART OF PROGRAMMING

I. Klaus has summed up 12 rules of the art of programming and building instructional frames:

1. Active responding. A learner learns from making a response and not from hearing or seeing it.
2. Proper context. The provision of proper cueing is the main difference between a test question and an auto instructional frame.
3. Appropriate context. This is the kind of stimuli that will be capable of evoking the desired response at some time in future.

4. Small steps. It is very desirable that there should be as any small steps as possible.
5. Sequence of topics. The topics of the subject-matter should be carefully sequenced so as to provide adequate motivation.
6. Frequent repetition. Cues associated should be changed and frequent repetition provided in frames.
7. Knowledge of subject-matter and technical accuracy. A sound knowledge of these is very necessary for preparing a suitable and effective programme.
8. Lecturing to be avoided. The learner should be helped to learn and this is possible in case we provide facts to the learner.
9. Evoking a relative response. Right kind of illustration should be used for evoking a response.
10. Providing cues in adequate number. Excess of cues will prevent the learner from making his own generalization and discovering principles.
11. Not assuming too much knowledge. The programmer should not assume too much knowledge on the part of the learner.
12. Presenting of facts in frames. Only one fact should be presented in one frame.

Effects Of Programmed Learning On The Teaching Process

1. Tutorial experiences are provided for individual learners on a large scale whereby the learner may proceed at his own rate.

2. Programmed instruction can exercise control on homework and individual study.

3. Programmed instruction can enable the learner to catch up the loss of absence from school.

4. Programmed instruction provides a technological solution to the problem of individual differences. Programmed instructional materials enable the teacher to gear up his presentation to what he senses is the average, too slow for the bright

student and too fast for the slow one.

5. The availability of instructional material of a programme and its powerful tools make the teacher much more a professional man than he now is.

6. By interpreting the feedback obtained through oral questions and discussions in the class, the teacher can intelligently vary the flow of information or further instruction.

7. A basic feature of teaching machines is immediate knowledge of results followed by immediate correction of errors and rewards for correct answers. It has been established by research that more frequent the rewards, the better the learner assimilates the material.

8. It eliminates cheating because the learner has to gain nothing by it.

9. The students like the use of machines than studying a textbook.

10. It eliminates the influence of teacher variable in research.

11. Immediate scoring promotes the learning process.

12. The technique is valuable in giving tests which can automatically be scored.

Professor John. Blyth and John Jacobson describe the following uses of a programmmg:

1. No class time is wasted on drill.

2. Examination of student's work on the programme can enable us to prepare for a class period with prior knowledge of the points that is needed for further clarification.

3. No time is wasted to locate and correct misconceptions the students may have through unchecked practices.

4. Classroom efficiency may increase by about 30 per cent. More material can be covered in less time.

5. Individual differences may be reduced to a considerable extent.

6. Difficulties of the students can be easily diagnosed.

7. Individual and class differences can be easily located.

8. There can be a great increase in interest and improvement in morals.

MERITS AND ADVANTAGES OF PROGRAMMED LEARNING

Programmed learning is considered to be a more efficient method of teaching learning. Its superiority is well established over the traditional. methods of teaching learning, It is increasingly being used in the advanced countries of the world. It is realized that the programmed instruction has potentialities to revolutionise the theory and practice of teaching. Following are the main merits of programmed learning.

1. A well-programmed instruction is a great thrust in the direction of individualised instruction, as it is tailed to the needs of the individual learner in the class.

2. It permits individual learner to progress at his own speed. An intelligent learner needs no longer to be bored or allowed to lose interest on account of his slow progress of other learners of the class. He can make progress, as he is able.

3. Since a programme requires continuous response from the learner, it overcomes the inertia and passivity on the part of the learner.

4. The teacher can give explanation in the classroom if the error is common or he may arrange individual conferences on specific points.

5. A well-programmed instruction is a great thrust in the direction of individualised instruction-as it is, tailored. to cater -to the, needs of the individual students of the class.

6. Learning material in a programmed instruction is presented in such a way that learning becomes an interesting game and the learner is motivated to meet the challenges set by his own capabilities.

7. Programmes are developed by experts. They are empirically tested and modified till they are standardised. A number of learners can use a single good programme 'and thus save textbooks.

8. In programmed instruction the learner is immediately reinforced to correct his response and this reinforcement sustains the motivation of the learner.

9. The self-instructional technique presents material in which its complexity is simplified through the analysis of the subject- matter into small and more easily assimilated segments of information.

10. The introduction of programmed instruction is of great significance for developing countries which are set on the path of educating millions of learners and are short of teachers.

11. Good teachers are freed from the boredom of routine classroom teaching and they are in a position to devote more time to more creative activities.

12. The progrmmned instruction has been used more successfully in teaching the discernment of the logic of various disciplines and inspiring students to creative thinking and judgment.

13. Certain motor skills and intellectual abilities normally taught by frequent drills and rote self-instructional devices could very efficiently teach memorization.

14. Self-instructional materials have been found to be very useful in the West in revolutionising the social setting of the classroom. Problems of discipline have been solved and a new hope for eliminating emotional and social problems has been generated.

15. Programmed instruction enables the teacher to diagnose the problems of the individual learner.

16. The introduction of programmed instruction is very helpful in certain situations where human instructors are not easily available in the required number, for instance small schools in the isolated or hill areas.

LIMITATIONS OF PROGRAMMED MATERIALS

Programmed materials have been severely, criticised as a threat to replacing the -teacher.

It is also argued that there is too much emphasis in learning facts and very little emphasis on the mastery of principles and concepts:

Some critics of programmed instruction maintain that the user of a programme does not know where he is headed to.

They also, point out that the learners are not aware of the organisation and programmed instruction is unrelated to other aspects of instruction.

It is also argued that the programmed instruction material is very costly and only rich nations can afford it.

It is also stated that the development and use of programmed instructional material require expert knowledge and training. An average teacher finds it very difficult to make use of this device.

THEOH.Y OF PROGRAMMED LEARNING

It is true that Sidney Pressy had actually designed several self-testing devices in the 1920' s but it was Professor Skinner who in his famous article "Science of Learning and Art of Teaching" published in 1945, pleaded for the application of knowledge derived from behavioural psychology to classroom procedures and suggested automated teaching devices as a means of doing so. He emphasized that to acquire or learn behaviour a students attention but, more important, the attention of students should actually be directed to what the teacher wants them to learn. Reinforcement, i.e., the knowledge of the correctness of the learning behaviour, must be immediate and frequent; the knowledge that student is right is sufficient reinforcement to encourage him to learn more. Professor Skinner also pointed out that "holding students together for instructional purpose in a class is probably the greatest source of inefficiency in education." In his view, if certain behaviour is expected of a student after the learning experience, he must be encouraged to perform in that manner during the learning session itself. A student learns better and is motivated to learn more if the step taken by him is confirmed to be correct, that is to say if the learnt behaviour has been reinforced. It is easier to learn one step at a time. If the behaviour to be learnt is analyzed into parts which arc properly' spaced and arranged in logical sequence, it would be easier to learn the whole desired behaviour by learning one step at a time. There should be few errors in the learning process so that the student practices correct responses and these responses are reinforced immediately by the knowledge of results so that he makes closer approximation to the responses which are desired outcomes.

CAN PROGRAMMED LEARNING REPLACE THE TEACHER?

Programme learning cannot replace the teacher. Any innovation in the school programmes and practices must remain in the hands of the teachers. The radio and T.V. did not displace the teacher. Similar is the case with programmed instruction. It is upto the enlightened teachers to take up the challenging task of preparing programmes. We have got a wide market. The programmes can be sold all over the country. A student who is convinced that he can learn better, achieve more with the help of this prgramme, will definitely prefer instead of buy this programme to buying a text-book. By taking up this challenging task we will not only help the cause of education, help our fellow teachers by setting them free from the routine task of information, giving help to the students to achieve more but we will be helping ourselves also.

It may also be remembered' that these gadgets can be used by in the cognitive field and possibly in the psychomotor field to develop certain abilities and ski] Is of the student as an individual. A teacher is something more than all these gadgets put together. Be has to bring about socialization of the individual- he has to promote socially desirable attitudes and interests and mould the personality of the students. The effective domain is almost reserved for his care. At present the teacher is not able to devote his energy and time to this important task as most of his time and energy is consumed by his routine job as an information giver we always talk of education for three 'H's'-the head, the hand and the heart. But it has almost remained a mere slogan. Programmed learning, teaching machines and other gadgets will set teacher free from routine work. These are labour saving devices for the teacher so that be may function more effectively in a field of his own choice.

Technique involved in programmed instruction can be used in teaching different subjects Teaching of mathematics, science, social studies and elements of Indian languages can' be done effectively with the help of this new technique. The teacher has to formulate objectives of teaching a particular subject, undertake content analysis of the subject matter in the light of objectives, frame a chain of question which will lead the pupils in the direction of he objective and present the questions to his pupils who are expected to try their hand at answering the questions independently. The teacher will. Have to play the role of a friend, guide and philosopher in the class when the p pits are engaged in solving the riddle and at the same time acquiring knowledge or skill. The question of class discipline may not arise as the pupils will be found busy doing the task assigned to them by the teacher. The teacher will have to do remedial or corrective teaching as the weakness of his pupils will be located in the very act of learning. The pupil wil1 also undergo a process of self-evaluation as he completes his work.

Role of the teacher in the changed context of Programmed Learning may be stated as under:

1. Teacher as an adviser in helping students in the selection of programme learning material.

2. Teacher as a discussion leader for focusing the attention: of the learners on important points.

3. Teacher as a guide to clarity doubts and elaborate on various points asked by the learner.

4. Teacher as an evaluator of the learning outcomes.

5. Teacher as a consultant to the various agencies engaged in production of programmed material.

Programmed Learning Approach In Normal Class-Room Teaching

The programmed learning approach can be adopted in normal class- room teaching in the following ways:

1. A teacher can make use of the principles of programmed learning such as active responding, minimal errors and confirmation while teaching various subjects in the conventional manner.

2. A teacher can define behavioural objectives in advance of teaching.

3. A teacher can validate the instructional systems of a class in terms of the performance of learners immediately after teaching is over.

4. A teacher can regulate questions and answers. The answer of a learner can be immediately reinforced by informing or telling whether it is correct or incorrect

5. A teacher can plan the entire instructional progrmmne of a class-room and can treat the terminal behaviour, the pre- requisite skills and content analysis in advance.

Komoski (1969) an expert has observed "Two thousand years ago the world's first public administrator, a gentleman by the name Quintilian wrote what might be called a handbook for teachers." In it he has one bit of advice which will serve as an excellent starting point-: for a -discussion of programmed learning and its potential uses.- His advice is: "Do not neglect the individual student. He should be questioned and praised."

Application of Programmed Instruction In India

Programmed instruction is still in its infancy in India. Programmed instruction as an optional or elective paper has been included at the B.Ed./M.Ed. evel in a few universities in India. It also form a part of the paper of Educational Technology/Educational Innovation. However, as regards its classroom use, it may be observed that it is almost nil. As far back as in 1966, the Kothari Commission suggested to develop programmed material in different subjects to test the suitability of the' technique in Indian conditions. An Association of Programmed Instruction has been formed to coordinate the research being done at different centres ill the country. The association also disseminates the information on new studies through its journal issued from time to time. The National Council of Educational Research and Technology has also done some work in. the field. In spite of allthese efforts, it may be stated that the application of progrmmned instruction has not yet made an appreciable impact' on our classroom teaching. Our methods of teaching still remain traditional, by and large.

Following are the important factors which stand in the way of introducing programmed instruction in Indian schools:

1. Resistance to change.
2. Lack of good programmes and progrmmners.
3. Lack of facilities

TYPES OF PROGRAMMING

As a result of experimental studies and research, following types of progrmmned instruction have emerged.

1. Linear or Extrinsic Programming.
2. Branching or Intrinsic Programming.
3. Mathetics Programming.
4. Rules System of Programming.
5. Computer Assisted Instruction.
6. Learner Controlled Instruction.

The first three styles-linear, branching and mathetics are the basic formats. The rules system represents the deductive and inductive approach to teaching. The other two types, Computer Assisted Instruction i (CAI) and Learner Controlled instruction (LCI) are not the basic format of Programming. They are, infact, the ways and means of providing instruction. Here we have taken up only the basic' type of progrmmning.'

LINEAR PROGRAMMING

B.F. Skinner is the originator of linear programming. It is also called a single-track programme. According to Skinner, a creature, a bird or a human being can be led to a desired behaviour by means of a carefully constructed programme consisting of small steps leading logically through the subject- matter from topic to topic, provided each-step is reinforced by some kind of favourable experience or reward: The increments in information which the learner is expected to absorb are small. The favourable experience, or response increases the probability of the same response to occur again in the future. The process of rewarding the correct response to a stimulus increases the general tendency to give' a response.

The process may be graphically illustrated as under:

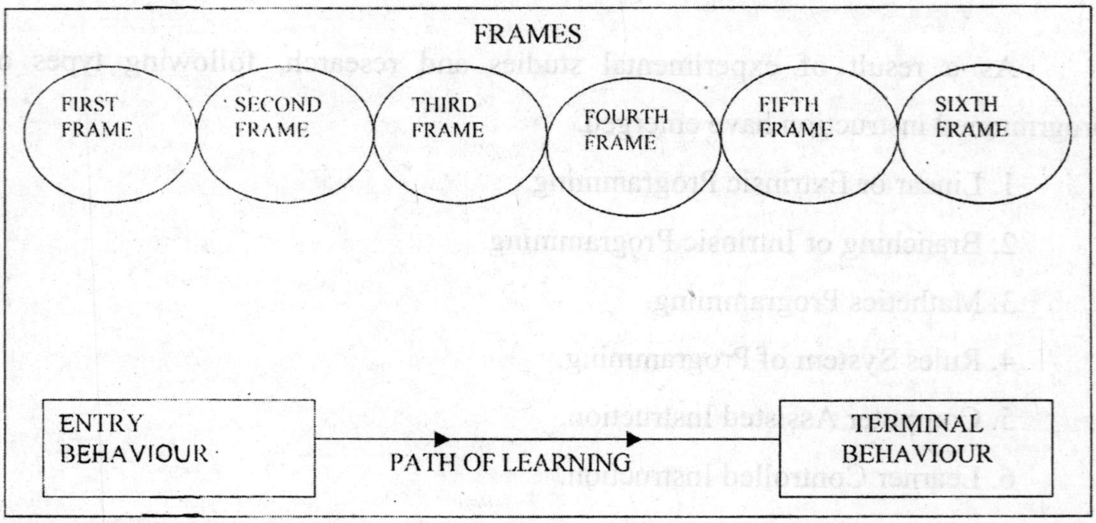

Fig. Arrangement of Frames in Linear Programming

As shown in the figure, the sequence of frames and path of learning in the programmed learning is systematic and linear. That is why, this type of programming is referred to as linear programming. Hence all the learners have to proceed through the same frames and in the same order.

In a linear programme, the programmer sitting at a distant place controls learner's responses externally. Hence linear progrmmning is also termed as extrinsic programming. In branching programming, learnr's response is controlled by learner himself internally. It is, therefore, also called intrinsic programming.

PRINCIPLES OF LINEAR PROGRAMMING

1. Principle of small steps.
2. Principle of active responding
3. Principle of minimum errors.
4. Principle of knowledge of results.

CIDEF CHARACTERISTICS OF LINEAR PROGRAMMING

1. A linear pogramme is a single track or a straight line programme.

2. In this programme, learning material is presented into a series of small steps (frames).

3. Every learner follows the same path in a linear progrmmne.

4. In linear programming, the content is broken into small units ranging from just one word to as many as 40 or 50 in length.

5. In a linear programme, the learner is given a small prograllline, the learner is given a small amount of information.

6. The sequence of steps remains unchanged.

7. The learner is expected to compose his won answer to each question.

8. The learner is expected to respond actively to each step or frame.

9. The responses of the learner get immediate reinforcement.

10. Linear Programming provides for self pacing i.e. one can learn according to one's own speed.

11. Linear programming moves slowly but steadily in leading a learner from initial to terminal behaviour.

12. Each of the unit constitutes a frame.

13. In a linear programme, the programmer controls the response of the learner.

14. In a linear programme, the learners learn by avoiding the error.

MERITS OF LINEAR PROGRAMMING

1. Immediate knowledge of results acts as a great motivator and releases anxiety and tension.

2. The smallness of the frames brings the sub-goals within the reach of the learner and thereby facilitates secondary reinforcement.

3. Repetition' strengthens the responses and ensures learning.

4. Easy nature of the programme provides 'success experience' to the

learner.

LIMITATIONS OF LINEAR PROGRAMMING

1. In linear programming, the learning process, becomes quite dull on account of the following reasons (a) Subject matter is broken into very small pieces (b) Responding is quite mechanical and restrictive and (c) The learning process is quite slow.

2. The use of-linear programmer is limited to some subjects and topics.

3. Linear programming cramps the imagination of the learner and initiative for creative integrative and judgement learning.

4. Linear, programming encourages guessing.

5. Linear programming does not develop the discriminating power of the students.

BRANCHING OR INTRINSIC PROGRAMMING

Branching or intrinsic programming was developed by Norman A Crowder (1954) an American: technician. According to Crowder, branching or intrinsic programme is one which adopts to the needs of the learners without the medium of any extrinsic device such as a computer. The progrmmner does not control it extrinsically.

Norman A. Crowder was a technician who was working in the United States Air Force. He was faced with the problem of efficiency of vocational training. His programme is based on institution. His approach at the most is practical. This type of programme employs multiple choice response patterns. The learner is required to select one right answer out of several responses presented to him.

CHARACTERISTICS OF A BRANCHING PROGRAMME

1. A frame may contain two or three related ideas or related sequences.

2. Each frame is of relatively bigger size as compared with the linear type.

3. With a vie\v to answering the question, the learner has to arrive at an answer by setting the relationship between one idea and the other and by filling up the gaps not fully covered in the frame. Only then he can select the correct alternative from the multiple choice.

4. The learner moves forward if his responses are correct but is diverted or branched to one or more remedial frames if he does not give the correct response.

5. Frames explain the matter afresh when: response is not correct. The frames ask the learner questions to elicit the right answer and reveal his previous mistakes. The learner, then, returns to the original frame.

6. The cycle goes an till the learner-'passes' through the whole instructional material at his own pace

7. B ranching; programme contains multiple choice of items 'where the learner' selects response whereas in linear programmes or Skinnerian style the response are constructed rather than selected.

8. In a branching programme, all? learners do not follow the, frame route Rather,' the route depends on, the response made by the learner. Thus, learners branch according' to their responses.

ASSUMPTIONS OF BRANCHING:

1. Learning takes place better; if the subject matter is presented in its totality.

2. Learning takes place better, if the subject-matter is presented in the form of meaningful, components or units.

3. Wrong answers do not necessarily hinder the learning of a correct

answer.

4. Multiple choice items help more in the learning process.

5. It is based on the possibility of detecting and correcting errors.

6. Basic teaming takes place during the learners exposure to the new material.

7. Learning takes place better if the learner is allowed sufficient freedom to take decisions for adopting the instruction to his needs.

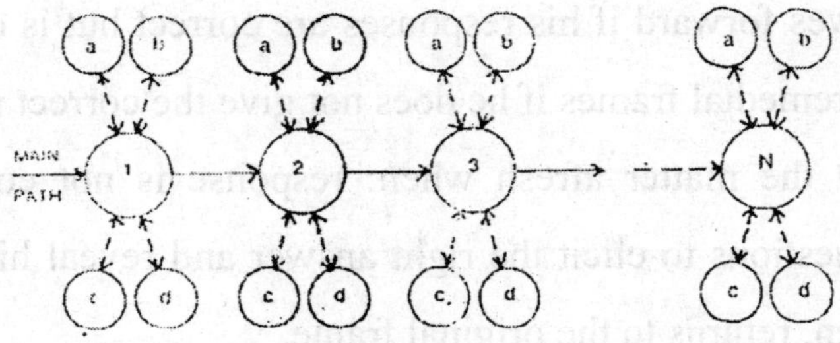

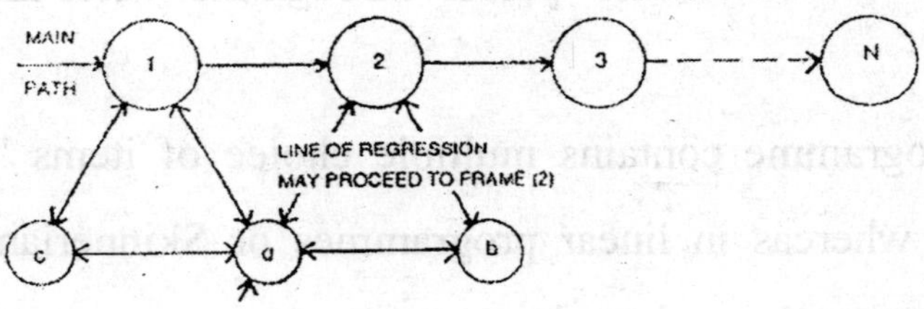

MERITS AND ADVANTAGES OF A BRANCHING PROGRAMME

1. Big size of a frame as well as the branching minimizes unnecessary repetitions and responding, thus reducing the amount of learning time and fatigue.

2. The pitfalls and consequences of erroneous logic are usually explained in the remedial frames so that the learner not only gets the correct response but also understands why some other response is not correct.

3. Instead of simple response it provides alternatives in the form of multiple choices.

4. Through its broad frames, branching programme provides for more freedom to respond and scope of choosing one's own path of learning according to

one's Peed. Thus it helps in maintaining the power of discrimination of the learner

5. Branching programme is helpful in the development of the interest and initiative of the learner.

6. Branching programme is helps in the development of creativity and problem-solving ability.

7. Branching is most useful in the areas beyond facts, definitions and basic skills.

8. The frames being of larger size contain a good deal of information and this may enable the programmer to enrich his style and expand his ideas.

9. The programmed material in branching programme may be employed in the form of programmed text or teaching machines. The material when presented in a book form takes the form of a 'scrambled book'.

Limitations and drawbacks of branching Programming

1. The multiple-choice questions provided in this programmmg may lead to guesswork on the part of the learner and he may not understand the subject matter of the frame.

2. The setting of appropriate multiple-choice questions suiting to the entire material of the frames proves a difficult task.

3. No branching method can provide infinite branching to take care of all possible needs of every individual student.

4. The cost of branching programme is very high when compared with traditional teaching approaches.

5. The branching programme is not suitable for small children as they are unable to express the symbolism.

6. The programme needs revision after every two years.

7. It is difficult to cover the entire subject-matter.

8. The diagnostic questions framed by the programmer mayor may not suit

the needs of the individual learner.

9. The programme cannot shape the behaviour of the learner.

Backward Branching. Backward branching is based on the principle of 'repeating the missed frames'. As shown in the diagram 'the learner of frame No. 1 of the main stream goes to frame No.2 of the main stream only if he makes a correct choice. But if he makes a wrong choice, he is led to a remedial frame wherein he is given some more help in understanding the concept and in solving the solution by a better logic. He will be then directed to the original frame No.1 so that he can, read it again and answer it correctly in the light of the remedial materials he has received. So the learner who has committed error goes though the same frame twice (once before the remedial material and once after the remedial material).

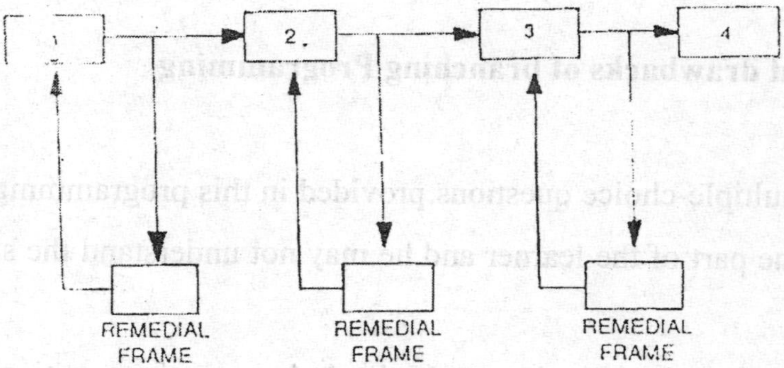

Fig. : Backward Branching.

Forward Branching. In the forward branching, whether the learner makes a wrong choice or correct choice, he will always be going to new pages, thus physically progressing from page to page.

The learner making a correct choice will go directly to the- next frame of the main stream. But the learner who had made a wrong choice goes to a remedial frame. wherein his mistake is fully explained, probably followed by another parallel question, from which he goes to the next frame of the main stream, So, even though he is wrong, physically he does not return to the original frame but progresses to a remedial frame, which is more logical and simpler and then joins the main stream.

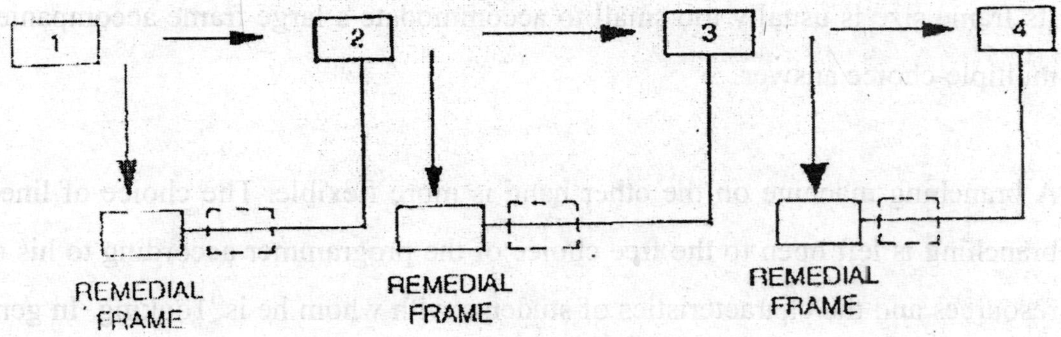

Fig. : Forward Branching

Forwardness or Backwardness of a Programme. We as programmers depend first on our previous knowledge and experience and if necessary let it be checked by a set of learners. This forwardness or backwardness of a programme is quite arbitrary but the only thing is that as long as we are successful in explaining the errors and consequently successful in inhibiting them, we are quite free to choose any of them.

Use of Linear-cum-Branching Programme. The style of programming depends on the topic programmed, population for which it is programmed and other multi-factors. Whether we are going to presentation a branching or a linear style, requiring' overt to covert responses, as long as it aims at taking the student through an elaborate and systematic path of self-learning and testing processes, thus facilitating the student to achieve the terminal goals, it serves its functions. It is very difficult to adhere rigidly to one type of presentation. A combination of the two may prove more useful. Thus an item on the main stream of the programme may follow branching pattern, but some of the remedial sequences may be linear to guide the learner in short steps through material, which he found difficult.

A linear, teaching machine cannot easily be adapted to take branching sequence. This type of machine is made 'cheat-proof by its technical construction. Its frame size is usually too small to accommodate a large frame accompanied by multiple-choice answer.

A branching machine on the other hand is more flexible. The choice of linear or branching is left open to the free choice of the programmer according to his aims, resources and the characteristics of students with whom he is '1ooking. In general, a linear programme will be of great use in the following situations.

1. When the programmer thinks that the learners cannot digest a large chunk of material, but may need small steps.

2. When the programmer thinks that the concepts or skills involved in the programme, are of such importance that the trainees must ensure their complete mastery;

3. When the, population of trainees has more or less the same entering behaviour, i.e., there is more homogeneity among the trainees.

4. When it is proved empirically (by way of individual and group try-out) that the very nature of the content demands linear format, e.g., in a subject, which is entirely hierarchical.

MATHETICS

Thomas P. Gilbert (l96L) is the originator of the concept of mathetics. According to him "mathetics is the systematic application of reinforcement theory to the analysis and construction of complex behaviour repertories usually known as subject-matter mastery, knowledge and skills. Mathetics, if applied diligently, produces materials that exceed the efficiency of lessons produced by any known method."

"The word' 'mathetics' is derived from the Greek work 'mathein' which means to learn.

There are two distinctive types of programming techniques: one stressing the subject matter and its treatment and the other stressing the behaviour. Matheties falls under the second category.

Mathetics is elective in nature but it is unique in application. It analyses tie deficiencies and tries to make them up. The success of task analysis depends to a great extent on the adequacy and reliability of data. The term task analysis suggests the breaking down of the'; task into' its constituent parts and involves detailed listing of component behavioural elements of a job or task. A task analysis is really an inventory to which knowledge, skills and attitudes are identified and isolated with a view to ultimately synthesizing them into a hierarchical organisation relevant to the writing of learning prescription.

The aims of task analysis may be stated as under:

1. Description of the task that the learner has to learn.

2. Isolation of the required behaviour.

3. Identification of the conditions under which the behaviour occurs.

4. Determination and generalisation of a criterion of acceptable performance.

Task analysis' is of three types' (i) Analysis of topic, (ii) Analysis of the job, and (iii) Analysis of the skills.

MAIN 'FEATURES OF MATHETICS PROGRAMMING

1. Like any other well-thought out instructional plan, a mathetics programme begins with, a detailed analysis. of what is to be taught.

2. In matheties, an exercise is the technical unit of learning instead of a

frame as in-linear or branching, programming.

3. No restriction is put of the size of an exercise.

4. The size of the exercise is determined by how big a step a learner can reasonably take at a moment.

5. Each exercise assumes the reinforcement value of accomplishment. In a mathetics style, a different, strategy of reinforcement i.e., other than the knowledge of results, which is the main source of reinforcement in the linear programming is employed.

6. This programme makes use of the techniques of retrogressive or backward chaining.

7. Learning prescription involves three principles: (i) Principle of discrimination, (ii} Principle of chaining, and (iii) Principle of generalisation.

The underlying rationale of mathetics programme is that closer the learner is to reinforcement when he is taught, the more effective the reinforcement becomes. The reinforcement, in this case, is the completion of the task.

Discrimination. Discrimination implies making a different label or name for a non-example, which shares some properties with previous examples. The three examples are reproduced from Gilbert.

(i) A colour band can have 10 colours.

Read thoroughly this list twice. . Learn the number for which each colour stands.

A five-dollar bill is *green.*

One *brown* Penny.

A red heart has two parts.

A white cat has nine lives.

Three *orange* oranges.

Seven *purple* seas.

A poor legged *yellow* dog.

Blue tail- fly has six legs.

An eighty-years-old man has *grey* hair.

(ii) List the number for which each colour stands. Red (heart), White (cat), Purple (seas), Brown. (penny), Green (bill), Grey (hair), Blue (tail-fly), Orange (oranges). Yellow (dog).

(iii) List the number for which colour, stands Black-Brown Grey Green-White Pur'ple-Red--Orange-Blue.

There is a correct response for each stimulus situation but there is no particular order in which these responses have to occur.

Chain. In a chain there is a fixed sequence of responses to be emitted, e.g., steps in division, order of words in a sentence;' opening or closing a bottle or tying or untying a shoe lace. Frames that follow indicate the chaining process.

In chains responses must occur in a fairly regular order. Each response produces some change in the stimulus -situation that sets the occasion for the next responses to occur.

The Retrogressive Chaining. It is based on the basis that closer the student to the reinforcement when he is being taught, the more effective is the reinforcement. In this case the reinforcement is the completion of the task. Each time the student performs, he completes the task.

The six- frame sequence that follows Retrogressive Chaining to teach a mathetical procedure is designed to teach one something by making one apply the knowledge one already has plus new information that this programme will supply.

Areas of behaviour most suited for shaping through mathetics programming

1. Behaviour requiring chain.
2. Skills and complex behaviour repertoires.
3. Behaviour, which shows dependence of one on the other.

Merits of Mathctics

1. It is ajob and task-oriented programme.

2. Results can be linked to concrete goals which we intend to achieve through a mathetics programll1e.

3. Its stress on learner-success at 90/90 criterion level of mastery motivates the learner.

4. It utilises the principle of backward chaining.

5. I t is relevant, significant, meaningful and valid in the eyes of the learner and the programmer.

6. It can be applied to a wide range of subject matter but it specifically suits the teaching of skills where the main objective is transfer of training of skills from one situation to another.

Drawbacks And Limitation Of Mathetics Programming

1. It is very technical in nature and as such demands a lot of skill, training and labour on the part of the programmer.

2. It is not suitable for learning the material of all subjects. Only concrete material and subject material involving psycho- motor skills can be gainfully programmed by means of Mathetics.

3. This programme makes inadequate provision for individual differences. All learners have to learn the same way.

4. It provides very little freedom to the learners as usually construct responses are required.

5. The learner encounters difficulty in constructing the last response or mastery response in the beginning.

6. Mathetics cannot be used for factual content.

7. Mathetics cannot be used for higher cognitive and affective learning

objectives.

8. Mathetics does not provide any remedial help for the weaknesses and difficulties of learners.

9. Mathetics is not based on any sound learning theory.

An Example Of Mathetics Programme

Do whatever the programme asks. If you come to the blank, (...) put the correct word, number, symbol or whatever in the blank.

When a response is required, you will find the correct response on the lower part of the page. Check your answer, and then go on to the next.

Programme Page 1

1 . To find the square of a two-digit number ending in 3.

(a) Multiply the number by its first digit and add to it the product of the two digits.

(b) Write 9 to the right of the result. No response in required.

Programme Page 2

2. To find the square of 16.

(a) Multiply the first digit (1) by the next consecutive number (2). 2

(b) Write 56 to the right of (2) 2 56

(c) Squareofl6is256.

No response required:

Programme Page 3

3. To find the square of 17.

(a) Multiply the first digit 0) by the next higher 2

Consecutive number :(2).

In the Mathetics Style, an exercise in the technical unit of

learning instead of a frame in the linear programming.

(b) Write 89 to the right of the result. (c) The square of 17 is 2 89

Programme Page 4

4. To find the square of 26.

(a) Multiply the first digit (2) by the next higher 3

3Consecutive number.

(b) Write 76 to the right of the result. (c) The square of26 is 6 76.

Program me Page 5

5. To find out the square of 21

(a) Multiply.. by ..

(b) Write.. to the.. of ..

(c) The quare of21 is ..

(i) Multiply 2 by 2

(ii) Write 41 to the right of 4

(iii) The square of 21 is 441

Programme Page 6

6. What is the square of: (a) 625.

(a) 25 ?....... (b) 3 5 ? .... (b) 1225.

Programme Page 7

Here each frame includes the entire process, part of it supplied by the programmer and part of it supplied by the student. Each frame of the programme increases the student's share and decreases the amount supplied by the programmer. .

Mastery Frame or Demonstration-In the above model, the first frame in mathetics is mastery frame, which is called demonstration. The mastery step completes the task or procedure to be learned.

Teaching frames follow teaching Frames-Mastery frame where prompts arc used to assist the learner to give the desired response.

Testing Frames-The testing frames in mathetics are called release where no prompts are provided. In the above model, the last frame is the release frame.

Comparison Among Liner, Branching and Mathetical Programming

	Liner Exponents	**Types of Programming Branching**	**Mathetics**
1	Exponents B.F. Skinner	Norman A. Crowder (1954)	Thomas F. Gilbert (1962)
2	Source of Origin Psychological laboratory experiments, application of operant conditioning learning theory to teaching.	Semi-industrial situation with emphasis on efficient instruction to improve job performance. Its origin is from human training technique.	To develop the mastery of content through retrogressive chaining.
3	Learning Theories It is based on the operant conditioning learning	It is based on configration theories	Connectionist theory of learning is

	theory its response centred approach of learning.	of learning i.e. problem solving approach. It is stimulus-centred strategy of learning.	used. It is also response-centred approach. Retrogressive chain or Reverse-contiguity is used.
4	Principles : It has five fundamental principles : small step, active responding, immediate confirmation, self pacing and student testing.	It employs three basic principles : principle of exposition, diagnosis and remediation.	It involved three principles : principle of chain, and discrimination and generalizations.
5	Assumptions : (a) Students learns better if content is presented in the small units. (b) Student's response should be immediately reinforced for learning. (c) Students errors hinder is learning (d) Student learns better if he gets the freedom to learn.	(a) Students learns better if the whole content is exposed. (b) Students errors help in diagnosis and does not necessarily hinder in learning. (c) Students learns better if the remediation is	(a) The prescription helps in learning (b) Mastery step can be placed any where in chain of learning. (c) Reverse-contiguity is helpful for the

		provided side by side for weakness of the learner.	mastery of the content. (d) Completion of task provided motivation to the students.
6	Frame Size : Small stem, may be one sentence of two in a frame	Large size, may be Para or page in frame.	Learning packages are developed in small steps
7	Frame Structure Three aspects : Stimulus, response and reinforcement	Three aspects : Exposition or presentation, diagnosis and remediation	It has also three aspects : Demonstration, prompt and release.
8	Types of Frames: Liner has four types of frames : Introductory, teaching practice and testing frames.	Two types of frames are used in instrinsic programme : (1) Home page : teaching and diagnosis (2) Wrong page : Remediation is given.	It provides three types of frames : demonstration i.e. prescription for the mastery, prompt to provide the response in exercise frames
9	Response : It employs the constructed	The multiple choice	The learner has to

	response. The response is controlled by programmed not by the learner. Response is the interal part of learning.	question is given to select the response. The response is controlled by learner not by the programmer. Response helps in learning as well as in diagnosis.	construct the response. The response is determined by programmer. The correct response is confirmed.
10	Reinforcement : This strategy is based on the theory of reinforcement. The confirmation of correct response provides the reinforcement to the learner. The continuous reinforcement is provided, the wrong response is ignored.	The correct response is confirmed and approved to provide the reinforcement. The wrong response indicates the weakness of the Learner and remediation is given the difficulties of the learner.	The completeness of task motivate the learner. The correct responses is also confirmed in the learning packages. The wrong responses are ignored.
11	Error : The student errors hinder in learning. The student will not learn of he commits error. The error-rate should be less than 10 percent in criterion programme.	The student errors do not necessarily hinder in learning but helps in diagnosing the weakness of the learning for which remediation can be	The discrimination can be taught effectively by learners error, but errors do not help in learning. Learning concentrates to

		provided. The error than 20 percent.	avoid the error. The error-rate should below.
12	Individual Differences : The principles of self-pacing or freedom of time facilitates the individual variation in learning process.	Each every learner according to Hos provides the branches own needs and requirements. Every learner follows his own paths of learning.	Learner has the freedom of time to complete his own task. Time factor facilitates the individual variation in learning not needs of learner.
13	Form Test : Linear programme texmois same the conventional book. The content matter is presented into small units.	Branching programme text is known as scrambled text. It is different from conventional books. The sequence of pages is not followed in it.	One concept if presented in a learning package. The sequence of pages is followed according to the conventional text.
14	Machine : Linear programme is presented usually through teaching machine. Very simple and cheap model of teaching machine is used.	It is rather difficult to use teaching machine presenting the intrinsic programme. A complex and costly model is required for this purpose.	Linear mode of teaching machine can be used effectively in presenting the mathetical programme.

15	Purpose or Use : (a) Modification of behaviour is the focus of linear programming. (b) It can be effectively used for secondary level of students. (c) Lower objective of learning can be achieved effectively. (d) It is very useful for average and lower intelligence students. It can be used for correspondence education lesson.	(a) The main focus to provide the remediation to the difficulties of the learner. (b) It can be used effectively for higher classes. (c) Higher objectives are realized by this strategy of programme. (d) Higher intelligence student liernes better by branching. Remedial instruction can be given correspondence students.	(a) Mastery of the subject-matter is main focus of mathetics. (b) Mathetics is also useful for higher classes. (c) It is much more useful for most motivating task. (d) Mathematical concepts can be developed effectively by this strategy.
16	Limitations : (a) It does not provide freedom to the student to respond or to learn. (b) It is based on learning theory which has been formulated by experimentation on	(a) It does not consider the learning process and its structure. (b) The sequence of pages are not followed; hence	(a) Main stress is given on mastery of concept rather than behaviour change. (b) The retrogressive chain is used which is not

	animals. Human learning is different from animals learning. (c) Every learner has to follow the same path. There is no remediation for wrong response.	students do not like to go through it. (c) It gives more emphasis on remediation rather teaching. Hence it is only tutorial approach of learning.	effective for terminal repertories. (c) It is difficult to develop the package of learning.

UNIT -3

Learning Objective

Modification of teaching behavior-Micro teaching, Flanders interaction analysis, simulation.

Communication process: Concept of communication, Principles, Modes and Barriers to communication, Classroom communication (interaction, verbal and non verbal) Models of teaching: Concept, Different families of Teaching Models.

MODIFICATION OF TEACHING BEHAVIOR

Modification of teaching behavior is an extension of the application of Behavior technology. Behavior technology is the application of principles of psychology, particularly those of learning of behavioral changes. Psychology is basically concerned with behavior. It has, right from the very beginning, studied three aspects of behavior- the cause, the change and the prediction of behavior. Education has been greatly benefited by the advances made in the field of learning psychology. Several devices of teaching-learning used in the field of education owe their origin to these developments is psychology. Behavior modification theory and practice have a long history behind it. But, its technology is not more than fifty years old. A brief background of this is presented as follows:

Behavior Modification: Historical Background: Skinner may be said to be the father of the science of behavior. He demonstrated successfully how behavior could be controlled. Working with the animals in the laboratory he was able to discover the principles which sere powerful enough to control behavior. The presented a detailed discussion of these principles in his book Beyond Freedom and Dignity and explained how behavior could be brought under control through the application of the principles of reinforcement and management of contingencies. He very convincingly said that a "technology of operant behavior" was possible to be developed. But, this was just discovering the principles and suggesting a science of behavior. It were his disciples who moved the science of behavior away from laboratory to the practicing fields. Then, the behavior scientists moving away from pigeons and rats in the laboratory started working with people in schools, prisons, hospitals, churches and mental homes and met with amazing success. The basic principles that guided them were the same as Skinner and his associates had formulated by observing the pigeons and rats in the Skinner box. The most basic principle was that behaviour is affected by its consequence, which was discussed in his first book The Ikhavior of Organisms (1939). Ten years after the publication of this book in 1949 P.K' Niter showed that human behavior could also be controlled in the same way. He taught an idiot to eaD1 food by raising his right hand to a vertical position. He used a "shaping technique", first reinforcing random movements of the arm and then, movements that brought the arm closer and closer to the vertical position. Ogden R. Lindsey and N. H. Azrin, both Skinner's students also demonstrated the same thing. Lindsey working with Skinner in 1950 at noston metropolitan State Hospital controlled behavior of psychotics, Azrin took a giant step into behavior modification in 1960 after he became the director of Behavioral Research at Anna State Hospital in Southerri Illinois. He brought 'T' Ayllon, a brand new Ph. D. student with him and treated a woman having a 9-year history of hoarding towels. Over the next few years Aytllon and Azrin developed Token Economy System of reinforcement and demonstrated its efficiency. They worked with large groups of persons. There were most significant achievements to date in human behavior control, The Token Economy system proved to be very effective and Ayllon-Azrin predicted that it would find great applicability in many different disciplines concerned' with human behavior. It came to be true as it was utilized for treating retarded children, slow learners, and juvenile delinquents. The system was discussed in detail in their book Token Economy (1968). It seemed at that time that Ayllon was moving in the direction of bringing about Skinner's "Walden Two", a fictionalized account of a community that was run on behavior principles.

Behavior modification is a catch-all term. In popular usage it refers to psychotherapeutic methods plus classical conditioning plus operant conditioning techniques. But, Leonard Krasner, a leading behaviorist used this term to cover What he calls evocative psychotherapies including psychoanalysis as well as the behavioral therapies. Albert Bandura, another major behaviorist discarded the use of this term and preferred the use of behavior therapy and Applied Behavior

Analysis (A B A). Applied Behavior Analysis is the direct descendent of Skinner's conditioning. The Behavior Analysts hold that if a person exhibits deviant behavior, the failure is in the social and physical environment that determines his behavior not in the individual. Changing the environment will change the behavior. If treatment is necessary the best place to do it is in the home or the school, not some artificial laboratory-like place. The ABA psychologists keep busy in writing prescriptions for change and producing results. The programme at Brvant School (Kansas State) is one of the numerous projects that make Kansas the world center of applied behavior analysis. The state leaped into behaviorism in a big way in 1965 when Lindsey, R. Vance Hall, Harris, Bijou, Wolf Baer and Risley many analysts gathered at Kansas University. They developed several programmes of training. Montrose Wolf developed a "teaching Family Model" of training parents to control behaviors of their children. Vance Hall developed a "Responsive Teaching Model" making it possible [or teachers to learn the technique in a weak-long programme. There was a terrific demand for such workshops and programmes" then. Todd R. Risley developed a "Living Environment Programme" in Kansas for young children beginning pre-school children, juvenile delinquents, adults, old men and woman. They used various methods such as tokens, modeling, desensitization and other techniques, which were found to be effective empirically. It is said that an ambitious plan to manage the behavior of a whole community was also under way it Prince Georges County. Maryland, a suburban area in the country under the direction of Harold Cohen, Director of International Behavioral Research (IBR) who hoped to convert the country's establishments (schools, police, courts, etc.) to behavior control methods such as the shaping technique.

In this chapter are discussed three strategies of behavior modification. These are (1) Microteaching, (2) Flander's Interaction Analysis and (3) Simulation. These are developed independently but seem to be based on the principles of behavior modification. The first two are, particularly; concerned with modification of teaching behaviors while the last one is a general training technique.

1. MICROTEACHING

Microteaching is not a method of teaching. It is' a strategy of developing teaching skills in the student teachers. It, therefore, comes within the teacher training programme.

Meaning And Nature: Training of teachers constitutes three, important components- development-' of knowledge, development of attitudes and development of skills 'which are essential for teaching effectively. Microteaching aims at developing essential teaching skills in the teachers. The usual practice for, achieving this objective had been to ask a pupil teacher to, prepare a lesson plan of 30 to 40 minutes and teach that in the actual class of a school to be supervised by a staff-member of the training college. This would be very time- consuming- this practice is in vogue even today in our country as well as in many other countries Microteaching is a newer technique of achieving the same purpose and having a number of advantages over the traditional training practice.

Microteaching is a teacher-training and teacher improvement technique, which was developed at Stanford University in the early sixties. It was developed originally by a doctoral candidate Keith Acheson who was working with Robert Bush and Dwight Allen for his Ph. D. and who found that a videotape recorder could be used more effectively for demonstrating to the trainee where he needed improvement in his teaching behaviors. Today, although videotaping is not an essential requirement of Microteaching it commonly involves videotaping a short lesson and playing the same back to the trainee. It is principally used in the preserve education of teachers. But, it can also be used for the improvement of teaching skills of in service teachers. It may also be used for research involving q1e study of the teaching and learning processes.

It has been defined by Allen (1969) as a "scaled down teaching encounter in class-size and period". It is scaled down in the sense that class size is kept very small, usually having 4 to 6 students. Again, it is scaled down in the sense that the teaching lesson is very short, usually of 5 to '10 minutes duration. Von Haden and King (p. 175) hold that microteaching commonly involves videotaping a short lesson, playing it back, making a critique of it, and repeating the operation to improve certain. components of the micro lesson.

Microteaehing is a skill-teaching technique. There are a number of skills such as explaining, introducing, the lesson, questioning, blackboard work, etc. which are essential for a teacher to learn and use for efficient teaching. Microteaching is a technique enabling the trainee teacher to learn them effectively and economically. Under, microteaching only one skill is practiced, but marc efficiently. Microteaching is a highly individualized training programme because only one single individual trainee is the focus of attention, guidance and learning at a time.

Microteaching is a specially contrived feedback device of establishing the desired behaviors in the trainees. The-trainee gets immediate information about how he has performed. If he performs well 'he gets appreciation, which strengthens his desired behavior. If he lacks something, this information stimulates him to correct himself next time. Thus, the feedback of this information controls his behavior and improves it. The feedback is real and rapid. The teacher himself can observe the performance or by him and his supervisor or by the colleagues. A record of the microteaching is kept so that original teaching performance maybe compared with subsequent re-teachings and improvements may be noted.

The feedback in Microteaching may be obtained either from the videotape or from the reactions of the students or from teacher's own observation and analysis and also from the suggestions of other observers. This review makes immediate and individual diagnosis possible and suggests ways of improving. Re-teaching can take place immediately after the review and critical analysis of the micro lesson.'

Procedure:

Microteaching runs through three phases. These are

1. Knowledge Acquisition Phase
2. Skill Acquisition Phase, and
3. Transfer Phase.

1. The focus of knowledge phase is on enabling the teacher under training to acquire knowledge of the skill, which he is required to learn. In other words, this phase is concerned with preparing the pupil teacher mentally for practicing the skill; it is a well-known fact that before something is done one must know what it is, how it is done, etc. For this reason the supervisor of the pupil teacher tells him about the skill and slows what it is. He gives a demonstration of that skill and the pupil teacher is asked to observe it: When the demonstration is over it is discussed with the teacher. An analysis of its major components or sequence or sub activities is made. This provides to the pupil teacher a sort of cognitive map of the skill to be practiced.

Thus demonstration of the skill by the supervisor and observation by the pupil teacher followed by an analysis and discussion of the same by the teacher and the supervisor constitute the major activities of this phase.

2. Skill acquisition phase involves practice of the demonstrated skill by the pupil teacher. He, for this purpose, prepares a microlesson, teaches or demonstrates the skill and, then, his performance is evaluated. If his performance has been videotaped, it is played back to him. He himself realizes his improvement. The supervisor also points out the inadequacies and gives suggestions for improvement. The pupil teacher, then, re-plans in the light of suggestions received and teaches again. Having finished his re-teach lesson there is, again, the discussion, analysis and criticism. Then again there is replanning. review and re-teaching, The cycle goes on like this till the teacher learns the skill sufficiently well.

3. Transfer phase refers to the application or use of the acquired skill by the trainee in the actual class of the school. It may he noted that microteaching is done in a simulated situation which is an artificially contrived teaching situation consisting of 4 to 6 class fellows of the trainee himself. Hence, the question arises whether the trainee can use the acquired skill in the actual situation of teaching also. The researches have revealed that it is not always the case. But, by and large, the belief is that skills are better learned through microteaching technique. Although it has not been without problems, it has had a great appeal.

Factors of Effectiveness: The effectiveness of microteaching depends on a number of factors and conditions, These should be taken into consideration while organizing a microteaching programme, They are as hallows.

1. Careful and detailed planning should be done before undertaking the microteaching practice.

2. The purpose of microteaching should be clearly understood and the technique should be defined in behavioral terms.

3. The supervisor and other teachers and trainees should have positive, helpful attitudes and manners.

4. The trainee must be responsive and free from any kind of threat. He should be willing and ready to accept suggestions and criticism. Trust and respect between the supervisor and the trainee is essential.

5. The supervisor must' be skilled and experienced having a good background of microteaching.

6. The trainee must be able to describe precisely the skill under study, know its purpose, recognize it and should know when and for what purpose under what conditions it is appropriate.

7. Micro lessons should be considered as devices for diagnosis of shortcomings and techniques of improvement rather than models of perfection.

8. Microteaching should be looked upon as a valuable aid to improving competencies, not as a complete programme.

9. Demonstration of the skill must be as perfect as possible.

Advantages of Microteaching: Following are seen the advantages of microteaching technique.

1. It focuses on specific behavioral acts of the teacher.

2. It is useful for studying the performance cf the teacher, reaction of the trainees and appropriateness of various activities such as analysis of the subject matter.

3. It is economical and more effective in terms of time and outcome respective]y as compared to the traditional student teaching programme.

4. The feedback- provided in this is more effective and powerful. The trainee can see for himself where he erred and in which direction he has to, improve his behavior. By comparing subsequent performance with earlier one, the process vividly portrays growth in skill and develops confidence.

5. When desired, alterations can be made readily in the various components

of the skill.

6. Comments of the supervisor can be made definite, understandable and relevant because they pertain to precise acts.

7. The system can be used for improving all aspects of teaching and student teacher relationships. It makes the trainee sensitive to both verbal and non-verbal behavior.

8. It reduces the complexities involved in the practice of teaching in the actual" classroom of the schools. It relieves many of the tensions experienced by the fresh trainee when he confronts a large class for the first time. By giving a trainee and the supervisor a chance to talk alone, it reduces the embarrassment common in classroom supervision.

9. It enables the trainee teacher to learn how to make the lesson more in cresting. motivate the students and be an enthusiastic teacher.

10. It quickens the interest of the student teacher in being a teacher and also stimulates the experienced teacher's desire for self improvement by making the improvement process enjoyable and observable.

11. It is equally effective for training teachers initially, for improving the skills of experienced teachers, and for enhancing the performance of teacher educators too.

Critical Evaluation:

In spite or its various advantages and its usefulness, microteaching is criticized on various counts. It is artificial and does not bring the student teacher into contact with the harsh realities and the complexities of the actual classroom teaching. Another difficulty felt by them is that it provides no guidance inn the integration of various skills taught separately for teaching in the actual classroom which calls for their use in an integrated manner. Sometimes, microteaching experience and student teacher criticism may be frustrating to oversensitive students particularly, when the supervisor becomes overcritica1. A major criticism of micro teaching is that it destroys the art of teaching by continuously concentrating on small segments of a lesson, and sometimes on trivial behaviors of the student teacher. More important aspects of teaching such as learning to teach concepts, problem solving, and creativity development are not taken into account.

These criticisms, however, don't seem to be very apt. Keeping in mind the limited purpose 'for which microteaching is used they seems to be just sweeping and too general. The fact is that because of its adaptability, its provision for feedback and reuse, and its focus on specific acts and skills microteaching has generated a great interest on .the part of trainees and supervisors. By reducing the complexities of the actual classroom of the school the teaching learning environment may be manipulated through the process of microteaching to direct attention to a limited number of specific behaviors, This is helpful to both the trainee and the supervisor, Although it is true that microteaching is somewhat artificial, it does promote learning through self- involvement of the trainee, his selJ-reJ1ection, and self-evaluation. Immediate knowledge of how he has performed reinforces his desirable behaviors and motivates him to modify the unwanted ones.

Keith Acheson, Dwight WAllen, W R. Borg, Robert N. Bush, James Olivero, Vv Warren ,Kallenbach of the U.S.A. have been a few leaders associated with the microteaching movement. In India the NCERT and professor B. K. Passi have popularized the technique

Skills Of Teaching

Since microtcaching is basically a strategy for developing teaching skills in the student teachers, it seems relevant to discuss the natureˌ and types of these skills. A skill is an organized and coordinated pattern of mental and/or physical activity in relation to some work or job. It is built up gradually in the course of repeated training or experience. It usually involves both receptor and effectors processes. It is serial in the sense that each of its components from second to second is dependent on the last and influences the next. Acquisition of skill is viewed as the integration' of activities' into a hierarchically organized structure. The following mnemonic device may help remember all the important teaching skills identified so far. Learn this name;

PEARLPASS BOM, S.Q.C.

Each letter of this name gives you the name of a skill as follows:

1. P= Participation of students in teaching-learning, How to involve students in teaching-reaming -is an important skill.

2. E = Explaining and illustrating, How to explain and illustrate the teaching concepts so as to enable the students to understand them is also an imp01 lant skill.

3. A= Attention getting and attention recognition. students should be attentive in the class. This is important. It is a skill how to know that students are attentive, who is not attentive and who is attentive. A skillful teacher can identify this from the expressions, movements and gestures of the students. Also the teacher should be able to seek attention of the pupils. But, this skill has to be learnt.

4. R = Reinforcement or motivation. how to reinforce the desirable behavior of students, when and where, at what time is also an important skill. Proper motivation goes a long way in achieving the goals of teaching. But, this is a skill which the teacher has to learn.

5. L = Lecturing. this is also a skill which needs to be learned.

6. P = Planned repetition. There are, always, occasions in every reaching lesson when the

teacher is required to repeat certain points, facts, explanations, principles, etc. in order to make students understand them thoroughly. But, this should be done in a planned manner. Um1ecessary repetitions may be waste of time and energy. This is a skill which has got to be learned.

7. A= Audio-visual aids. How to use, identify and procure audio-visual aids is-also an imp0l1ant skill.

8. S = Set Induction. In ordinary language it means preparing the students mentally and emotionally for the lesson. Set means a state of preparedness. Before starting teaching development of this state of mental preparedness in the pupils is necessary.

This is also a skill to be learned by the teacher.

9. S = Stimulus variation. to sustain the interest of the students it is very necessary that the teacher should sometimes ask questions, sometimes use blackboard, draw diagram, use charts, maps, illustrate, give assignment, move a little, or even should keep silent for a while. Going at the same speed, continuously lecturing or speaking in the same- way is monotonous for the students, Hence, changing the activity is necessary. But, this should not be in a way that makes the teacher a laughing stalk: How to do it has to be learnt. This is an important skill.

10. B= Blackboard. This is the simple skill relating to the use of the blackboard.

11. 0 = Objectives. This refers to the skill of identifying the objectives of teaching and stating them in behavioral terms.

12. M=Managing the class. This refers to teacher's capability of controlling students and maintaining discipline in the class.

13. S= Silence. There are occasions when a teacher is required to keep silent in the class. Teacher's silence can be used as a tool for achieving certain important purposes. If the students are noisy and the teacher just stops teaching, keeps

silent staring at students for a minute they will stop making noise immediately. The teacher asks the students to think over a problem and himself has to keep silent, During this period using non-verbal cues he can encourage, correct, reinforce, direct the behaviors of the students. But, how to (in all that successfully has got to be learned.

14. Q- Questioning. Questions serve various purposes. They, are used for directing students' thinking, directing students ability of analysis, leading discussion, developing understanding, arousing interest, curiosity and inquisitiveness, involving students in learning, providing students an opportunity to talk and make their own contribution. There are various types of questions asked at different stages of teaching. Framing good questions and handling answers of the students is a very important skill. Very few teachers are able to frame and ask divergent questions and higher order questions or probing questions. This is what the teachers have to learn.

15. C= Closure. Bow to wind up the teaching session or a unit of that is also a skill.

Finishing the lesson abruptly is not effective.

Ending with a few most important points repeated by way of summarization in an interesting manner is more effective.

There can he other ways also. But, this is to be learned.

2. FLANDERS INTERACTION ANALYSIS

Teaching may be viewed as a system of interaction between the teacher and the pupils. Educational researchers have been working on the problem of describing teacher's classroom behavior in a systematic manner for several decades. They have used two systems for this purpose (1) sign system, and (2) the category system. In case of the sign system the isolated events to be observed arc determined and frequencies of occurrence of each of them is recorded, for example, the number of times a teacher asks questions, number of times he praises the student, number of times he issues instructions, etc. In case of the second approach, the category system teacher's classroom behavior is classified and put into one of the predetermined categories e.g., convergent or divergent, integrative or diminutive, etc.

Meaning And Nature of Flanders Interaction Analysis Category System (FIACS):

Flanders Interaction Analysis system is a category system. In this an attempt is made to observe and record systematically the spontaneous act of the teacher teaching in the classroom and scrutinize the process of instruction by taking into account each small bit of interaction. It is particularly concerned with the influence pattern of the teacher. It is concerned primarily with verbal behavior of the teacher. The assumption is t at the verbal behavior of the teacher is an adequate sample of his total behavior and also that verbal behavior patterns of teachers and pupils are significantly related to teaching effectiveness.

Ned A. Flanders developed it in 1963. The beginning of classroom interaction analysis maybe traced to early research by Kurt Lewin, Ronald. Lippitt and Ralph White. But, the Flanders system of verbal interaction analysis the best known and most widely used.

The Procedure : The first step of the procedure is to encode the Behaviour of the teacher teaching in the classroom. For this the observer sits in the classroom in the best position to hear and see the participant. He observes closely the behavior of the teacher. At the end of each 3-second period he records the communication event, which is completed by writing down the number of the category to which it belongs. There are ten categories in all. The observer decides to which of these categories the behavioral event belongs. He writes this category number down while simultaneously assessing communication in the next period. For example, if the teacher asks the students to answer a question, he immediately writes down 4; when the student answers the question, he puls down h and so on. He continues in this way at a rate of 20 to 25 observations 'per minute(His record is, thus, a sequence of numbers written in a column, top to bottom with the result that the original sequence of events is preserved. Occasionally, marginal notes are put to explain the class formation or any unusual circumstances When there is a major change in class formation, the communication pattern. or the subject under discussion, the observer draws a double line and the time. When the observations have been completed, he goes to a nearby room and writes up a general description of each separate activity period. This includes the nature of the activities, the class formation, and the position of the teacher. The observer also notes down any additional facts that seem pertinent to interpretation and recall of the total observation period. In case of doubt the behavioural event is assigned to the category which is farthest from 5, for example, if it is not certain whether the event should be classified as 6 or g it is which is recorded Similar if the doubt is between 2 and 4, it is which is chosen. Intentions and biases are put as? and not as 2. All e1tegorics of behavioural events occurring during the 3- second interval are recorded. If the behavioural event continues even during the next three seconds, the saner category is repeated.

The Categories: There are ten categories in the system. Seven of these are assigned to teacher talk and two to student talk. The tenth category covers pauses, short period of silence, and the talk that is confusing or noisy. The following table described the category system:

TABLE-I

CATEGORIES OF FIACS (1959)

T	In	1	ACCEPTS FEELING : accepts and clarifies the tone of
E	di		feeling of the students in an unthreatening manner. Feelings
A	re		may be positive or negative. Predicting or recalling feelings
C	ct	2	are included.
H	in		PRAISES OR ENCOURAGES : Praises or encourages
E	fl		student action or behaviour. Jokes that release tension, but
R	ue		not at the expense of another individual, nodding head or
T	n	3	saying "um hm"? or "go on" are included.
A	ce		ACCEPTS OR USES IDEAS OF STUDENT : Clarifying
			building, or developing ideas suggested by a student.
	Dir	5	LECTURING : Giving facts or opinions about content or
	Ec		procedure; expressing his own ideas, asking rhetorical
	T	6	questions.
	In		GIVING DIRECTIONS : Directions, commands, or orders
	Flue	7	which students are expected to comply with.
	Nce		CRITICIZING OR JUSTIFYING AUTHORITY :
			Statements intended to change student behaviour from
			unacceptable.
Student		8	STUDENT TALK-RESPONSE : Talk by students in
talk			response to teacher.
		9	STUDENT TALK-INITIATION : Talk initiated by student.
			If "calling on" student is only to indicate who may talk next,
			observer must decide.
Silence		10	SILENCE OR CONFUSION : Pauses, short periods of
			silence, and periods of confusion in which communication
			cannot be.

*There is NO scale implied by these numbers. Each number is classificatory designating a particular kind of communication event. To write these numbers down during observation is merely to identify and enumerate communication events, not to judge them.

Of the seven categories assigned to teacher talk, category 1 through 4 represent indirect intluence and category 5,6,7 direct intluence. Indirect" intluence encourages participation by the students and increases their' freedom of action. When the teacher asks a question (category 4), it means'" he provides an opportunity to students to participate and express their ideas, opinions or facts. Similarly when the teacher accepts, clarifies or uses constructively the ideas and opinions of students (category 3), they are further encouraged to participate this is a way of recognizing the students which is a very satisfying experience to them. Again when the teacher praises or encourages student participation directly (category- 2) it solicits even more participation by way of reward. Category I implies a very important skill of the teacher. By accepting students' feelings, using them constructively, reacting to their feelings and clarifying them the teacher can mobilize positive feelings for motivating the students and can' control their negative feelings. All the behaviours of the teacher falling into categories: 1 through 4 increases and reward student participation and provides greater freedom of action for the students.

Direct influence means active control of the teacher. It is an attempt on seeking compliance. The lecture (category 5) seeks students' attention on ideas chosen by the teacher. The intention of directing or commanding (category 6) is to direct the activities of the class; and again, to seek compliance. Category 7 concentrates authority in the hands of the teacher. Thus, direct influence means authoritative teacher and restrained students. Restriction of student's freedom results into students' compliance. In any case it results into less freedom of action for the students.

Direct teacher influence is associated with less student talk. This is generally the result of responses to the teacher (category 8), Category 9 reflects a pattern of indirect influence and is associated with more student talk. The division of student talk into categories 8 and 9 provides an automatic check on freedom of student action. Category I should be used only to indicate the student's' spontaneous expression of his own ideas.

The purpose of category 10 is to record short pauses, silences, and periods of confusion. If this continues for more then two minutes, it is not to be recorded. It serves no purpose. The system of categories is meant for use in situations in which the teacher and the students are actively engaged in discussion. It is not applicable in a situation in which communication is discontinuous separated by long periods of silence. It is only spontaneous interaction for which this system is used. If two-way communication does not exist, the observer must stop and make a note to this effect only with its. reasons and should resume making record when spontaneous interaction begin to take place.

Decoding: Having completed the observations and having recorded the categories, they arc first put into pairs and are transferred on to a 10X 10 matrix table. In order to put them into pairs a category 10 is added at the top as well as the bottom of the column of the observed categories as shown below in figure -1

Figure-1

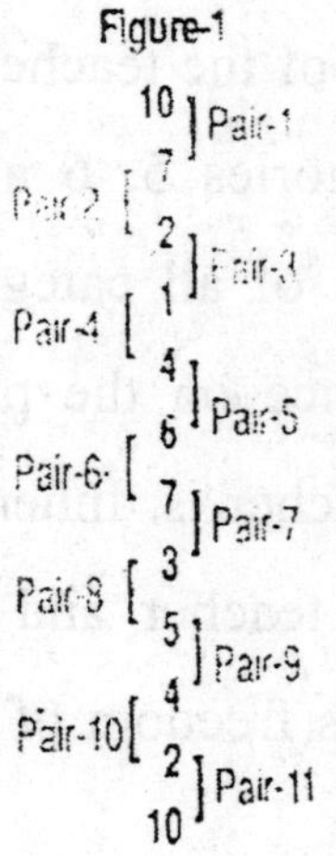

ROWS	1	2	3	4	5	6	7	8	9	10	Total
1				1							1
2	1									1	2
3					1						1
4		1				1					2
5				1							1
6							1				1
7		1	1								2
8											0
9											0
10							1				1
Total	1	2	1	2	1	1	2	0	0	1	11

Having put the categories into pairs as shown under figure-I, each pair's position is marked in the cells of the matrix as shown in table-2. The first category of the pair is taken on the row side while the second is taken on the column side; for example first pair (10-7) is marked in the cell which is formed by 10th row and 7th column. In this way ail categories are transferred to the matrix. Row wise and column wise totals are made which must be equal to one another if there is no error. This interaction matrix or teacher behavior matrix is, then, used for analysis and interpretation. For this purpose various kinds of ratios are calculated. Some very useful ratios are:

1. Teacher Talk Ratio: This indicates the extent of teacher's being active in the class, i.e., how much he talks or how dominant he is. This is calculated by adding all the frequencies of categories 1, 2, 3, 4, 5, 6 and 7 and dividing the total by the total number of frequencies of all categories (N) and multiplying the dividend by 100. The formula is expressed as

$$\text{Teachers Talk Ratio (TTR)} = \frac{f(I+2+3+4+5+6+7)}{N} \times 100$$

F = frequencies

2. Direct Talk: This represents direct influence or control of the teacher. It is the ratio between the sum total of the frequencies of. categories 5, 6 and 7 (i.e. lecturing, directiil g, criticizing) and the total frequencies of all categories (N). This kind of teacher behavior often, stimulates compliance on the part of the students. The high ratio may tell h9w authoritarian the teacher is. Inherent in the high ratio of this talk is increased participation of the teacher and increased restraint on students' behavior. It may be interpreted as less freedom of action for the student. This is calculated by using the formula:

$$\text{Direct Talk} = \frac{f(5+6+7)}{N} \times 100$$

3. Indirect Talk: Indirect talk refers to the sum total of frequencies of categories 1, 2, 3 and 4 (i.e. accepting feelings, praising, accepting or using student ideas and asking questions). In terms of ratio it means

$$\text{Indirect Talk} = \frac{f(1+2+3+4)}{N} \times 100$$

This ratio represents indirect influence of the teacher which encourages student participation and allows greater freedom of action to students. It may be taken as an index of teacher's permissiveness. Teachers high on this are able to motivate the students and control successfully their negative feelings. This is very close to democratic/quality of the teacher.

4. Indirect-Direct Ratio (ID-Ratio): This is the ratio between the direct and indirect influences of the teacher which reveals whether a teacher is authoritarian or democratic, whether he is self oriented or student- oriented, whether he allows freedom to students or tries to dominate over the class. It is calculated as follows:

$$\text{I/D Ratio} = \frac{f(1+2+3+4)}{f(5+6+7)} \times 100$$

5. Pupil Talk: The student talk is divided into categories 8 and 9 which provides an automatic check on freedom of students' action within the system of categories. This is calculated as follows:

$$PT = \frac{f(8+9)}{N} \times 100$$

6. Pupil Initiative Ratio (PIR): The student talk is divided into two categories 8 and 9. Category 8 is associated with direct teacher influence indicating less student initiative. I n the same way category 9 is associated with indirect influence of the teacher indicating more talk by the student. Thus, pupils initiative is judged by taking the ratio of category 9 to categories 8 and 9 both combined together, It is calculated in the following manner,

$$PIR = \frac{f(9)}{f(8+9)} \times 100$$

In the same way some more ratios are calculated. Some of them are: 7. Silence or Confusion Ratio (SR or CR): The formula for this

$$SC = \frac{f(10)}{N} \times 100$$

8. Teacher Response Ratio

$$(TRR) = \frac{f(1+2+3)}{f(1+2+3+6+7)} \times 100$$

This refers to teacher's willingness to react to the ideas and feelings of the students.

9. Teacher Question ,Ratio (TQR): It is computed by using the formula:

$$TQR = \frac{f(4)}{f(4+5)} \times 100$$

10. Content Cross Ratio (CCR): This tells whether the teacher is more subject or discipline- oriented or student- oriented aiming at student motivation and interest. It is calculated as

$$CCR = \frac{f(4+5)}{N} \times 100$$

Besides these, a Jew researchers have given some ratios. But, these' are more of research interest than of practical use.

Implications Of Interaction Analysis:

Interaction analysis is based on the premise that the verbal behavior patterns of the teachers and pupils in the classroom are significantly related to teaching effectiveness. The, analysis provides a common ground for the teacher and the analyst to consider the teacher's directive and non-directive verbal influence. It should not be thought that all direct behavior is bad, or that all indirect behavior is good. The system is well suited to analysis of both, preserves and in-service Performance. But, as is the case with microteaching its purpose is not evaluation or fating of teachers. Rather it is designed as a tool to provide an objective basis for analysis and subsequent improvement of instruction. It provides to the teacher concerned a rapid feedback, which results into improvement of his teaching behavior. Several qualities of his teaching improve; for' example, questioning ability, ability to ensure student participation in teaching, skill of motivating, ways of communicating with students are some of these qualities which improve. Classroom interaction analysis .of this kind is a strong motivating force for both teachers and pupils. It develops in them a sense of inquiry, creative thinking and experimentation. The system of analysis makes the teachers and the students aware of the value of active participation, which helps pupils to achieve, feel successful and develop better attitudes. It provides the teachers with definite; systematic data regarding their performance and its influence on the behavior of the pupils. In fact, it improves the total learning climate.

In spite of the advantages and the implications of interaction analysis as discussed earlier, it is criticised on several counts. Some of the points raised by its critiques are:

1. In general its reliability is not quite satisfactory. Recording of teacher's and students' responses in the form of categories can not be considered very objective Judgment may be made after too few visits or too little observation.

2. It covers a very small territory of what goes on in the classroom. There are many aspects of teaching that are not touched by this system of analysis. Hence, it has very limited scope of its application.

3. Many "a time the behaviors, statements or questions of teachers are

found to be difficult to fit into a classification system.

4. It requires a well trained and a very skillful person to use the system. The process cannot benefit everyone.

5. Teachers, generally, do not like to be analyzed in this way.

6. It is very time- consuming.

7. Interpretation of the categories and various ratios is not easy. The whole system is too complicated and unwieldy and difficult to explain to teachers.

8. It ignores non- verbal interaction which is equally important.

9. It is too atomistic and destroys the wholeness of the teaching act. Teaching, apart from being a science, is an art also. And that art of teaching is disregarded by the system.

Final 'Remark: several of the above criticisms have little relevance. Although research evidence of the value of Flanders Interaction Analysis is not conclusive it has proved itself as a method of gathering a kind of data and summarizing it, It has established itself as a good tool for diagnosis and improvement. It is an objective way of knowing about what the teacher does in the classroom; and what influence his actions, his performance has on pupils and on the overall classroom climate. The criticism that FIACS takes into consideration only the teacher's verbal behavior ignoring nonverbal and other aspects is not relevant because that is the purpose for which the, system has. been developed. No system can be all inclusive. It should not be doubted that FIACS contributes quite significantly to identification of teacher's verbal patterns of behavior that affect learning, both positively and negatively.

3. SIMULATION

Meaning And Nature:

Simulation is a teaching procedure that uses a model of a real system to provide a life-like representation to stimulate and aid learning. The representation of the real world may be physical or symbolic. But, they are designed it introduce realism into the learning environment. Symbolic models are usually verbal or mathematical. The mathematical models are often used to express qualitative relationships in quantitative terms. Simulations are used for learning or training “off the-job" or "off the real situation", what is simulated may be the equipment, the material or solutions representing the real ones. Gagne (pp. 91-94) has described three important features of simulation. These are: (1) it represents the real situation in which the operations are carried out; (2) it provides its users with certain controls over that situation. (3) it is designed to admit certain parts of the real operational situation. The crucial components of the real situation are incorporated into the constructed model and are presented as verbal descriptions, diagrams, pictures, and other symbolic representations. The real environment is limited and simplified so that it can be more readily manipulated. Time and space are usually compressed and significant aspects of reality are selected.

Simulation has been used in various fields and in various forms for learning and training purposes. One example of simulation of equipment is aircraft simulation. One can see different types of car simulators also. Trains and ships arc also the areas where simulation is used for learning certain skills. Simulators in these areas represent car's, tram's and ship's displays and controls with films being shown of traffic situations. Examples of simulation of material are found in dentistry and tailoring. Dental students may be found using 'phantom heads' for practicing various skills. Paper or old worn-out cloth is used for learning cutting for various kinds of dresses. Simulation of behavioral components, for example, social skills is frequently used" in service industries concerned with person-to-person interactions. Hotels, travel agencies, air transport, education, management of organizations all have tasks of this kind, e.g., sales transaction, watering, marketing teacher training, etc. The skills involved here are' customer contact skills', 'teaching skills', 'social skills', etc. Role-playing is used in a big way in these areas for developing certain specific skills and behavioral components. Role-playing involves playing the part of a job incumbent, e.g. hotel receptionist or an insurance agent or a medical representative. The trainer or another 'trainee plays the role of customers, etc. They act out a situation that can be videotaped and replayed with suitable comment and suggestion from trainer. In management training business games are used as simulators, In teacher training colleges training situations are simulated for developing teaching skills In the student teachers.

Advantages of Simulations: The operational situation is often not the best place for teaching the required skills or performing the task. For various reasons it may be inconvenient or improper. These reasons may be (1) costs and consequences of error, (2) poor availability of needed feedback, (3) environmental stresses, (4) constraints of time, i.e., the operational situation may be time-consuming, (5) lack of provision of part-task simu!ation. (6) paucity of needed facilities in operational situation.

The early stages of learning and training are characterized by errors which in job situations may not be tolerable. Learning to fly, for example, is one such job, in case of which small error may result in huge loss in terms of man and material both. Costly apparatus may be damaged and the trainee may lose his life. Simulation can reduce these costs to a very great extent. Simulation provides a situation in which the feedback in the form of knowledge of one's performance can be managed more effectively as and when desired. For example, when a pupil teacher is practicing teaching in the actual classroom of 30 to 40 students, it is not possible fix the supervisor to tell him on the spot that he was wrong or he should not have done something. But, in a simulated class of 5 to 1'0 pupil teachers it is possible to discuss, then and there, where he was wrong and what he should have done. The simulate can give extrinsic feedback on the spot. On the job it may snot be, possible. Another advantage of simulation is that the task maybe performed in an environment which is free from the stresses of the operational situation. For example when a newly recruited student teacher is asked to teach a large class he is under various kinds of fears and stresses such as fear of being unable to handle the apparatus, fear of being judged to be a poor teacher and so on. In a class of his own class fellows which is a simulated situation he knows that he will commit mistakes only to be corrected and guided by the supervisor, The situation is not so stressful for him. He is in the "sheltered" situation. The situation is not so stressful for him. He is in the "sheltered" simulated situation. Again, simulation permits practice of more components of the job than possible in the actual operational situation for example, in a simulated teacher training situation it is possible to demonstrate ho",: to do model reading on the spot while in actual classroom practice of teaching it is not possible. On the spot demonstration of several teaching skills is not possible in actual classroom teaching practice. It is possible in case of the simulated classroom teaching. The full period actual classroom teaching practice does not permit "part- task" learning and training. It is the whole task which has to be practiced in real situation. But, in case of simulated situation it is possible to practice learning of any number of separate and individual components of the task. For example, in case of simulated teacher training it is possible to simulate training in any of the fourteen teaching skills separately. Even attitude development and development of social skills can be simulated. Such separate "part-task" simulation is not possible in ease of real task training. Simulation, therefore, provides relatively economic and simple devices of teaching, learning, and training.

Besides the above, simulation is "appealing, motivates intense effort and increases learning". It is held by some experts that simulation is particularly effective with under motivated persons. It enables the trainer to control extraneous factors allecting performance adversely which exist in the real situation, thus, simplifying the complexity of the real situation. Simulated situation can be adjusted to wide range of individual differences. Optional starting and stopping are additional advantages. Success or failure is rapidly and readily recognized by the trainee as well as the supervisor. Simulation, by and large, generates deep emotional involvement bf the trainee in learning the task and, thus, prevents alienation of the learner.

Criticism of Simulation: However simulation is criticised on several counts. He is agreed by many that simulators developed and used are generally, narrow in their applicability. It is also said that they suffer from low degree or fidelity meaning thereby that the transferability of the acquired skill is poor. They do not provide the experience of the real feel of the job; hence they are superficial exercises .of learning and training.

Simulation In Teacher Training: The most common forms of simulation have' computerized models. War games have existed or hundreds of years: Chess is, often, considered as the oldest of the war games. Much of the early work in simulation has been done in the field of social studies with attention being focused on group interaction. In the field of teacher education simulation is widely used for practice of teaching, particularly for developing certain skills of teaching in the student teachers. Microteaching is largely practised in simulated situation in which the class consists of 4 to 5 pupil teachers only. The whole procedure is designed in as simplified a manner as possible. Being a "scaled down" simulated situation it is very convenient, comfortable and controlled situation.

Simulation in teacher education can be used for developing essential social skills also, particularly the skill to deal with pupils, colleagues, subordinates and super ordinates. One such model has been developed by Cruicksshank (p. 23-26) which is known as Simulated Social Skill Training (SSST) in which the actual classroom situation is simulated in such a way that the student teachers themselves constitute the classroom and- they themselves play the role of the teacher and thought a controlled feedback device the desirable social behaviors are established in them. But, this is not the only model which can be used for training teachers. In the psychology, sociology and management training there are several simulated designs of teaching and training which are used Their use has been discussed in detail by Guetzkow (1962), Raser (1969), Rogers (1970), Sachs (1970) and Tansey (] 969). Though they are not commonly used in training teachers, they can be successfully utilized for developing special skills. Role- playing, T-group Training, Transactional Analysis, Sensitivity Training, etc. maybe used after designing them appropriately.

How To Use Simulation Effectively: Simulated teacher training programmes can be made more effective by taking a few precautions. Suggestions to this effect are as follows:

The supervisors must take the programme seriously and must plan it carefully with the purpose and focus clearly understood. The skills to be practiced must be objectively defined and effectively demonstrated. Feadback must be real and genuincana used judiciously. Accurate information and facts are essential. An open climate should be maintained free from the domination of the supervisor. Threats to the ego of the trainee should be avoided.

In spite of their limitations simulation techniques of all kinds are in a stage of rapid experimentation and utilization. In schools of America, simulations are becoming alternative methods of instruction to the lecture, discussion, group and other methods of teaching. Using physical, verbal and mathematical media, the simulators are employed in the teaching of information skills, values, attitudes and behavioral changes.

COMMUNICATION

Communication is a very important sub-system of education. Every educational organization, the university, the school, the department of education depends for its effective functioning, on this sub-system. The following discussion will throw light on communication relationships and processes that occur among people at various levels in the educational system, such as the administrators and the supervisors. The discussion will be exclusively confined to communication as related to teaching,

Meaning: Communication is the transfer of information and understanding from one person to, another person. It is a process through which a person reaches other person with knowledge, ideas, facts, thoughts and values. Merrihue (p. 5) defines communication as a process of "mutual exchange of thoughts, ideas, facts and emotions". It is a "process of getting across ideas and information to another person, meaning thereby, that a person presents, in some from, some information while the,- other person or groups of persons receive it. It is through this process that people relate themselves to other people. In away this is the process which, builds a bridge or-meaning and understanding between two or more persons.

Communication is a process which always involves two people, one the sender of information and the other the receiver of the information. The existence of the receiver is essential in the process of communication as one, person alone cannot communicate. The process of communication takes rise at the level of the sender, the communicator and terminates at the level of the receiver, some other person or the group, who receives it and acknowledges it.

COMMUNICATION PROCESS

Elements:

There are six steps, elements or components involved in the process of communication. These are:

(1) The **Message** or the information, any idea, thought or meaning

(2) The **Encoder or Encoding** i.e., rendering that message into words, charts, pictures, diagrams or any other suitable symbol for transmission. These serve as signals of information used by the sender, transmitter or the encoder. In the context of teaching the teacher and the students both play the role of the sender depending on the situation. When the teacher explains a concept to the students he plays the role of the sender or encoder of the message. But, when the student seeks some clarifications and asks the teacher to explain something the student assumes the role of the encoder.

(3) Transmission, which means that when the message to be communicated is finally decided the sender selects an appropriate mode or way of communicating or transmitting these signals to the receivers. At this stage the sender takes several relevant-decisions find precautions. Particularly, he has to make efforts to control "noise" and eliminate the various kinds of barriers to effective communication.

(4) The Receiver: This means the person who receives the information, decodes it and uses it. In order to receive the infol1nation he may listen it (if it is oral), write it (if it is dictated), observe it (if it is something of the diagram form). If the receiver does not function efficiently the message is lost. In case of instruction largely the students but quite often the teachers also function as receivers of the information. When the information flows from the teacher the students receive it and when it flows from the students the teacher receives it.

(5) Decoding: This is the fifth step in the process of communication. The receiver having received the message decodes it so that it comes meaningful to him The sender wants" the receiver to understand' the message exactly-in the way it was meant which is not the case many a time because the sender and the receiver are two different persons Due to "the differences in personal? and environmental characteristics of the receiver the message communicated is not decoded and understood by him in the same way as it was understood by the sender. In case of class room teaching the students receive the, information from the teacher. But, all of them do not understand the same equally well as desired by the teacher for students may have their own differences. The teacher can make the students listen; but it is not easy to make all of them understand also. It is the students only who choose whether to understand or hot to understand. Many teachers think that teaching something to student in the class is sufficient, while the fact is that communication is not truly successful until there is understanding. This is known as "getting through" to a person. The teachers, therefore, should ask themselves every time in the class" Am I getting through to my students".

(6) Use: This is the last component of the communication process. The infor.nation having been received and even decoded (i.e understood) it is not necessary that it will be used by the receiver as desired by the sender. Several options arc left with the receiver, He may ignore it, store it , add to it, subtract from it, do as desired or do something else. But in case of teaching certainly there are predetermined goals to be achieved through classroom communication. Hence, the teachers need to communicate, inside as well as outside the classroom, with the students and other 'concerned persons with great care.

The following figure is illustrative of these components.

PROCESS OF COMMUNICATION

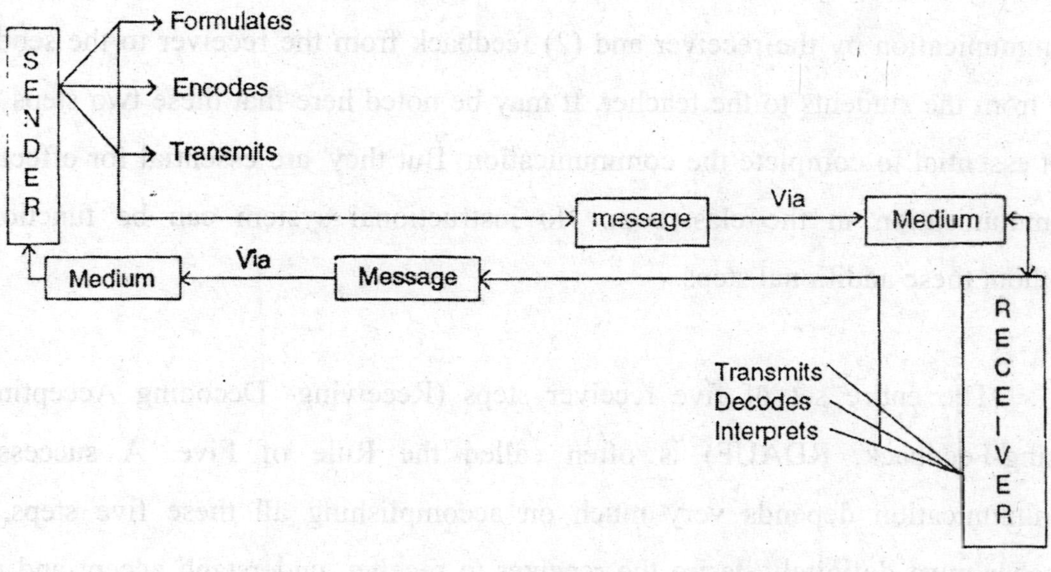

Fig. 1

PROCESS OF COMMUNICATION

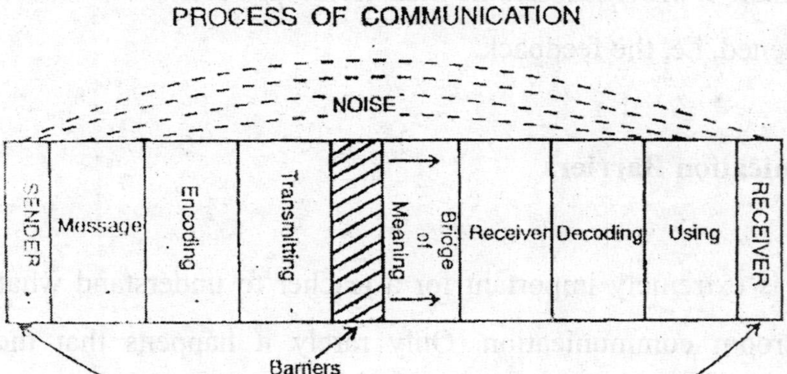

Fig. 2

Two additional receiver steps are considered necessary in situations of teaching-learning particularly. These are (1) acceptance of the message or communication by the receiver and (2) feedback from the receiver to the sender, i.e from the students to the teacher. It may be noted here that these two steps are not essential to complete the communication. But they' are essential for effective communication in the classroom. No instructional system can be functional without these additional steps.

The entire set of five receiver steps (Receiving- Decoding Accepting-. Using-Feedback, RDAUF) is often called the Rule of Five. A successful communication depends very much on accomplishing all these five steps. A teacher must definitely desire the receiver to receive, understand accept and use the information provided; and he must he deeply concerned with knowing how all this happened, i.e, the feedback.

Communication Barriers

It is extremely important for a teacher to understand what interferes with his classroom communication. Only rarely it happens that the students fully understand what the teacher wishes to communicate to them. There are a number of interferences which limit students understanding of what the teacher communicates to them. These interferences are known as Barriers to communication which may entirely prevent a communication, filter some part of it out, or' give it an incorrect meaning. These barriers are classified as follows:

1. Personal Barriers: - These constitute the personality variables of the students and the teachers. They arise from human emotions, perceptions, attitudes. skills. values and a host of other personality traits. This is common experience of all of us that many a time our feelings and emotions limit or distort our communication with others. Human emotions act as filters in most communications that occur between people. It is a. common phenomenon that people see and. hear what they are emotionally tuned to see and hear. The psychological variables can not be banished from the scene of communication.. What the teacher says or does in the class is perceived and made meaningful by the students in the context of their own feelings, attitudes, interests and purposes. The teacher communicates, but what it stands for is determined by students own interpretation which is coloured by their. preexisting personal variables. For example the teacher tells his students "what I am going to discuss today is very important"; but that may not be a thing perceived by the students as important.

2. Physical Barriers: - These constitute the environmental factors which interfere with the communication. The noise outside the classroom, lack of discipline and order, conditions prevailing in the classroom, the lighting and ventilation conditions, the condition and availability of the blackboard and other needed facilities, poor- socio-emotional climate of the classroom all are factors that may interfere with the classroom communication.

3. Semantic Barriers -These relate to limitations in the symbols which are used: in communication. Symbols usually have a variety of meaning. Sometimes, the teacher may choose the wrong meaning and misunderstanding occurs. If the teacher says "You are a clever boy", the use of the word "clever" may have a meaning which annoys the student. This blocks further communication. Students may misinterpret words, inferences, pictures, charts and actions all. When it happens it interferes with the communication. If the teacher asks questions to only one or two students repeatedly, this may be misinterpreted as teacher's favouring those students which may cause some students to dislike the teacher further blocking the communication. Words have multiple meanings depending upon the contexts in, which they a1 used, A word appropriate in one context may not be appropriate in another context.

4. Barriers of Communication: - Kimball Wiles (p. 58-61) widely known in the field of supervision discusses in detail the following factors that distort the meaning of message and reduce its accuracy.

1. Differences in the meanings of words and symbols used by people.
2. Differences in the values held by people.
3. Differences in the perceptions of the problem.
4. Emphasis on status.
5. Conflicting interests of people.
6. Making decisions by majority vote rather than by consensus.
7. Trying to keep feelings out of discussion.
8. Using such words, which prevent thinking.
9. I.ack of, desire to understand other person's point of view or his feelings, values and purposes.
10.' Refusing to accept diversity.
11. One-way conception of co-operation
12. Feelings of superiority
13. Vested interest;
14. An obvious attempt to push one's ideas.
15. Feelings of personal insecurity.
16. Differences in the role-concepts of the sender and the receiver of the message.
17. Negative feelings about the situation etc

Informal And Formal Communication

Teaching may be considered a specialized form of communication between the teacher and the students. This communication, however, may be formal as well as informal. Formal communication is a designed and contrived way, which takes lace in a well-regulated setting for achieving, specified objectives according to standard rules and procedures. Classroom teaching is formal communication that is organized in a deliberated manner to be conducted according to predetermined timetable by predetermined set of teachers. Both the teacher child the students know well what the theme of communication has to be and what purposes both have to achieve. Most things of the setting are defined and a significant deviation is not possible. Parameters of formal communication in the teaching - learning setting are knowledge of the subject (message), methods 01' teaching (channels' of communication) and objectives of teaching (receiving, decoding and using by the students). This formal communication in a teaching context is a conscious, deliberate, designed and purposeful way of interaction.

In formal communication on the other hand, is passing of an underhand message of which the teacher is not generally aware. It is unintentional, unplanned, indefinite flow of ideas, feelings, and attitudes from teacher to the students. From student to student inside the class and outside the class. Grapevine is one form of this kind of communication. It occurs by the way in the class, outside the class, in small groups of students or in the whole class. This may take the form 0,1' the criticism of the teacher, appreciation of his teaching or personality, also condemnation of certain of his behaviour. All these reactions of students, which f1oat freely among the students inside and outside the class take, rise in the 'Nay the teacher interacts with the students. They may include all kinds of students attitudes, satisfactions and dissatisfactions generated about teacher's formal communication and informal interactions with the students. But they are important as they give a colour to the socio- emotional and academic climate of the classroom. An insightful teacher keeps constant watch over this i1ormal communication and consciously tries to control it in the interest of effective teaching. He should keep his eyes and ears open to keep himself abreast of students feelings and attitudes, classroom groupings of students and their motives, the grapevine they spread and should try to correct if something is found undesirable through positive and constructive ways of communication. What a teacher communicates to the students informally is as important as formal communication.

COMMUNICATION FEEDBACK

To be sure that the message (knowledge of the subject) has reached the students (the receiver) with the same meaning, purpose and intention as was desired, the teacher has to get some acknowledgement from the students. Feedback is the process that ensures this. This can "take the form of a nod, an acknowledgement, or doing something as expected by the students. Feedback provides a learning opportunity to the-teacher and the students both as it mirrors where the communication has gaps or inadequacies indicating the corrective action to be taken. In case of classroom teaching such feedback is essential for effective teaching. On -the other hand if students act in conformity with the communicated items, they also need to know this from the teacher. This kind of feedback loop is the most essential principle of effective teaching. Positive and negative both kinds of feedback are necessary. They should, however be focused on specific action rather, than on the individual student. Comments related to behaviour are accepted more easily than those relating to an individual's personality, attitudes, feelings etc. But it is necessary to tell the students where they are wrong. If they are not told this, the wrongs may perpetuate. Feedback, which is provided "here and now", is more meaningful than the delayed one. It is more effective to provide a feedback as a way of sharing information rather than insisting on the right way of doing things. For that reason the teacher and the students should study the problems and the situations together, evaluate various alternatives and choose the best. This motivates the students and allows. them to feel that they are the important link in the process of teaching - learning.

IMPORTANCE OF COMMUNICATION

Importance pf communication in teaching - learning can hardly he overemphasized. If the instructional system is to operate effectively, the teacher must understand the fundamentals of communication process as teaching is just communication and nothing else. Communication is the basic necessity for teaching- learning. It is a tool to achieve the instructional goals. Hence, the teacher is required to understand what ıt is and how it works. This is true that a teacher should know his subject of teaching well but still more important for him is to put that in the minds of the students which is ensured only by the process of communication. A teacher can not be effective without being a good communicate or He needs skills in getting his thoughts, ideas, understandings, facts, concepts and principles inherent in his teaching subject across to his students. And this is what communication means. It is through communication that he fails or succeeds in changing the attitudes and skills of his students. It is communication which he uses for motivating the students to generate good or bad human relations in the classroom giving a particular shape to classroom climate. It may be students feelings of alienation or satisfaction, students morale or frustration, students interest in or apathy to learning, students understandings or misunderstandings, all, in one way or another, are outcomes of some kind of communication.

PRINCIPLES OF EFFECTIVE COMMUNICATION

A teacher who desires to be successful, who wishes to be effective must learnt that art of communication. Words have great power, and the way they are expressed has still greater power. No teacher can succeed in his mission if he lacks the ability-to express his ideas in an effective manner. In this section, a few principles a few considerations are stated which, if followed may help the teachers in achieving success in. this art of communication.

1. Focus: - Before saying something or discussing or organizing a conference, its purpose should be clearly identified and this should be kept, in mind constantly while speaking or discussing. This focus should guide the communication of the teacher.

2. Understand the Receiver: - This means that the teacher must analyze and understand the abilities, interests, values, motives, educational and experiential background of students, their fears and anxieties, their intentions and purposes and should try to keep them in mind while passing the message to them. He must try to adjust as far as possible to these individual differences existing among the' students of the class.

3. Planning and Designing of the message:- The needed adjustment described above requires planning and designing of the message with utmost care. The choice of words and expressions, the choice of material, illustrations, etc. all need to he made in the light of the characteristics of the students and the objective to he achieved. At every stage the teacher must question "how will this be received by the students

4. No losing the heart: - If the students do not understand his point of view and argue illogically or begin to be restless or mistrust him or their fellows, he should not lose heart as, in view of many kinds of psychological differences existing among 'them, they are hound to perceive the problem differently. It is, part of human nature. Hence no need to be upset or frustrated.

Similarly some students may be interested in getting a decision made in their own interest and they may oppose or may not see the point being made by the teacher. Considering that all these things are a natural phenomenon of group life, the teacher should not get discouraged. He may use more relevant and vigorous approach to make the students see his point of view.

5. A variety of media to be used: - The teacher should use a variety of approaches messages and media in order to appeal to different students in the calls. The same technique, method or way of approach may not be effective in case of all the students. Hence, he has to be dynamic and flexible.

6. Keep in mind five things: - Of whom you speak, to whom you speak, what you speak, when you speak and where you speck as these variables will require you to choose specific and different ways and media for communication in order to produce desired effects.

7. Develop genuine interest in the purpose and the people - - Identification with the task to be completed or the objective to be achieved and a genu111e interest in the students is very necessary for effective communication. In the absence of this genuine words, expressions, methods and techniques will not be available to the teacher. His genuine, spontaneous feelings will not come out of his inner world. His performance will remain superficial. The students may not be impressed, moved, stirred-up in that case. The communication in this situation will remain ineffective. A liking for students. a genuine interest in them should be reflected in the overt behaviour of the teacher. The same should be reflected in regard to the objectives to be achieved. This will enable the' teacher to have at his disposal more meaningful and relevant words, expressions, gestures, illustrations, methods and media. The communication will then become more effective.

8. Be Knowledgeable and well-informed: - This is important as only when the teacher has these qualities he will be perceived by the students as a competent person This kind of perception is necessary for releasing prestige suggestions to the students. In that case, the students will unwillingly accept whatever is aid or desired by the teacher. The teacher in order to be effective and influential must read constantly and keep himself abreast of the day-to-day developrnents taking place in the field of education and teaching. In other related fields of knowledge also he should have up to-date knowledge.

9. Let others feel you are well-informed: - Just reading latest literature and keeping himself well-informed in posses-Jon of up-to-date knowledge is not ,enough. Students around should know this fact about you. Only then, they will be impressed and have regards for you. They know about this quality of yours when you play an active role in the classroom, conferences, discussions, suggesting innovations and programmes of curriculum and instructional improvement. "Remember that unexpressed ideas are of no more value than the kernels in a nut' before it is cracked" (Marks, p.132) this is necessary for effective communication.

10. Have poise and balance in heated discussions: - Control over emotions is essential for effective communication in all situations, particularly in a situation of heated discussions. The teacher, in the interest of effective communication, should never use sarcasm, derogatory remarks, insulting words or language as this will immediately reveal to the students his inner weakness and they will not be influenced by him. He should display in his behaviour high degree of tolerance, regard for students, poise and balance. These qualities should be manifest in his tone of voice; facial expressions, volume and rate of speech. posture and approaches to answering students questions.

11. Prepare hard for conveying your message: - A good preparation for teaching discussion, conferences, meetings etc. is necessary. For explaining things, showing their importance, convincing students of these, making them accept these, it is necessary that illustrations should be given, facts and data should be presented, trends should be shown, arguments should be substantiated, and so on. This requires a good prior preparation.

12. Be brief and precise: - As emphasized by Mark Stoops and Stoops, (p.132), in order to be an effective communicator the teacher should be brief and precisc. He should not bite off more than he can chew or more than his listeners can digest, should omit long and unnecessary explanations, should select his point and get to it, should use short sentences, should be economical in his use of words, never using three or four where one would do. This is important for facilitating listener's understanding and absorbing the message in his mind.

13. Communicate with your eyes: - It means looking directly and straight at the students. This is actually "talking with eyes". "Sweep the audience gently with a warm, friendly gaze, allowing your glance to rest here and there for a brief second or two". Looking at the faces of the students the communicator can easily understand whether he is being understood or not, whether his impact is being felt or not, whether he is reaching the students or not. The faces of the students will tell the teacher where he went off the track or where he was cut-off the students. Then, he may try to return to the point and make more vigorous efforts to carry the students with him.

14. Talk less, listen more: - An effective communicator listens to the other person carefully and tries to understand what he said. The teacher should develop the habit of being an attentive listener. Only then he will bring the students closer to himself, otherwise he will alienate them from himself. The alienated students will never accept or do what the teacher is aiming at.

15. Banish the "I" from the discourse: - Use of "I", "mine", "me" should be avoided. This indicates lack of maturity on the part of teacher. It does not, at least, produce a good impression on the students.

Keeping these points in mind while interacting with students or having a conference with them the teacher will improve the quality of his communication, and thus, will be more effective as ah instructional leader.

CLASSROOM COMMUNICATION

Classroom communication is very important in teaching-learning as it is the chief means by which the teacher and the students work together. In the words of R.E. de Kieffer and Lee W. Cochran, "Effective teaching and communications are synonymous, for good teachers are clear communicators and good communicators as effective teachers.... Our society today has a vast array of modern media of communication....These modern media are among the tools, the education profession uses to mould and shape human minds." Good teaching, infect is intercommunication. There must be reaction and interaction with constant feedback.

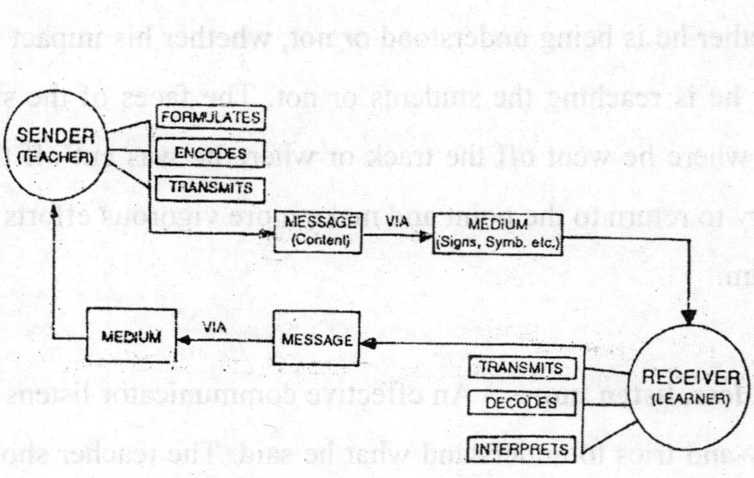

Fig . Classroom Communication

The message conveyed by the teacher and or the educational media may be verbal or visual and the receiver may listen, see or examine and react in other ways. The communication channel in the classroom should ideally carry both messages and counter messages.

Verbal and Non-Verbal Communication. Classroom communication between teacher and the students can be categorized broadly into two : (i) verbal communication, and (ii) non-verbal communication. The influence of verbal behaviour is mostly audible, while non verbal behaviour have a vision-based impact on the listener.

Communication

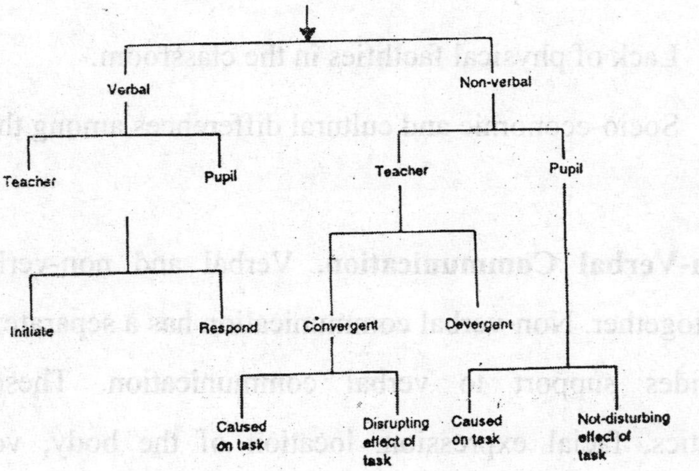

Fig. Type of classroom communication

Fig. Communication interaction

Barriers to Verbal Classroom Communication. These are as under :

1. Inaudibility of speech.
2. Abnormal speech of speech.
3. Unfamiliar pronunciation of the teacher.
4. Use of unfamiliar words and technical terms without explanation.
5. Lack of understanding of the basic knowledge of the students-known as referent confusion.
6. Day dreams on the part of the students on account of their inattentiveness.
7. Unsystematic presentation of the subject-matter.
8. Lack of scope of immediate feedback.
9. Lack of physical facilities in the classroom.
10. Socio-economic and cultural differences among the students.

Non-Verbal Communication. Verbal and non-verbal communications should go together. Non-verbal communication has a separate impact of its own. It also provides support to verbal communication. These include physical characteristics, facial expression, location of the body, voices, gestures, and powers etc.

EFFECTIVE CLASSROOM COMMUNICATION

Following factors may be considered in effective classroom communication.

1. Two-way communication. Two way communication instead of one-way communication is needed. One-way communication, i.e. lecturing or telling or demonstrating by the teacher denies the facility to the students to seek classification. The learners remain passive listeners. Two-way communication has a built-in-system of feedback. It ensures that further information, clarification etc., are provided whenever possible. The receivers or the learners get opportunities to understand the message or the content.

2. Effective Feedback for Efficient Teaching. Feedback ensures that the message has reached the receiver. This can take the form of a nod, and execution of the behaviour suggested in the communication. Thus the feedback provides a learning opportunity to the sender and the receiver because it mirrors the consequences of behaviour. In addition if the behaviour has been found to be incongruous with the message it feedback it would be difficult to ascertain whether communication has been received as intended or not. Positive and negative feedbacks may be used. When a learner does something commendable, a useful acknowledgement is made.

3. Communication and Principle of Clarity. A communication possesses clarity when it is expressed in language and transmitted in a way that can be comprehended by the receiver. Clarity requires literary approach to languages and familiarity with languages patterns of the learners.

4. Development of Motivation. The learners cannot listen or read with understanding unless they concentrate. Listening by fits and starts, listening inattentively or ignoring or skimming, out written words ensures lack of understanding. Adherence to the need for attention will gradually overcome certain barriers to communication, inattention, loss in transmission and poor attention. Motivation on the part of the learners will increase the quality of learning and they will certainly feel encouragement for their efforts.

5. Use of Technology/Instructional. Teaching technology should be made use of in providing effective communication in classroom teaching.

6. Teaching Strategies and Skills. They should be fully exploited to make communication inspirational and pragmatic.

COMMUNICATION AND INFORMATION TECHNOLOGY REVOLUTION

Just as previous centuries experienced their technological revolutions – the agricultural and industrial revolutions that radically changed the worldwide patterns of production and distribution-so the twentieth century is said to have experienced a communications revolution that is affective the world situation, not least the world of learning.

At the center of that revolution are communication technologies . Some are long established, like radio, television and telephones. Other such as satellites, optical fibre, microcomputers and video recording on tape or video disc are quite new. Among the older ones, radio and television broadcasting have been improved, adapted, put to new uses or linked with newer communications technologies. The result is wider distribution, greater accessibility and more clarity, consumer control and economy. They have also been improved by techniques that enhance recording, text screening and printing and the editing and manipulation of recordings.

There have been spectacular recent developments in telecommunication links that carry signals for telephone, broadcasting and other purposes. The range has been extended by the use of satellites to achieve worldwide links, covering even the remotest islands and overcoming difficulties of terrain or distance to unify countries hitherto fragmented by their geography. Satellite , microwave, optical fibre and other forms of telecommunications linkage give speed and dependability that, in their turn, permit new forms of communication to occur, notably the flow of digitally controlled data from computer to computer. The rapid evolution of computer technology resulting from developments in microchip technology has made possible the storing of information at levels of complexity, and its transmission at speeds, that challenge the imagination. Development costs have been high but widespread applications, user-friendly operation and miniaturization of larger components have brought mass sales and diminishing unit costs. An increasing proportion of the workforce of all countries (but especially in the technologically advanced and fastest developing countries), works in the communication/information sector, updating, recording, transmitting, analyzing accelerates as new products result from using the information technologies themselves.

To-day we see technology being applied to every department of civilized living. It comes in many forms and its applications are limitless. Technology is revolutionizing training. However in India its impact has yet to be felt adequately.

Information revolution implies the use of technology especially electronic devices communicating information, knowledge and skills.

INTERACTION

Mutual or reciprocal influences between individuals or groups, usually with special reference to social and emotional behaviour e.g. teacher-pupil interaction.

Group dynamics term for a systematic analysis and recording of the reaction of each person in a group to each other member of it.

Interaction process analysis is a technique for studying social behaviour in groups (e.g. classroom behaviour of pupils) where all the explicit interaction is carefully recorded according to systematic classification and analysis. Various devices may be used for timing different types of behaviour.

Interaction motive is a design tool used in arranging plant layouts, activity relationship etc. particularly where physical positioning is a key consideration.

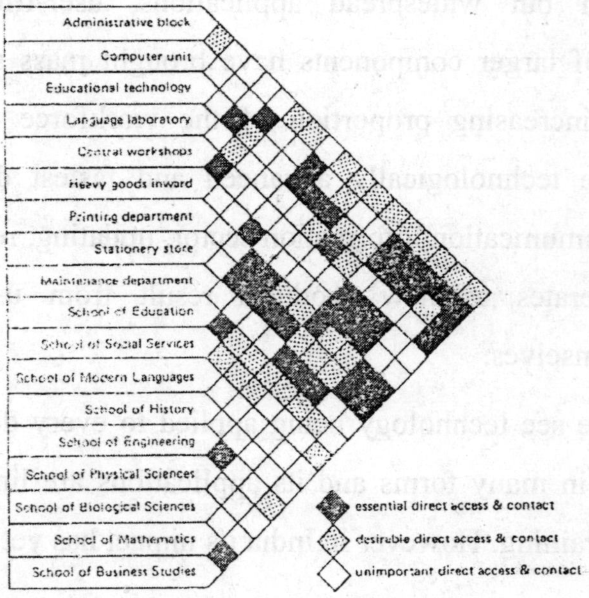

INTERACTION MATRIX

Verbal communication : A Two Way Process :- Classroom teaching or instruction is two-way communication process, The teacher transmits the message and the receiver, the students return feedback to the teacher. Thus there is a completed communication circuit. There is continuous flow of message from teacher to the students and back from the students to the teacher. This flow of message or Information back and forth is called a feedback-loop or communication-loop. One great advantage of this two-way communication is that the teacher gets an opportunity to adjust to the needs of the students which is not there in case of one-way communication as it happens in straight-jacket classroom lecture. The two-way process of communication provides a better understanding to both the teacher and the students.

The noise in the communication stem or the process of communication means all those factors and conditions which affect the communication adversely or reduce the accuracy of the communication. In the context of teaching it means all those factors that stand in the way of students understanding of what the teacher teaches or explains. Noise in classroom communication of the teacher interferes with the achievements of the goals of teaching. These factors constitute the barriers to effective teaching.

Thus, to sum-up briefly, the whole process' of communication can be describes as al1 interaction among three major components-who, what and whom, i.e, who communicates what to whom.

NON-VERBAL COMMUNICATION

Non-verbal communication is a channel of communication in which the message is sent without "words. Such non-verbal messages are present is all situations of people meeting other people. In teaching it is of great significance because it can either reinforce or minimize the verbal message and persi4s longer even after the verbal message is over.

Kinds of Non-verbal channels of Communication: - These consist of such events as facial expressions, posture, gestures, movement etc, which are sometimes known as the body language also. Sometimes, arrangements of space or objects around-may-also function as channels of non-verbal communication. One's actions constitute a powerful channel of this kind of communication. We all may have heard that "actions speak louder than words" meaning thereby that how we say something can be as important as what we .say. In the classroom-teaching session many such non-verbal communications occur. for example, a child's' shrugging his shoulders and saving "I donot know" is more than simply saying "I do not know". There may be inherent in that some frustrations, some surprise, some feeling of being ashamed, some efforts on defending oneself.. For a teacher it is important to know what it is exactly. If a student is asked to sing and she says "I do not sing well" when she sings well, this may mean that she would like to sing. Many gestures and facial expressions symbolize our deepest feelings. Eyes alone may beacons or reject. Teacher's just looking at a student silently while he does some mischief may immediately tell the student that he is caught and his action is disapproved. The very look of the teacher may tell many things to the students. His way of dressing, talking, walking etc, may tell them that he is a teacher by accident or a teacher committed to his profession.

The teachers may or may not be aware of, but the fact is that a lot of non-verbal communication takes place in every class of the teachers. Method of checking students assignment, asking questions to students, appreciating or criticising students, the time and mode of teacher's travelling in the class, moving close to or away from the students, teacher's control manners such as placing finger ,to lips to ask the students to keep quiet, standing with hands on hips and stare at students in silence, scanning room to see who is not working, teacher's being incongruous, i.e not being honest in appreciating or encouraging students, for example saying 'good' when the praise is false, etc, are numerous behaviours and actions which along with verbal message send non - verbal message also. Improving classroom non-verbal behaviour is difficult. but this should be the conscious goal' of all teachers and they should remember that "non - verbal communication is behviour that conveys meaning without words. It can be symbolic, non- symbolic, spontaneous or managed. It can be expressive, transmitting emotion; or it may be informative transmitting facts. It can be as specific as a gesture or as general as the atmosphere or a room" (Golloway 1968).

MODELS OF TEACHING

(Concept and Select Psychological Models)

Teaching is an act of communication with students with a view to bring about change in the cognitive affective and psychomotor behaviors of the student. Effective communication, however, calls for a definite strategy or methodology.

Teaching does not ensure learning by students essentially and automatically. In other words it means that teaching is an attempt 0.11 the part of the teacher to help and enable the students to learn. In fact teaching amounts to creating an appropriate situation in which desirable and durable learning can take place. In the past vast amount of research has been conducted in the U.S.A., England and Europe in search of that appropriate situation. Many experts in the field have tried to identify and define what that appropriate teaching situation can be, how that situations can be structured, and so on. Consequently a totally new insight has emerged in this respect. An entirely a different approach to teaching learning has been formulated. In this approach what is unique is the focus on integrated view of all aspects of teaching. The objectives, the curriculum, the teaching methods, etc. all are taken into consideration as related to one another in an integrated manner in a situation of teaching. They start with questions such as what is the objective to be achieved, how is it related to the curriculum, how best it can be achieved, what supporting material and facilities will be needed, how the teacher will act and how the students will be required-to-act. Taking all these into: consideration, a comprehensive, specific, functional and compact strategy is, then, developed. Like this for achieving different objectives a number of specific strategies of teaching have been developed. Since all the objectives of teaching can not be achieved just in one and the same way, there have to be different and several strategies. These strategies so developed are termed as "models of teaching".

THE CONCEPT OF MODELS OF TEACHING

A model is a design or a paradigm of something which is prepared on paper or in the mind prior to the coming into existence of that something. It is a pre existing blueprint of the execution of an activity. Before an activity is undertaken for achieving some purpose, an attempt is made to prepare a complete plan to which one has to conform to while executing the work. Hence, a model is a complete map which shows what will have to be done, when, for what purpose. Exactly that is the meaning of model of teaching too, which describes what is the objective of teaching, what activities will have to be carried out by the teacher in order to achieve that objective, what behaviors will the students be required to adopt, what teaching facilities will be needed, what kind of enviroml1ent will have to be created and so on; and all these are considered in an integrated manner in relation to one another. The decisions taken in regard to these entire phases 0,' teaching are never arbitrary. They are based on sound theoretical principles. They are rationally determined.

Thus. models of teaching are just different approaches or strategies of teaching learning. They describe who focuses on 'what'. This simply emphasizes that depending_upon the objectives to be achieved there have been constructed different models of leaching. As expressed by Joyce (1972) yodels of teaching are specific combinations of'learning_goals, environmental manipulations and other processes., When an educator' possesses identifiable focuses and a frame of reference which rationalizes them, he has a model of teaching. A model of teaching is a comprehensive theoretical position about teaching learning defining and describing goals of learning, curriculum, setting and procedure. It consists of guidelines for selecting educational experiences and structuring the most appropriate learning environment for providing these experiences to the students. They describe how a more relevant teaching situation can be constructed. They contain proposed specifications of all q1mponents of teaching in an integrated manner.

Models of teaching are specific plans to teaching which have been developed by people who worked in different fields. They are the outcomes of empirical research work, theories and experimentation. Some of the persons whose theories and researches have contributed to the development of different models are Erikson, Maslow, Ausubel, Bruner, Skinner, Hunt, Kohlberg and Piaget. Bruee Joyce and others developed ways of making the theories operational. Each model has a rationale that justifies it and describes what is relevant and why. The sound theoretical bases backed by experimental trials have made them very popular as strategies of teaching.

It should not be understood by the foregoing description that there are models for achieving every object of teaching or that the models developed are the only ways of effective teaching- learning. Still very little is known about how children learn. There can be myriad kinds of ways in which they can grow. We, therefore have to think in myriad ways to help them grow. And teachers have to develop their own models. They can draw upon, for this purpose, many a source such as developmental psychology, sociological theories, behavior modification theories, systems analysis etc. The most basic idea underlying the development of a model of teaching is the unifying way of looking at curriculum and teaching i.e., content and the process, curriculum strategy and teaching strategy. They reflect the optimum relationship among educational objectives, curriculum design and instructional design as a one-to-one relationship. They arc in balance when they support the same educational ends. In the past these three facets of educational design have been "out-of-joint with one another.

Definition And Meaning Of A Teaching Model

Teaching models have been defined in a number of ways. Some of the important definitions of a teaching model are given here to have a wider perspective of this concept.

Allen and Ryan (1969): Modelling is an individual demonstrating particular pattern which the trainee learns through imitation.

Bondura (1969): Modelling demonstrates that virtually all learning, phenomena resulting from direct experiences can occur on a vicarious basis through observation of other person's behaviour and its consequences for them.

B.K Passi L. C. Singh and D. N. Sansanwal (1991): A model of teaching consists of guidelines for designing educational activities and environments. Model of teaching is a plan that can also be utilised to shape courses of studies, to design instructional material and to guide instruction.

Joyce and Weil (1972): Teaching models are just instructional designs. They describe the process of specifying and producing environmental situations which cause the student to interact in such a way that specific change occurs in the behaviour.

Joyce and Weil (1972): Teaching model is a pattern or plan, which can be used to shape a curriculum or course to select instructional materials and to guide a teacher's actions.

N. K. Jangira and Ajit Singh (1983): A model of teaching is a set of inter-related compone'nts arranged in a sequence which provides guidelines to realise a specific goal It helps in designing instructional activities and environmental facilities, carrying out of these activities and realization of the stipulated objectives.

Paul D. Eggen et al (1979): Models are prescriptive teaching strategies designed to accomplish particular instructional goals.

Weil and Joyce (1978): A model of teaching consists of guidelines for designing educational activities and environments. It specifies ways of teaching and learning that are intended to achieve-certain kinds of goals.

Poul D. Eggen and others (1979): explain the meaning of a model in these words." An engineer, in considering a. project, first identifies the type of structure to be built, e.g., a building, a bridge or a road. Having done this, he selects an appropriate design or blueprint to follow in building that structure. The specifications of the blueprint determine the actions of the builder takes and the kind of building that will result. The particular type of blueprint or model chosen depends an the type of structure to be built. In a similar manner a teacher considering the choice of a teaching model first identifies what is to be taught and then selects a model in accordance with that goal. The model chosen is specifically designed to achieve a particular set of objectives and will determine in large part of the actions of the teachers."

Educators and psychologists have designed several types of teaching models which provide suitable guidelines, to the teachers for modifying the behaviour of the learners.

As a matter of fact some sort of models of teaching have been in existence since times immemorial.

In simple language a model of teaching may be defined as a blueprint designed in advance for providing necessary structure and direction to the teacher for realizing the stipulated objectives.

MAIN CHARACTERISTICS OF A TEACHING MODEL

Some common identifiable characteristics of a good model, are given below:

1. Specification of learning outcome. All models of teaching specify what the students should perform after completing an instructional sequence.

2. Specification of environment. A teaching model specifies in definite terms the environmental conditions under which a student's response should be observed.

3. Specification of criterion of performance. A model of teaching specifies the criterion of performance which is expected from the students.

4. Specification of operations. A model of teaching specifies the mechanism that provides for the reaction of students and interaction with the environment.

5. Scientific, procedure. A model of teaching is based on a systematic procedure to modify the behaviour of the learner. It is not a haphazard combination of facts.

FUNCTIONS OF TEACHING MODELS

1 . They help. in guiding the teacher to select appropriate teaching techniques, strategies and methods for the effective utilisation of the teaching situation and material for realizing the objective.

2. They help in bringing about desirable changes in the behaviour of the learners.

3. They help in finding out ways and means of creating favourable environmental situations for carrying out teaching process.

4. They help in achieving. desirable teacher-pupil interaction during teaching.

5 .they help in the construction of a curriculum or contents of a course.

6. They help in the proper selection of instructional material for teaching the prepared course or the curriculum.

7. They help in designing appropriate educational activities.

8. They assist producers of materials to create interesting and effective materials and learning sources,

9. They stimulate the development of new educational innovations.

10. They help in the formation of a theory of teaching.

11. They help to establish teaching and learning relationship empirically.

12. They are useful to develop social efficiency, personal abilities, cognitive abilities and behavioural aspects of the students.

Effects of Teaching by Modeling

Bandura and Walters mention three kinds of effects in teaching by modelling. These are: (i) A modelling effect (ii) An inhibitary and disinhibitary effect and (iii) An eliciting effect.

1. A modeling effect. A modelling effect can be seen when a teacher demonstrates to a student how to hold a pencil or write Capital A etc. and thus shows a new behaviour. Here a student learns new kinds of response pattern.

2. An inhibitary and disinhibitary effect. An inhibitary or disinhibitary effect takes place when through modelling we let the student know that it is not possiblc to look at pictures of nudes, in an art book.

3. An eliciting effect. The eliciting effect takes place when a teacher through modelling tries to teach students to rise whelJ. a lady enters the room and thus provides a cue eliciting a response neither new nor inhibited.

Modelling and other similar terms. Among those in common use are 'modelling', 'imitation', observational learning', 'identification' , 'copying' , 'vicarious learning', 'social facilitation', and 'role playing.'

Gagne feels that learning through imitation seems to be more apprcpriate for tasks which have little cognitive structure.

Miller and Dollar also plead for learning by imitation. There is no doubt that modelling plays an important role in the development of our personality. Imitation contributes immensely to the learning of values, beliefs, attitudes and sentiments.

It is because of this that great stress is laid on the selection of right type of teachers who in turn must be very careful in selection learning experiences in the class.

Three stages of modelling. Three stages in the development, of a model are:

(i) Analysis of a particular skill.,

(ii) Identification of the key elements in it.

(iii) Exposition of the elements in such a way as to exemplify satisfactorily the skills under consideration.

FUNDAMENTAL ELEMENTS OF A TEACHING MODEL

A teaching model has six fundamental models: (i) Focus (ii) Syntax (iii) Principles of reactions (iv) The social system (v) The support system (vi) Application context.

Focus. Focus is the central aspect of a teaching model. Objectives of teaching and aspects of the environment generally constitute the focus of the model.

Syntax. Syntax includes the sequence of steps involved in the organisation of the complete programme of teaching.

Principles of reactions. This element is concerned with the way a teacher should regard and respond to the activities of the students. These responses should be appropriate and selective.

The social : System. It is related to the description of the following: (i) Interactive roles and relationships between the teacher and the students. (ii) The kinds of norms that are observed and student behaviour which is rewarded. The support system. The support .system relates to the additional requirements other than the usual human skills or capacities of the teacher and the facilities usually available in the ordinary classroom. These requirements refer to special skills, special knowledge of the teachers and special audio- visual material like films, self-instructional material, visit to special places etc.

Application Context. Several types of teaching models are available. Each model attempts to describe the feasibility of its use in varying contexts-goal achievements-cognitive, co native and effective.

SOURCES OF MODELS OF TEACHING

Four important sources from which all the models of teaching have been derived arc given below:

1. The Social Interaction Sources. The model of teaching of this category emphasis's the importance of social relationship of the person and are based on the assumption that social relation is the vehicle of education.

2. The Information Processing Sources. The other source of a model of teaching is the information processing capability of the learner which means the way in which people handle stimuli, organise data, sense problems and solve them., The model of this category emphasises the use of specific strategies within academic disciplines which lead to the development of creativity and general intellectual ability of learners.

3. The Personal sources. Personal and emotional life of the individual and their internal organisation as it affects relationship with this environment are the sources of this category of models.

4. Behaviour Modification. As a Source. The operant conditioning theory built by B.F. Skinner is the. origin of this type of model which is purely a psychological model and is used in most of the teaching strategies developed in the last two decades.

ASSUMPTION OF MODELS OF TEACHING

1. Each model is based on the assumption that teaching is the creation of appropriate environment and various components of the environment are interdependent.

2. Environment system consists of the content, skills, social relationships, instructional roles, activities and physical facilities etc All these elements interact.

3. Various combinations of the different elements of the environment create

different types of environments and elicit different outcomes.

4 .Models of teaching create environment.

Components of Models of teaching: Every model of teaching is a theoretical construction which describes in specific terms its various components which facilitate translation of its theory into practice. These components. or concepts are.

1. Focus
2. Syntax
3. Principles of Reaction
4. Social System
5. Support System

1. Focus: Every model of teaching is highly specific in the sense that it is constructed for achieving certain definite and well defined objective. It cannot be used for achieving any other purpose. Focus of a model of teaching, therefore, means the specified objectives which a model of teaching, intends to achieve. Once the focus has been described, all other aspects of teaching are determined in relation to only this focus. Thus, focus of a model is the nucleus of all the teaching dforts and activities that are to be carried under that. It is the integrating, determined factor of all that goes under that model of teaching. The focus of a model of teaching determines the whole of the strategy of teaching.

The objectives or the focus of a model is theoretically derived. Research done by experts pertaining to that area provides a background for deriving the focus. However, once the overall focus is determined, it is split out into speci fic behavioral terms. The focus of a model may he development of intellect and acquisition of information; or it may be development of essential social skills; or it may be development of a certain select personal qualities or modification of behavior in a certain direction. Keeping either of these focuses in mind all other related aspects of teaching are accordingly determined.

2. Syntax: syntax of each model is determined in the light of its focus. Since every model has its own focus, its syntax also has to be unique. Syntax refers to the prescribed f10w of actions of a model. It is described in terms of a sequence of events which are called phases. Each model has a distinct flow of phases. 1n a '\lay syntax may be said to be the structure of the model specifying the various phases of activity and the purpose of these phases along with the relationship between phases of activity. The syntax of model describes the whole sequence of the activities, programs and experiences which the teacher is required to follow or provide while teaching in the class. It is a set, predetermined way of what the teacher will do, and how he will do in order to achieve predetermined objectives. The syntax provides the teacher well considered guidelines for actions to be taken by him, the beater paths he has to follow to each fixed destinations.

3. Principles of Reaction: In classroom teaching there is essentially an interaction between the teacher and the students. The students behaviour and responses are manipulated by the teacher. Each model, in view of its focus, prescribes specific ways how this function is to be performed. Treatment given to the students by the teacher is not left wholly to the teacher. It is guided by the principles laid down by the model concerned. Differenl models lay down different rules in this connection. Thus, principles of reactions means those principles which are incorporated in the model for providing guidelines to the teachers for handling the response and behaviours of the students. They tell how the teacher should treat the students in the class, how he should respond to what the student does. They tell the teacher or the materials maker how to program his behaviour while developing a unit or performing an activity. In the words of Joyce (. 238) they mean "the principles which govern the reactions or responses of teachers to the activity of the learner," For example some models require the teacher to be corrective reshaping the behaviour of the student along a predetermined line. While using a particular model of teaching the learner is not free to treat and manipulate the students as he likes. Rather he has to follow the principles specific to the model.

4. Social system: in order to achieve the objectives specific to the model of teaching the classroom social structure is required to be created in a manner relevant to the activities to be carried out under that particular model. In some models the teacher is required to be permissive, reflector or a facilitator of "group activity. In others, he is the director and controller of all activities and students are just followers of what he ask them to do. Still in some others hc is to act as a counselor or 'a guide. In some models teachers play the dominant role, while others the students determine the tone of the classroom.

5. Support System: This refers to the conditions which may be cjl1sidered necessary for the successful operation of the model. Many programs fail because they are not provided the essential support system in the form of additional requirements. Optimal support system is needed to facilitate the activities of the teachers and the learners. These additional requirements may be various kind of audio-visual aids and teaching material, tnoney and manpower facilities, equipment, specially trained personnel, needed cooperation of colleagues and authorities, and so on. Different models of Leaching require different kinds of supporting conditions and material. For example, Inductive Teaching Model used for teaching history requires sets of original documents, Human Relations Model may require a trained leader, Non Directive Model may require a particular type of personality. Similarly, Computer assisted Model will require equipment like computer and other related accessories.

A model of teaching is incomplete if it does not specifically describe all these components. Success of any model of teaching depends on meeting all these specifications.

CLASSIFICATION OF MODELS OF TEACHING

Joyce and Weil (1972) have discussed in their book Models of Teaching a number of models of teaching which have been constructed by different experts for achieving different purposes. It is not possible to describe all of them even in brief. However a classification of a few most important of these is presented below. These have been grouped according to the purpose they serve into four groups:

1. Information processing models
2. Social interaction models
3. Personality development models and
4. Behaviour modification models

Joye and Weil discuss these all the four families of models of teaching in Models of Teaching. Within each family there are a number or models of problems and uses verbal and non-verbal symbols. Some of them are concerned with the ability of the learner to think productively. In one way or the other all of them are concerned with learners cognitive development and knowledge acquisition. A brief account of some of the models of this family is presented below:

INFORMATION - PROCESSING MODELS

	Model	Major Theorist	Focus
1	Inductive Teaching Model	Hilda Taba	Designed primarily for development of inductive mental processes and academic reasoning of theory building but these capacities are useful for personal and social goals as well.
2	Scientific Inquiry Model	Joseph Schwab (also much of the Curriculum Reform movements of the1960's)	Designed to teach the research system of a discipline, but also expected to have effects in other domains (sociological methods may be taught in order to solve social problems).
3	Concept Attainment Model	Jerome Bruner	Designed primarily to develop inductive reasoning but also for concept development analysis.
4	Cognitive Growth Development Model	Jean Piaget, or Irving Sigel Edmud Sullivan	Designed to increase general intellectual development especially logical reasoning, but can be applied to social and moral development as well.
	Advance Organizer Model	David Ausubel	Designed to increase learner's efficiency of information processing capacities to meaningfully absorb and relate bodies of knowledge.
	Memory Model	Jerry Lucas	Designed to increase capacity to memorize.
	Enquiry Training Model	Richard Suchman	Designed to develop inductive mental processes and academic reasoning or theory building.

2. Social Interaction Models: these models emphasize the social development of the learner, particularly the relationship of the individual to the society and to other persons. They focus on the process by which the individual understands the social reality.

Development of insight into social relationship, social adjustments, appreciation of social dependence and social perspective of living are some of the goals of these models. In one way or the other every model of this family aims at social integration of the learners. Some of the most important models of this family are:

3. SOCIAL INTERACTION MODELS

Model	Major Theorist	Mission or Goal Intended
Jurisprudential Teaching Model	(i) Donald Oliver (ii) James P. Shaver	Group problem solving, cooperation, social interaction skills.
Group Investigation Model	(i) Herbert Thelen (ii) John Dewey	Development of skills for participation in democratic social processes.
Social Inquiry Model	(i) Byron Massialas (ii) Bengamin Cox	Social problem solving skills
Laboratory Method Model	National Training Lab (NTL), Bethel Maine	Development of Interpersonal and group skills

3. Personal Development Models: The focus of the models of this family is the development of the personality of the learner. These models are oriented to the self- development of the learner, particularly aiming at the emergence and development of insight into one's emotional life. They concern themselves with the development of such aspects of personality as capacity for self- instruction and self-understanding., self-responsibility and self- exploration, self-awareness and self-extention. Some of them aim at increasing learner's personal complexity and personal flexibility. All of these models share an orientation toward the individual and the development of selfhood. They emphasize the process by such individuals construct and organize their unique reality. Teaching through them is expected to develop in the learners a sort of emotional maturity and the capacity to view themselves as capable persons. Some of these models are as shown below:

3. PERSONAL DEVELOPMENT MODELS

Model	Major Theorist	Mission or Goal for Which Intended
Non-directive Model	Teaching Carl Rogers	Emphasis on building the capacity for personal development in terms of self-awareness, understanding, autonomy and self-concept.
Awareness Training Model	Fritz Perls William Schulth	Increasing one's capacity for self-exploration and self-awareness. Much emphasis on development of interpersonal awarness.
Synectics Model	William Gordon	Personal development of creativity and creative

Model	Major Theorist	Mission or Goal for Which Intended
		problem-solving.
Conceptual System Model	David E. Hunt	Designed to increase personal complexity and flexibility
Classroom Meeting Model (Social Problem Solving)	William Glasser	Development of self-understanding and responsibility to oneself and one's social group.

4. Behavior Modification Models: These .models have evolved from attempts to develop efficient systems for sequencing learning tasks and shaping behavior by manipulating reinforcement. These, models are supported by the reinforcement theory anc 1 operant conditioning theory of learning propounded by Skinner. They are domain-free and are of general applicability. They assume that by manipulating reinforcement in a predetermined manner and by using shaping and token economy techniques any behavior can be modified, any desirable behavior can be established. These principles and techniques have been applied to a 'wide variety of goal-achievements in education and other areas ranging from military training to the improvement of interpersonal behavior and even to therapy. There are a member of models which come within this family: Some of these are media based while others are oriented to interactive teaching A few of these are presented below:

4. BEHAVIOUR MODIFICA TION/CYBERNETIC MODELS

Model	Major Theorist	Mission or Goal for Which Intended
Programmed Instruction Model of Training	B.F. Skinner	Facts, concepts, skills
Managing Behaviour Model	B.F. Skinner	Social behaviour/skills
Relaxation Model	Rinn, Wolpe	Personal goals (for example, reduction of stress, anxiety)
Anxiety Reduction Model	Rinn, Wolpe	Substitution of relaxation for anxiety in social situations
Assertive Training Model	Wolpe	Expression of feeling in social situations
Silulation Model	Link, Guestzkow Glasser	Concepts anddecision-making skills
Direct Training Model	Lumsdaine	Pattern of behaviour skills

These families of models of teaching are not entirely different from one another. They are neither antithetical nor mutually exclusive. For example, information-processing models are also concerned with social relationships and personal development. Similarly social interaction models emphasizing development of social relationships and social insight are similar to other models like personal development models as they are equally concerned with the development of social relationships. Not only in focus, the various models of teaching have many things common in other aspects also.

In the following pages a few models of teaching are described in greater detail. For this purpose only following models have been selected.

1. Concept Attainment Model.
2. Enquiry Training Model.
3. Advance Organizers Model.
4. Operant Conditioning Model of Teaching.
5. Glaser Basic Teaching Model.
6. Computer-based Teaching Model

1. THE CONCEPT ATTAINMENT MODEL

This is a model, which is derived from the cognitive processes which are used by human beings in collecting and organizing information. The process was studied over several years by Bruner, Goodnow and Austin (1956). These are the processes, which the people use for forming concepts of categories or concepts which enable them to describe things or relationships. These categories or concepts make it possible to "manipulate the confusion world". There are certain definite advantages of concepts or categories thus formed. Firstly, they reduce the complexity of the environment; secondly, they enable us to identify objects in the world; thirdly, they reduce the necessity of constant learning; fourthly, they give us direction for activity, i. e., what we should do in a given situation. The process of categorization is known as the process of concept attainment. This is the process by which we discriminate the attribute of things, people. events and places and put them into categories. There are three types of concepts: (i) conjunctive, when the category is defined by the joint presence of several attributes or characteristics. (ii) Disjunctive, when categories are formed on the basis of relationships between defining attributes and (iii) third type is known as relational concepts.

The Concept Attainment Model describes how concepts can be taught more effectively.

Elements of Concept Attainment Model:

1. focus : The, focus of this model is to teach concepts.

2. Syntax: There are two strategies involved in the process of this model. These arc (i) Reception and (ii) Selection. The syntax of each of these is as follows: (Passi, Singh, Sansanwal, 1985).

1. Syntax Of Selection Model

Phase-I: presentation of data and identification of attributes

Teacher presents unlabelled exemplars.

Students inquire which examples are positive.

Students generate and test hypotheses.

Phase 2: Testing Attainment of the Concept.

Students identify additional unlabelled examples.

Students generate examples.

Teacher confirms hypothesis.

Phase 3: Analysis of Thinking Strategy

Students describe thoughts.

Students discuss role of hypotheses and attributes.

Students discuss type and number of hypotheses.

2. Syntax of Reception Model

Phase 1: Presentation and Identification

Teacher presents labelled exemplars (both positive and negative).

Students compare the attributes.

Students generate and test hypotheses.

Students name the concept.

Students state a definition.

Phase 2: Testing Attainment of the Unlabelled Exemplars.

The pupils generate exemplars.

Phase 3: Analysis of Thinking Strategies Discuss thoughts.

Discuss the role of the hypotheses.

Discuss the type and the number of hypotheses

Evaluate strategies.

3. Principles of Reaction

During the initial stage of the lesson the teacher should support the students hypothesis emphasizing, however, that they are hypothetical in nature. Later she needs to turn the-students' attention toward analysis of their concepts and their thinking strategies. The teacher should encourage analysis rather than attempting to seek the one best strategy for all people in all situations.

4. Social System

While using the Reception Model of Concept Attainment the teacher selects the concepts, organizes and labels the material into positive and negative examples and sequences the examples. The pupils are required to study the attributes of positive and negative examples and frame hypothesis. The teacher supplies additional examples when needed.

When using the Selection Model of Concept Attainment the teacher presents unlabelled examples and she has no control over the sequence of the examples chosen by the pupils. Further the pupils have to frame a hypothesis regarding the concept and then select an example and ask the teacher whether it is a 'yes' of a . no'.

5. The Support System

Concept Attainment lessons require material that has been so designed that concepts are embedded in the material. The material must be so organized that positive and negativc exemplars are pointed out to the students.

Utility of the Model: This model of teaching is very useful for teaching of concepts or various subjects. Much of the language-learning, in fact, is concept attainment. The same is true in the learning of the vocabulary of a foreign language. Linguistic structure consists of relational concepts of various kinds that need to be attained. In the same way every discipline uses thousands of concepts in presenting its subject matter Hence, learning the structure of any disciple amounts to attaining the concepts of that discipline. Learning of concepts constitutes the foundation of all learning's including the learning involved in the school curriculum. Concepts attained are the bricks of which the grand mansion of knowledge is built. Efforts should be made at every level of education to enable the learners to acquire these concepts as efficiently as possible.

Next is described the Enquiry Training Model.

2. ENQUIRY TRAINING MODEL

J. Richard Suchman developed this model of teaching when he was at the university of Illinois. This was based on his earlier book **The Elementary School 'Raining Program in Scientific Inquiry (1962)**. Suchman also derived this model from information processing theories of cognitive behavior. it comes partly from a model of scientific enquiry, but has been generalized, no more remaining confined to science. The model is described in detail as follows:

1. The Focus: The model is specifically meant for developing mental, powers which are used in research, enquiry or investigations. Suchman himself describes the objectives of this model as follows:

(A) To develop the cognitive skills of searching and data-processing and the concepts of logic and causality necessary for enquiring autonomously and productively.

(B) To give the learners a new approach to learning which is helpful in building concepts through the analysis of concrete episodes and the discovery of relationships between variables.

(C) To capitalize on two intrinsic sources of motivation, the rewarding experience of discovery and the excitement that is inherent in autonomous searching and data processing.

Suchman's aim was to have a teaching strategy which should consist of activities which are mostly. autonomously controlled and intrinsically rewarded (p. 28). The critical element in the model is to put the learners into a situation where they would have t6 try to find out the answer to a puzzling situation.

Thus the focus of this model is to help the students develop an intellectual discipline and skills .necessary to raise questions and search out answers stemming from curiosity.

Inquiry training begins by presenting before the students a puzzling event. Suchman holds that faced with such a problem the students are naturally motivated to solve the puzzle.

We can use the opportunity provided by natural inquiry to reach the procedures of disciplined searching. He deliberately selects episodes that have sufficiently surprising outcomes to make it difficult for students to remain indifferent to the encounter.

After the presentation of the puzzling situations the students ask the teacher questions. The questions, however, must be answered by a 'yes' or a 'no' by the teacher. Whenever they phrase a question that cannot be answered by a 'yes' or a 'no' the teacher reminds them of the rules and waits until they find a way of stating the question in proper form. Comments such as "Can you restate the question so that I can answer it with a yes or a no?" are common teacher responses when students slip out of the inquiry mode.

Syntax:

The following are the five phases of Inquiry Training Model:

Phase 1: Encounter with the problem

Explain inquiry procedures.

Present discrepant event.

Phase 2: Data Gathering: Verification

Verify the nature of objects and conditions.

Verify the occurrence of the problem situation.

Phase 3: Data Gathering :Experimentation

Isolate relevant variables.

Hypothesize (and test) causal relationships.

Phase 4: Formulating and Explaining

Formulate rules or explanation.

Phase 5: Analysis of the Inquiry Process

Determine Inquiry Strategy and develop more effective ones.

Principles of Reaction

1. Ensure that the phrasing of the 'yes' and 'no' questions is done correctly. There should be no double barrel questions.

2. If the above is true, the teacher must ask the students rephrase his or her question.

3. Make sure that the other students take-off from questions already asked and that there should be no repetition. The teacher should also point out points which are not valid.

4. Use the language of the inquiry process.

5. In the process of the model the students will come up with hypotheses. The teacher must avoid evaluating the students' theories.

6. Ask the students to make clear statements of theories and provide support for their generalization.

7. Encourage interaction.

Social System:

The teacher selects or designs the puzzling situation and presents it to the students. However, during the enquiry session teachers and students participate as equals. As the students learn the principles of inquiry, the teacher guides them to use the resource material and perform experiments and conduct discussions with other students.

Once the students are trained in the principles of enquiry they are given freedom to select or design their own puzzling situations and play the game on their own or on their peer group.

Support System

All the specific conditions required for the smooth running of all phases of the model are called the support system. These would include books, films, posters and apparatus required for experimentation etc.

3. ADVANCE ORGANIZERS MODEL OF TEACHING

This model of teaching was propounded by the psychologist David Ausubel who set forth subsumption theory of learning (Ausubel,1965). Subsumption theory of learning is concerned with meaningful reception learning in which the entire content of what is to be learnt is presented to the learner in final form. The learner has to internalize the same so that it may be reproduced when needed. Meaningful reception requires the learner to use a meaningful set. Material to be learned should also be potentially meaningful. It is different from discovery learning in this that in discovery learning what is to be learned is not given and is identified by the learner himself while in case of subsumption learning the material to be learned is presented before the learner the teacher; and the learner tries to assimilate that into his already existing cognitive structure.

Ausubel like Bruner (1961) holds that each discipline of knowledge has a structure of concepts that can be identified and taught to the learner. He, in addition to this, says that the organization of the content in the subject fields should be governed by the important principles. One of them is progressive **differentiation** that, means that the most general and inclusive ideas should be presented first and then, they should be progressively differentiated in terms of detail and specificity (Ausubel, 1963, p.79). He assumes the presence of a hierarchical structure of knowledge in the mind of the learner in which the most inclusive concepts occupy a position at the apex of the structure which subsume progressively less inclusive and more highly differentiated sub-concepts and factual data. Ausubel feels that for the purpose of teaching if the material is organized in conformity with this hierarchical structure, learning becomes "optimum" and it is retained better and longer. Theoretical organization concepts, thus, becomes a principle of teaching according to him.

The second principle of Ausubel is **"Integrative Reconciliation"** which means the way the new' ideas are reconciled and integrated with previously learned content. Thus, sequential arrangement of material is emphasized so that "successive learning builds on what has gone before". Ausubel suggested a model of teaching based on this principle and called it **"Organizer Technique of Didactic Exposition",** In this he emphasized that the content to be learned should be organized sequentially so that each segment of learning material is preceded by a conceptual organizer, better called the "advance organizer", which means a higher level of abstraction, generality and inclusiveness of the material. The advance organizer should not be confused with an overview or summary. The organizer is an idea, a general idea which functions cognitively to organize the material and provides a conceptual framework into which the learner will integrate the material.

Ausubel recommends that the learner should be presented with such general expository organizers to which he can relate the new material. .

ELEMENT OF THE MODEL

1. The Focus: The focus of the model is to enable the learner to acquire knowledge in a meaningful way, to conserve the learned material in the mind in a sequential hierarchical manner so that it may be retained better and reproduced as and when required. The meaningful and efficient learning is the goal of this model of teaching.

2. The Syntax: the first phase of the activity is the presentation of the organizer which is more general and inclusive as compared to the material that is to follow. It may be a broader concept which covers or implies many more facts, sub concepts and smaller points. The second phase is the presentation of the material itself, which the teacher wants the learner to acquire. The teacher, thus, has to proceed from general to particular. The first organizer and the subsequent material should. be hierarchically woven into the fabric of knowledge. The beginning concept may be more abstract and, then, generally, more and more concrete material should be presented.

3. Reactions By the Teacher : The teacher plays the dominant role. He constructs the 'whole situation of teaching. He presents the organizer and the material to be learned He puts questions to students to evaluate whether they have understood. He controls the total environment. Students are allowed to seek clarifications, but only within the context of the material presented. But, teacher's role is important, as he is to help the learners to see the relationships between the material presented and the organizer. The teacher with planned material controls the whole activity of teaching. Everything is centered on the teaching material as planned by the teacher. Students role is to acquire and understand the concepts and the material presented.

4. Social System : Since the purpose of this model of teaching is to acquire knowledge and retain it in a systematic, meaningful way as planned by the teacher the social system is controlled entirely by the teacher. The teacher himself defines roles and prepares norms of behavior. The students have to act according to the intentions of the teacher. Students responses are controlled by the teacher. They have to accept the authority of the teacher, Thus, the model prescribes a teacher-dominated social system. But, it should, certainly, not mean that the, students are not allowed to reveal their difficulties and seek clarifications freely. There they have freedom. But, freedom to seek clarifications is regulated by the teacher.

5. Support System : The. most important thing needed is a thorough preparation and planning for teaching. Arranging the whole material in a hierarchical order with major advance organizers and sub organizers requires a lot of thinking and organization. It is also necessary that the students have a cognitive structure already existing which is needed for receiving and integrating new knowledge.

Application of the Model : this model of teaching was basically prepared for teaching verbal material. But, the model is "extremely versatile" in the sense that it can be applied to any kind of material for teaching. The lecture can be made well structured and well-organized arid more meaningful. It can be helpful in the analysis of expository materials which involve abstract ideas. Its greatest value lies in suggesting that in order to make the learning-material meaningful it should be organized and structured or a hierarchical order, proceeding from general to particular and from abstract to concrete.

4. OPERANT CONDITIONING MODEL OF TEACLING

This Model belongs to the family of behavior modification models. It is based upon Operant Conditioning Theory of Learning set forth by B.F. Skinner. Conditioning theory has value in explaining how behaviour may be changed with no intention on the part of the learner to modify his behaviour. Principles initially derived from conditioning experiments are applied to the development of the: s model. The principle is that when a reinforce follows the behaviour of an individual, there is a tendency for the behaviour to be repeated again. A satisfying consequence or reinforcement immediately following a response facilitates permanent acquisition of the response: Thus, the principle of reinforcement constitutes the foundation stone of this model. A few other psychologists have asserted the importance of this principle also. But, Skinner has made its application directly to classroom learning situations.

ELEMENTS OF THE MODEL

The focus: the focus of this model is to bring about a change in the behaviour of the individual. Behaviour may be cognitive, affective or co native, i.e. skills. It can be applied to teaching knowledge (for example program learning), changing attitudes and teaching skills.

Syntax: the structure of the model consists of three phases. the first phase is concerned with the presentation of the stimulus which is capable of eliciting the desired behaviour. For example, in case of programmed instruction prompts frames are used for this purpose. There can be various kinds of stimuli which can be used for eliciting the behaviour which is desired to be learned. If the terminal behaviour is to be brought under the control of a stimulus, this stimulus must be relevant and effective. The second phase of-the model consists of the response which is to be learned and which has to be emitted by the learner. The third phase consists of reinforcement of the response or behaviour shown by the individual'. It may take any form such as the knowledge of result or any of the method of reinforcement schedules whichever is relevant in the situation. It is only the desired behaviour which is reinforced.

Social System: The social system under this model is highly structured. The model requires that it should be used in a controlled situation. The teacher manipulates everything. The learner is expected to show the behaviour which is desired. He is not free to act as he may wish. There is no open-ended discussion. The learner is treated like a machine that must operate as handled by the instructor. Impersonality is the hallmark of the social system of this model.

Support System: In order to make the system work following supports are considered necessary:

(1) Stimulus must be relevant and sufficient to elicit the desired behaviour.

(2) Reinforcement provided must he satisfying and must be administered effective]y according to judiciously selected schedule.

(3) Factors that can interfere with learning should be controlled.

Applicability: the greatest use of this model has been in programmed instruction, particularly the linear program.

But, the model has its utility in all areas of learning. Behaviors iii the affective domain can be shaped quite successfully by using this model. The model has probably, the most applicability to the affective domain. But, its utility in developing cognitive knowledge and psychomotor skills has also been well-established. Its techniques of Token Economy and Shaping have been effective in developing attitudes and skills. Some of the training programs developed in the U.S.A. use this model with satisfactory results.

5:PSYCHOLOGICAL TEACHING MODELS

The models discussed in the foregoing pages are also psychological models of teaching as they are derived from the psychological base provided by the theories of learning and studies of cognitive processes. But, Dececco and Crawford discuss specifically three models of teaching under this head which are (1) Robert Glaser's Basic Teaching Model, (2) a Computer-based Teaching Model, and (3) Flanders Interaction Model. Flanders interaction model has been presented in chapter- VI separately. The two remaining models are discussed in the following sections.

6:GLASER'S BASIC TEACHING MODEL

In the language of DeCecco and Crawford (p.8) this is said to be a stripped down" teaching model which probably means a strategy of leaching which splits the whole process of teaching-learning into its basic component parts and directs how they should be managed separately and in relation to one another. The model was developed by Robert Glaser (1962). It views teaching-learning as a system composed of four basic parts each having its own specific function and all put together in achieve some specific teaching learning objective. It clearly explains the teaching learning process in terms of its most essential aspects. DeCccco and Crawford (p.9) hold that "it provides an uncomplicated, yet fairly adequate conceptualization of the teaching process". The model, in fact, suggests how essential activities of teaching process such as identification and management of inputs, identification and management of process and identification and management of outputs can be best organized so as to achieve a specified goal. It is a simple model, but helpful in several ways. In very simple and clear terms it answers the question "what is teaching".

Components of the Model: The model splits the whole process of teaching learning into four components as follows:

1. Instructional Objectives
2. Entering Behaviour
3. instructional Procedures
4. Performance Assessment

1. Instructional Objectives: The model requires that before selecting and using a teaching procedure it is essential for the teacher to identify the objectives of teaching. These can be of various types depending upon the topic. But, what is important about them is that they should be attainable by the students. They should be specific and defined in behavioral terms. How to do this job is discussed in detail in another chapter.

2. Entering Behaviour: This component of the model refers to' the existing status of the learner, his previous background of knowledge, his level of intelligence and other required mental abilities, requisite skills, etc. In a way the model requires that the teacher before starting to teach should examine and see that the learner possesses all those abilities, skills and knowledge that are required for acquiring proposed learning. It is a very broad concept defining the state of "readiness" or "preparedness" of the learner for acquiring new knowledge. It takes into consideration all aspects of learner's personality including even socio-cultural aspects. All these should be assessed and known precisely and instructional procedures should be adjusted according to these. Only then the specified objectives can be achieved.

3. Instructional Procedures: This component refers to the methods, techniques and procedures which should be used in order to achieve the specified goals. These should be appropriate in view of the learners entering behaviors and the already specified objectives. They have to be different and specific depending upon the objectives and the entering behaviour of the learner. All objectives cannot be achieved through one single technique or method. Procedures for teaching facts, concepts, rules, problem- solving, skills have to be different. Thus, the teacher has to select the most appropriate ones.

4. Performance Assessment: This is the last and most important component of the model. This is the component that tells the teacher how well he has identified and managed all the previous three components. It functions as the feedback device that tells the teacher whether the specified goal has been achieved or not. It directs the teacher to take further-action. If the assessment of learner performance reveals that the objective has not been achieved or it has not been achieved satisfactorily, the teacher tries to find out where the discrepancy lies. He, then, corrects it by either changing the objective or by selecting a more appropriate procedure of instruction. This kind of adjustment is necessary and is made possible by performance assessment only. For this purpose the teacher uses all kinds of tests, examinations, tools and techniques. The results of performance assessment are related to each of the other component in order to find out the discrepancy. This kind of feedback operates as a searchlight within the system.

The important feature of the model is integration of the four components, an emphasis on their relationship and interaction. They should all be in harmony with each other, each synchronizing with' the other. How the teacher achieves that depends on his knowledge, skills and wisdom. In order to teach well he must manage these components.

5: COMPUTER BASED TEACHING MODEL

This model of teaching may be considered as based on extension of the theoretical concepts described and used by Glaser in constructing his basic Teaching Model. Hut, it is much more complex than that. It was developed by Lowrènce Stolurow and Daeniel Davis (1965). This model is base on the use of the computer. It is not the teacher, but the computer that teaches and takes decisions about the instructional procedure. The model has following two phases.

1. The Pretutorial Phase, and
2. The Tutorial Phase

The Pretutorial Phase : It is the phase which precedes actual teaching. Its single purpose is to identify the most suitable teaching program for a particular student for enabling him to achieve a particular goal. At this stage the computer is asked to make certain decisions regarding the (a) instructional objectives (b) the entering behaviours of learner. Three factors have to' he taken into consideration while taking decisions about instructional objectives. These are: (i) final level of performance; (ii) subject matter or the topic to which the performance is related, and (iii) the time within which the objectives have to be achieved.

Decisions about the entering behaviors have also to be made during this phase. The model lays down in this connection that two aspects of the learner's status should be taken into account while determining the entering behaviors (a) the apperceptive mass of the learner which means the previous knowledge or the achievement level of the learner, and (b) the aptitude level or set of skills required for achieving the specified objectives.

The computer identifies taking these things into consideration an appropriate instructional strategy. When these factors are, thus, considered the computer may reach the following conclusions:

1. Just one appropriate strategy is available. If this is the case, teaching is done according to this strategy.

2. More than one strategies or programs may be found suitable. In this case, further considerations are made as to which of them may be more economical in terms of time and money. The one which is more economical is finally selected.

3. No program may be found suitable and applicable under the circumstances. In this case the computer suggests to bring about changes and adjustments in the entering behaviours or the objectives to be achieved. Even the learner may have to be rejected. If the entering behaviour needs to be modified, the computer presents revisional exercises and gives more practice in order to enable the learner to attain those abilities, aptitude and competencies that are needed to acquire the specific objective. If that is not the case topic may be changed or even the acceptable level of final performance may be changed.

The Tutorial Phase: This is the stage of actual teaching, i.e., presenting or operating the program which has been selected after critical evaluation during the pre-tutorial phase. Two functions are performed at this stage. (a) the teacher function, and (b) the processor function.

The teacher function means operating the selected program. The program is put to work. The professor function includes several activities. It is a manipulating function, if new situations are; it has to take decision as to what further action has to be taken. If it is found that the program is not working satisfactorily. It takes decision regarding change to be made similarly; if on the basis of learner responses some alteration is required it t vies to make most suitable adjustments.

Utility : The model has all the advantages inherent in the Basic Teaching Model as this is an extension of the same with certain added functions. Stolurow and Davis believe that "only computers have the capacity to make-all the decisions and acc6mmodations an enlightened pedagogy requires,".

UNIT -4

Learning Objective

Designing instructional system: Formulation of instructional objective, Task analysis, Designing of instructional strategies: Lecture, Tean1 teaching, Discussion. Seminars, Tutorials and Brainstorming sessions.

Development of Evaluation tools: Norm referenced. tests and Criterion referenced tests

Application of Educational Technology in Distance Education: Concept of Distance Education; Distance and Open learning system, Student supports service, Evaluation strategies in Distance Education; Counseling in Distance Education.

DESIGNING INSTRUCTIONAL SYSTEM

Much of the public enterprise in every country is concerned with education. "Education", said Alfred North Whitehead, "is the acquisition of the art of utilization of knowledge". This constitutes "micro educational" part of the whole ,system of education which focuses on schools and the classroom and al l that happens. there. This part of the system is mainly concerned with the structure of knowledge, its imparting to pupils and its receiving by the pupils. In other words construction of curriculum. process of learning and process of instruction-along with the human element involved in these constitute major subsystems of this micro-educational system. Even each of these sub-systems consists of still smaller subsystems. This chapter concerns itself with a discussion of the subsystem known as the instructional system.

Meaning of System: The meaning and nature of a system has already been discussed in detail in chapter-II. Here it suffices to say that a U stem is an integrated whole of a few components constituted to serve a specific purpose. The components are inter-related and by inter-acting with each other they contribute to the achievement of the purpose. The components are so arranged that they forma unity or an organic whole, an orderly way of doing things. Achievement of the goal is determined by the characteristics of the components and effectiveness of their interconnections in the system. If something goes wrong with any of these components it affects adversely functioning of the whole system. System theory, therefore, emphasizes proper selection or construction of these components, proper placement of these in' the system and ensuring that functionally they are. synchronized with each other so as to enable the system to achieve the purpose for which it was constructed.

Meaning and Nature of Instructional System: Instruction can be viewed as a system since it has a definite purpose to achieve with-the-help of a number of other interacting sub-systems such as the learners the teacher, the curriculum, the technology .off instruction, the goals to be achieved all of which interact with each other with an orientation to achieve the overall purpose for which it is designed an established. Designs of instructional systems vary from country to country depending upon their socio- political climate and goals to be achieved. It is obvious that the whole system of instruction for its efficient functioning depends on the efficient functioning of its components, their characteristics and interactions. These parts interrelate and interconnect so as to form a total entity, which is more than the sum of these parts, a definite structure. The major components of this instructional system are the foals of instruction, the process of instruction, the instructor, the learner. The goals "or objectives constitute the immediate learning tasks in the system. They may pertain to cognitive, affective, co native or psychomotor domes The process of instruction as a subsystem refers to the media and technology of communication and interaction between the instructor and the learner. The instructor is the person' who operates the instructional system, who puts power input into the system and moves it in preferred directions. He makes the system to achieve the goal and is the central figure in the system. He is the decision-maker and makes choices of ways and means for implementing plans and decisions. The learner is the target where the system as a whole has to strike, the material to be manipulated and treated for shaping it according to the goals. The output of he system eras system into the changes that are brought about in the learners through its functioning. This brief discussion brings out the fact that for an instructional system to be effective, it is necessary to think carefully about each of these components, strengthen them and manage them optimally taking into consideration specifically their required interactions with each other. In other words it makes it imperative to design the system of instruction with meticulous care after scrutinizing every detail pertaining to each component, and the. whole system. A detailed and objective analysis of the functions of each component, the input, output and, processes involved in the whole system are what are implied in designing of instructional system.

Designing And Instructional System - This is the process which has two elements involved in it, (i) an analysis of each or-the component and taking decisions about the way they should be shaped and arranged, (ii) developing a new or improved system accordingly. It means arranging the various components into input-process-output system and describing in detail how these three systems should be coordinated with each other how their operations should be managed in order to achieve the specified goals, i.e., the predetermined output. There is not one way of achieving this. In the past experts in the field have suggested three main approaches to designing instructional systems. These are

1. Training Psychology Approach
2. Cybernetic Approach
3. System Development Approach

This is to be noted in this connection that these in themselves, are not the instructional designs. They are, in fact, the approaches to designing instructional systems, specific ways in which instructional structional systems have to be prepared.

1. THE TRAINING PSYCHOLOGY APPROACH

Training psychology is not a branch of psychology. It is not even the applied psychology. It is an approach which was developed independently by the psychologists of the defence department during the World War-II, particularly in America in response to military needs. It was developed as a result of researdl on complex training (in other- words learning) situations. The problem faced by the defence psychologists was how to train people efficiently and quickly for performing on jobs in which great precision was required. The principles of learning derived from theories of learning could not help then in this regard. Consequently they evolved through practice and experience their own way of achieving the purpose. The methods and techniques that they evolved proved to be more successful. Having found them to be more practical and useful the educationists recommended their use in designing instructional systems also.

Salient Features: The focus of training psychology is on (i) designing performance goals, or tasks, (ii) breaking these tasks down into component or sub-tasks, and then (iii) developing training components, (iv) arranging these training components into entire learning' situation with proper sequence like behavior-shaping psychologists. Like behavior modification psychologists training psychology also recommends the use
and manipulations of reinforcements and feedback. The training psychology also manipulates variables like "task definitions" "task analysis".

Task-Analysis

Task analysis is the most important element in the training psychology approach to instructional designing. DeCecco and Crawford (p.33-35) draw a distinction between the two terms which are generally, confused with one another. To them the two terms "task description" and "task analysis" have different meanings. Task description stands for "full description of terminal performance". Robert Mager (1962) has developed a method of task description, which emphasizes to identify and describe the terminal behavior along with the standards (minimum or maximum) and the necessary conditions required to achieve that performance behavior. According to Mager task description stands for instructional objectives, which are defined in measurable and attainable terms.

Meaning of Task Analysis: Task analysis, on the other hand, refers to classes of behavior which are needed to be performed in order to achieve the performance goals or instructional objectives and are different at different stages and from objective to objective. Once the instructional objectives have been identified and defined, a description of those activities and behaviors has also to be prepared which need to be performed for achieving the objectives. These are prerequisites, essential behaviors which must exit or be developed in order to achieve the terminal goal performance. That means that the terminal performance is the end result of a sequence of activities or behaviors which need to be developed first before the final objectives can be achieved. Analysis of the final instructional objective, task description or goal to be achieved into its component parts is what is meant by task analysis. It consists in breaking the final task into its subtasks which must be learned to learn the final task. Every task is a series of subtasks each of which must be learned before the final task can be performed. What are those subtasks? Task analysis answers this question. For example, if the final instructional objective (job described) is that the child must be able to say "this is a dog, when he sees a dog on the road," this composite behavior may be broken down into subtasks or component behaviors as (i) the child must have the concept of 'dog'; (ii) the child must be familiar with the Hindi (or mother tongue) equivalent of dog; (iii) he must know the meaning and use of the English word 'this' 'is' and 'dog'. If these component behaviors or anyone of them are missing, the final performance objective can not be achieved. this kind of breakdown of any composite task into its unitary component parts is known as task analysis. Task analysis serves as a guide to identify what should be done for reaching the final goal as well as a diagnostic tool to identify where the missing link responsible for failure lies.

For designing an instructional system some kind of task analysis is necessary. Before decisions are taken about the required inputs and needed processes for producing the particular output, it is quite essential to define the output, i.e., the performance objectives. The content of the instruction is derived from this. In different fields different terms are used for the same operation: for example, job analysis, task-analysis, skill analysis with some difference all mean the same thing. They all refer to identifying the instructional or training needs and determining their content. The Glossary of Training Terms defines task or job analysis as the process of examining the job in detail in order to identifying its component tasks. The same glossary of terms defines task analysis as systemic analysis of the behavior required to carry out a task with a view to identifying areas of difficulty and the appropriate training techniques and learning aids necessary for learning. Annett ; say that the most general way of looking at task analysis is as the process of collecting information necessary to reach decision about what to train, how to train, even how well to train and perhaps how much to spend on training. In short task analysis should lead directly to a training design specifying not only what is usually called "course content" but also the output or criterion performance and the method or methods of training by which this can be achieved. The same is true about designing any kind of instructional system.

It is a sort of audit or inventory. In this knowledge, skills and attitudes are identified and isolated with a view to ultimately synthesizing them into a hierarchical organization relevant to the writing of a learning prescription. One way of doing this is to think of a topic or job as a hierarchical organization of - levels or components each of which describes the job in successively greater detail. This hierarchy may include topic, sub-topic, task and element (rule). A rule is a statement of generality, a definition, a fact or an item of information e.g. metals expand when heated. They should be complete in themselves and should contain only one fact or idea. They are critical and essential to the task. They are arranged in a hierarchical order to make a task. Tasks lead to sub-topics and sub-topics to the topic, e.g.

Topic: Theory of conservation of Energy.

Task : (i) Concept of electrical charge,

(ii) Concept of electrical current.

Rules: 1. Electric charge is produced by friction"

2 Electron is the basic unit of electrical charge.

3 .Electron is an impractical unit of charge.

4. Coulamb is the practical unit of charge.

5. Current is a flow of charge.

Techniques of Task Analysis: There is not one uniform way of task analysis. In different fields this is done in different ways. However, they employ some way of categorizing and, classifying the sub-components. Thus, there have been different taxonomies of describing these behavioral skills and unitary performances that compose the final task. Depending upon the field and purpose for which task analysis is done, there have been different taxonomies used for this analysis. Mainly, there are three more popular taxonomies or ways of classifying these sub-components.

These are:

1. Miller's (1967) taxonomy of psychological demands of tasks.
2. Gagne's (1970) taxonomy of eight different categories of learning.
3. Annett and Duncan (1967) hierarchical task analysis.

Miller (1967) asks what performance behaviour the robot will have to have in order to make him behave like a human being performing a particular task. He then lists these categories as (i) concept of purpose, (ii) scanning function, (iii) relevant cues function, (iv)' interpretation of cues, (v) short-term memory, (vi) long-term memory, (vii) decision making and problem solving, (viii) effect or response.

Gange. (1970) has developed a different type of taxonomy. He calls these categories as categories or conditions of learning. These are. (i) sign learning, (ii) stimulus-response learning, (iii) chaining, (vi) verbal association, (v) discrimination learning, (vi) concept learning, (vii) rule learning, (viii) Problem solving. Gagne's taxonomy is unique in the sense that his categories are arranged hierarchically. For example, one can acquire concept only when he has already developed discrimination learning.

Annett and Duncan (1967) at Hull University developed a technique of taxonomy which is known as hierarchical task analysis According to this technique tasks are broken down into "Operations" which constitute units of analysis and are defined as units of behavior. These operations or units may be long or short in duration. simple or complex in structure. But, they should be defined in terms of their objective. Any operation can be further divided into rule-operations; and these can be. again. subdivided. This technique can be applied to a wide variety of tasks and proceeds -hierarchically. Each operation clearly specifies the (a) input required, (b) action that needs to be performed during the operation, and (c) feedback that tells the operator how adequately he has performed.

Planning Evaluation and Review Technique (PERT) that constitutes an important aspect of management science also utilizes task analysis for planning and programming. In this the whole task is analysed in detail in terms of its sub-activities or sub- components. The task is, then, sub-divided until the desired level of detail is reached. The breakdown structure takes the form of a pyramid, its apex being the total task or project followed by the major components as its first level and the tasks within each major component as the second level. PERT was developed in 1958 by a research team appointed by the United States of America's Navy Special Projects Office for developing ballistic missile.

Sequencing Operation: When an operation or task is broken down into subordinate operations the analyst states how the subordinates are related to one another, i.e., the ,order or network of their relationships is also stated. This is known as preparation of network design or sequencing of operations. All priorities of tasks and components with their relationships and interdependences are shown in the structure of the network. The basic elements of the network are events, activities, and constraints. Events represent the start or the completion of an activity. They arc shown as circles, triangles rectangles and squares in the graphical network design. They are connected with each other by arrows which represent activities. Events don't use personnel or consume resources and time. Activities are real which are shown by continuous straight lines and also dummy which are shown by dotted lines. Real activities are those which are personnel resources and time. Dummy activities involve no use of personnel, resources or time. They only show dependency of one event on another. A constraint means when an activity can not take place until all preceding events and activities have been completed.

Application in Education: Task analysis is a general technique or approach which can be applied in any field, though its structure and details vary from one field to another. It assumes a very sophisticated form in industry and management science. In education it does not go so deep into the details as in other fields. But, sprit of task analysis remains uniformly the same in all fields. A concrete example of its application in the field of education is Georgia University's Proficiency Modules (PM) prepared for training elementary school teachers, The university team into following three components at the first level broke down the task of training elementary school teachers.

1. Identifying and stating general objectives.
2. Identifying and stating pupil learning behaviors.
3. Identifying and stating teaching behaviors.

Alter analyzing the job they prepared a job-analysis flow chart for training elementary school teachers. At the second level breakdown each of the above component was trai1slated into performance specifications which took the form of proficiency or performance modules (PMs). They were. then, published along with a guide which was designed to direct individual student learning behavior. The performance modules (PM) prepared by the team were a series of learning activities designed to achieve specific performance criteria. Another example of this kind of task analysis is the Wisconsin University Model.

Task analysis has, now, become a general and common approach to preparing a program for achieving some specific purpose. It is more objective and scientific way of doing things.

Formulation of Instructional Objectives

In the beginning of this chapter it was emphasized that an instructional system consists of several components such as (1) the goals and objectives to be achieved, (2) the process of instruction, (3) the instructor, and (4) the learner. It is obvious from this that for designing an instructional system one has to identify and define these components as objectively as possible. identifying and defining the instructional objectives or performance goals is, in fact, the first step of designing an instructional system. But, there is a lot of confusion in this as a number of terms are in use. It seems necessary, therefore, to clarify the meaning of these terms.

De Cecco and Crawford (p. 25) distinguish instructional objectives from school objectives and teacher objectives. School objectives are very broad goals which the nations and the communities establish for being achieved through their system of schools or education. The governments from time to time specify them by formulating their educational policies. The government of India did it by issuing their National Policy on Education (1986). These goals relate to various aspects of national development such as education for democracy, education for social and emotional integration, education for citizenship, and so on. School objectives, thus, reflect economic, political and social philosophies of the nations and the communities. Teacher objectives are narrower in scope than school objectives. These objectives guide the teacher in selecting the. content, method and activities that have to be followed while teaching in the class. These are defined in terms of teacher's behaviour, i.e., what the teacher will do. These may be considered as the sub-categories of school objectives. In order to achieve the school objectives, the teacher has to make' efforts; and the efforts he .makes define his objectives. De Cecco and Richards (1974) bring in another term, "the student objective" in the discussion. These, as they hold, refer to the "opinions and plans expressed and pursued by students." For example, introduction of vocational courses, development of certain specific skills, imparting knowledge which may help students in taki1 1g competitive examinations, etc

Another way of defining instructional objectives is to identify the end product of construction in terms of observable performance of the student. From the point of view of effectiveness of teaching, this way of identifying and stating instructional objectives is considered more important. This set of objectives. thus identified and defined, is known as Behavioral objectives. The following pages will be devoted to the detailed discussion of behavioral objectives.

BEHAVIORAL OBJECTIVES

Behavioural objectives are specific behaviours (more -correctly terminal performances) of students. They are the end products of (earning indicating whether or not a student has learned something as reflected in his specific behaviour as a result of teaching-learning. What is most significant in case of these objectives is that they should describe observable terminal performance. This means that the objective must be stated in the form of the specific behaviour which can be observed and measured. For example the objective that "The students will enumerate five important facts leading to the civil war" or "The students will write the word 'believe' correctly" or " The students will tell the meaning of 'to be skeptical', etc. are behavioural objectives. But, on the other hand if we state these objectives as "The students will know the facts leading to the civil War "or" The students will learn the meaning of the word skeptical "or" The students will learn the spelling of the word behaviour, they can not be considered behavioural objectives. "Knowing" and "learning" are not the observable behaviours. Nor they can be measured. They are internal conditions or processes of the organism, which can be known only when they are reflected in overt behaviour.

A behavioural objective is an observable criterion of performance. "It is a clear, precise statement of the students behaviour which is accepted as an evidence. of his having achieved what he and the teacher set put to accomplish." (Haden and King, p. 43) Some of the most important characteristics of a behavioural objective are' (i) It should be a precise statement, (ii) it should be observable performance, (iii) it should state what the students will do after completing the learning activities, (iv) it must be based on the needs of the pupils and society, (vi) it should be consistent with the philosophy of education. Behavioural objectives state how a learner is to act think or feel.

Taxonomy of Instructional Objectives: For long teachers stated their objectives in broad and general terms which were vague and could not be measured. This was quite frustrating to some experts. Hence, a group of psychologists met in 1948 to establish a common language for classifying human behavioural characteristics. After a brief investigation this group under the leadership of Bloom (1956) came to the conclusion that instructional objectives could be classified into three categories or domains such as cognitive. affective and psychomotor domains. The group constructed a taxonomy based on the assumption that objectives could be arranged along a continuum from concrete to abstract and from simple to complex. Bloom and his associates prepared the taxonomy of objectives pertaining to cognitive domain only. Later on Krathwohl (1964) published taxonomy of objectives pertaining to affective domain. An abbreviated form of these is presented below.

Cognitive Domain (Bloom)

1. Knowledge
2. Comprehension
3. Application
4. Analysis
5. Synthesis
6. Evaluation

Affective Domain (Krathwohl)

1. Receiving
2. Responding
3. Valuing
4. Organization-conceptualization and organizing a value system
5. Characterization by a value or a value complex

The psychomotor domain.

1. Observing 2. Imitating
3. Practicing 4. Adapting

Each of these levels of all these domains has been explained in the following sections.

COGNITIVE DOMAIN

1. Knowledge: This is the lowest level of learning and includes recall and memory. At this level the student is expected to recall specific facts such as dates, events. persons, places, basic principles and generalizations.

2. Comprehension: This is the lowest level of understanding. The student is expected to use facts or ideas without relating them to each other (e.g. paraphrasing or interpreting something gained form reading or listening). At the highest level of this category the student may be able to extend thinking beyond the data. For example in science class a student may draw conclusions 'from a simple experiment. The student of psychology may predict consequent behaviour from aggressive face.

3. Application: This intellectual skill entails the use of information in specific situations. The psychology student, for example, may explain various kinds of anti-social behaviours of people in the society.

4. Analysis: This skill involves taking apart information and making relationships in order to discover hidden meaning and the basic structure of an idea or fact. The student is able to read between the lines, to distinguish between fact and opinion and to assess degree of consistency or inconsistency.

5. Synthesis: At this level the student is able to reassemble the component parts of an idea in order to develop new or creative ideas.

6. Evaluation: This highest level of cognition involves making judgments on the materials, information or method. It represents the end process of cognition. This is the basis of decision- making.

The five levels of affective domain objectives are explained as follows:

AFFECTIVE DOMAIN

1. Receiving: At this level the student becomes only aware of an idea, process or thing and is willing to listen to a given communication. For example, the student listens for rhythm in poetry- or prose read aloud.

2. Responding: This level involves displaying an interest in the subject. He makes a voluntary response and has a feeling of satisfaction. For example, he reads poetry for personal pleasure.

3. Valuing: The student values a thing, phenomenon or behaviour. He, then, is said to "hold the value". He is motivated to appreciate the behaviour. At the lower end of the continuum the student might be said to hold the belie f somewhat tentatively. At the other end- his-or her value becomes one of conviction, certainty "beyond the shadow of a doubt".

4. Organization: The student organizes values into a system at this stage which forms the basis for making choices, a set of criteria for guiding behaviour.

5. Characterization: At this level, the internalization process is complete.

Values are integrated into some kind of consistent system. Thus, the person is described as having certain controlling tendencies and a recognized philosophy of life. This becomes his stable character.

CONATIVE DOMAIN

A third major instructional domain is the development of mental and motor skills, such as those needed in reading, pronouncing, speaking, explaining, collecting data, playing tennis, drawing, dealing with people, working together etc. Simpson, Harrow and Hoover have classified these skills or "psychomotor behaviours" as they are called by them into 7, 6 and 4 taxonomic levels respectively. Hoover's model has four levels. These are:

1. Observing: At this level the student observes a more experienced person performing the activity.

2. Imitating: At this stage he follows directions and sequences under close supervision and makes an attempt to imitate the model.

3. Practicing: The entire sequence of steps is performed repeatedly at this level. Performance, then, becomes more or less habitual in nature. He has, now, acquired thc skill.

4. Adapting: This means adapting minor details that, in turn, influence the total performance the student or the teacher may initiate these modifications. This leads to perfection of the skill. There is always room for greater perfection.

Writing Behavioral Objectives:

Behavioral objectives are stated in a way different from that of non-behavioral objectives. Since the behavioral objectives are observable terminal performances, the have to be stated in terms of behaviors that are observable, which are concrete, overt and expressed. For example, if we say "the child will know", the knowing behavior is such as it can not be observed; it is covert and unexpressed. How can it be confirmed that the child has known something unless the "knowns" are expressed in overt behavior which anyone can see or observe. However, if we say "the child will tell the meaning of", this becomes a behavioral objective as 'telling' is an oveli, expressed, concrete behavior which can be observed and measured or tested.. 'the difference between the behavioral and non-behavioral way of writing objectives lies mainly in the use of the verb. While writing objectives in behavioral terms, we use action verbs, for example, will tell, will name, will identify, will enumerate, will draw and so on. Use of such verbs as 'will understand', 'will draw', 'will appreciate', etc. indicating behaviors which can not be observed or seen is discarded for writing objectives behavioral terms. "Understanding", "appreciating", "knowing", etc. by themselves are meaningless unless they are manifest in actual concrete behaviors.

Mager (1942 has suggested that in stating specific learning outcomes the statements should include three elements: (1) the specific student behaviour (ii) the condition under which the behavior is to be, shown, and (iii) the standard of acceptable performance. For example, "out of ten causes of civil war explained to the students in the class, they will reproduce, at least, eight of them". In this "reproduce" is the specific behavior which can be observed, "explained in the class" is the condition and "at least eight" is the standard of performance expected.

A few action verbs or key terms, which are, generally, used in writing objectives in behavioral terms, are as follows

1.	Recognizes	6.	Gives an example
2.	Identifies	7.	Exlpains
3.	Distinguishes	8.	Predicts
4.	Selects	9.	Formulates, etc.
5.	Describes		

Use of these verbs in the statements renders them to be statements of behavioral objectives. When an instructional system is required to be designed- its general objectives are converted into behavioral objectives.

Criticism and Advantages of Behavioral Objectives: There are experts who are quite critical of behavioral objectives. Their criticisms are mainly as follows: (i) behavioral objectives lead to neglect of broad concepts, principles and understandings, (ii) behavioral objectives focus on parts of the whole and the trivia to the detriment of integration and unity, (iii) behavioral objectives ignore affective teaching and learning, and overlook reasons underlying concepts, (iv) behavioral" objectives undermine improved and qualitative thinking processes, and so on.

Some of these criticisms do have some truth in them. but, with little more care some of these limitations of these objectives can be eliminated. On the whole, from several points of view, behavioral objectives are very useful. Their main advantages are:

1. Ralph Tyler (1964) and Robert Gagne (1965) have given three important reasons of using behavioral objectives. First-Js that writing objectives in behavioral terms provides guidance to teachers in the planning of instruction. For

example, if a teacher does not know where he has to take his students to, he may very well reach a point where did not want to. Hence, it is extremely important to very clearly and specifically determine what the student will do at the finish. This will enable the teacher to take all the precautions and steps which lead him to his destination. Thus. stating objectives in behavioral terms helps the teacher in identifying and selecting the most appropriate instructional procedures too. It is these objectives which help the teacher in selecting the appropriate level and amount of the teaching material.

2. Another great advantage of behavioral objectives is their use in the assessment of performance of a students. (valuation or assessment of student performance is an integral part of teaching-learning. but, it is not possible to do so reliably and validly unless it is known specifically what is to be assessed. Behavioral objectives provide the most objective and specific guidance in this regard. They specify the behaviors which are expected to he shown by the student as a result of learning. Since this learning is expressed in terms of observable. and specific behaviors, it becomes easy to construct reliable and valid tests for measuring them. Since evaluation determines, to a large extent, what the teacher will teach and what the student will learn, a more objective and valid valuation is bound to result into more efficient learning and more effective teaching.

3. The clear, specific and meaningful objectives stated in behavioral terms provide guidance to the students also. If they know if well in what terms, on what specific behavior they are going to be assessed, they can adjust their studies accordingly. This focus will prevent them from making irrelevant efforts, from going into unwanted directions, from wasting their energy and time on what is not going to be the part of their evaluation.

4. Stating objectives in behavioral terms makes it possible to develop

innovative and more effective strategies or programs of learning. For example, programmed learning has been possible only on the basis of behavioral objectives. Without defining and stating objectives in behavioral terms construction of teaching machines, computer-based instruction programs of educational T V and multimedia-based programs of teaching would have never been possible. Any relevant program of measurable quality such as PPBS, Performance Contracting, Voucher System etc. will have to be based on behavioral objectives.

5. Curriculum planning and program revision, program evaluation, etc. can not be done meaningfully in the absence of behavioral objectives.

6. Even quality research cannot be possible without defining the objectives behaviorally.

All that goes before, however, does not mean that all instructional objectives in all cases should be defined in behavioral terms. There might be certain areas of learning which may not be amenable to be translated into behavioral terms. Simi1arly behavioral objectives need not be atomistic and trivial. Tyler (1964) suggests that the behaviors to be learned by the students should be described at the "most useful level of specificity and they should be purposeful and meaningful to the students".

Thus, task analysis and formulation of instructional objectives constitute two most important aspects of training psychology approach to instructional designs.

STRATEGIES OF TEACHING

The main focus of teaching is to bring about a desirable change in the behaviour of the learner. It is brought about by the teacher using teaching strategies to active his objectives. But traditionally we have been using teaching methods for content presentation. In order to increase the effectiveness of the presentation, the audio-visual aids are also used.

The teaching is much more difficult task. It requires different type of methods, techniques and teaching aids. The selection of these methods and techniques depends upon the nature of task, learning objectives, learner's abilities and student's entering behaviour.

The learning objectives and task analysis provide the basis for effective presentation of teaching. In order to bring desirable change in the behaviour of the learner, teacher has to employ the devices-Teaching strategies and teaching tactics. These terms have been defined in the following ways

Meaning and Definition of Teaching Strategy

'Teaching strategy is the means to achieve learning objectives'. E.Stones and S.Morris have defined the term 'Teaching Strategy' comprehensively in the following manner:

"Teaching strategy is a generalized plan for a lesson which includes structure. desired learner behaviour in terms of goals of instruction and an outline of planned tactics necessary to implement the strategy. The lesson strategy is apart of a larger development scheme.

This definition of teaching strategy involves two aspects-(1) a generalized plan for the persecution of lesson and (2) it includes desired learner behaviour in terms of goals of instruction. He has further explained the meaning of a lesson. It a part of a development scheme of the curriculum and plan includes an outline of tactics of teaching which help in implementing the strategy.

Teaching strategy seeks to establish the relationship between teaching and learning in view of achieving the objectives.

Teaching strategies includes broad method instruction, e.g.., elector strategy - a case -study strategy programmed instruction strategy. They can be regarded as a broad and away of operation.

Definition of Teaching Method

Teaching method is a style of the presentation of content in classroom. M. Varma has defined the term method in the following manner:

"Method is an abstract as logical entities that we can distinguish between manner and method, in realty, they form an organic whole and matter determines method. analogously as objective determine means; content and spirit determines method. The common teaching matter may be three of literature".

M.Varma has presented broad meaning of the. term method. According to him matter is important for determining methods can be classified under three heads:

(1) Telling Method-Lecture, Questioning, Discussion, etc.

(2) Showing Method-Demonstration. Excursion, etc.

(3) Doing Method-Project, Role playing, Practical, etc.

Broady (1963) has stated that, "Method refers to the formal structure of the sequence of acts commonly denoted by instruction. The term method covers both strategies and tactics of teaching and involves the choice of what is to be taught, and in which order is it to be presented".

Method is more general, it includes techniques also. The teaching techniques are ways of implementing a method. Different techniques may be employed with in one method.

Difference Between Teaching strategy and method

Teaching strategies and methods are used for the same meaning but they are quite different from one another. Some points of difference have been discussed here:

(1) Teaching method is based on classical theory of organization task centered whereas teaching strategy is based on modern theory of organization tae k centered.

(2) The content and mode of presentation are the main elements of teaching method. The matter determines the method (telling, showing and doing). The bebavioural objectives and learning conditions are two basic' elements of teaching strategy. The objective determines the strategy of (Cognitive, Affective and Psychomotor) leaching.

(3) The term strategy has been borrowed from military science (technology) and n1ethod is the term of pedagogy.

(4) The assumption regarding teaching strategy is that teaching and methods uses macro-approach to teaching.

(5) Teaching strategy employs micro-approach to teaching and methods are implemented by techniques are concerned with mode of presentation and nature of content.

(6) The strategies are implemented by tactics of teaching and methods are implemented by techniques of teaching. The tactics are more concerned with learning structure whereas techniques are concerned with mode of presentation and nature of content.

(7) The effectiveness of teaching strategy is evaluated in terms of achieving objective by administering criterion test. The teaching methods are evaluated in terms of mastery over the subject matter by using achievement test.

(8) The main focus of teaching strategy is to achieve the objective by creating appropriate learning conditions. The teaching method aims at the effective presentation of subject-matter to have the mastery over it.

Some teaching methods are also termed as teaching strategies, e.g., lecture is used both method as well as strategy. The lecture strategy refers to realizing some specific objectives but lectured method refers to mode of presentation of some specific content. In selecting appropriate teaching strategy task analysis, learning conditions and learning objectives are crucial factors, but subject-matter determines the method though the same subject content can be used for achieving different types of objectives.

Meaning and Definition Teaching Tactics

The teaching tactics are the ways of implementing a teaching strategy. Different types of tactics are used in the same teaching strategy. The tactics are more concerned with creating appropriate learning structure.

E. Stones and S. Morris (J 972) have defined the term teaching tactics in the following

"Teaching tactics is good linked influenced influencing behaviours of the teacher the way behaves in the instructional situation in working towards the development of the strategy; units of teacher behaviour through which the teacher, the students and subject matter interact."

A tactics, strategies is a unit of teacher behaviour which is helpful for achieving instructional objectives. A tactics may range from non-verbal behaviour of a teacher behaviour are purposeful or goal linked influence.

In preparing an instruction, attempt is made to establish relationship among tactics, strategies, teacher-behaviour, objectives of education and the learners. The instructional behaviour consists of chain three links- observing, accepting and acting functions of teaching.

The Structural Approach of Teaching

The structural approach of teaching was revolutionized the whole process of education. It lays down the great importance of teaching acts and learning situations. They can be used as the basis for selecting appropriate teaching tactics. Structure is a primary factor in most of teaching tactics. It has the following advantages for teachers and students.

(1) It Enables a Teacher to

(a) Select appropriate teaching tactics, depending upon the classes of structure involved in the task.

(b) Demonstrate the relationship between different classes of learning objectives and different classes of structure.

(c) Increase ,his student's depth of understanding by using the innate structure of the task as a media for presenting facts and incorporating additional facts in student's repertory.

(d) Present the information in such a way that it is more likely to be remembered.

(2) It Enables a Student to

(a) Select appropriate learning involved in the task.

(b) Perceive the relationship between the different classes of learning objectives .arid different classes of structure.

(c) Increase his depth of under standing by using the innate structure of the take as a Vehicle for learning facts and incorporating additional facts in to his repertory.

(d) Remember the information once he has learnt. It must be remembered, however, that optimal structure of a body of knowledge, is absolute but relative, and must constantly related to the needs student and the objectives to be achieved.

Type of Teaching Strategy

A teacher organizes his activates of teaching to bring about the desirable change in the behaviour of the learner. Thus the students are: forced to achieve learning adjectives. Most of the teaching strategies in terms of their effectiveness in achieving different kinds of learning objectives. These are the means for realizing the learning objectives. Teaching strategies can be classified under the following two heads:

(A) Autocratic Style-It includes the following strategies

(1) Lecture, (2) Lesson demonstration, (3) Tutorials, and (4) Programmed Instruction.

(B) Permissive Style-It includes the following strategies

(5) Question -Answer, (6) Heuristics, (7) Project-strategy, (8) Review, (9) Group discussion, (10) Role playing, (11) Assignment, (12) Discovery, (13) Computer Assisted Instruction, (14) Bain storming, (15) Independent study, (16) Leaders less group (17) Sensitivity Training.

The tutorial strategy is included in both types of strategies- automatic and permissive style of teaching strategy. The detailed description of these strategies has been provided with the following paragraphs:

[A] AUTOCRATIC STYLE OF TEACHING STRATEGIES

The autocratic style of teaching strategies is traditional. These strategies achieve different objectives more than permissive style of teaching strategies. The autocratic style strategies are content centered and teacher remains more active and students are like passive listeners. The autocratic -teaching strategies realize cognitive objective while permissive teaching strategies tend to achieve affective objectives.

The strategies do not consider the student's abilities, interests and personality of the learner. There is no freedom for the learner in teaching process. these are highly subjective and conventional style of teaching strategies. A detailed description of such strategy have been given in the following paragraph

(1) Lecture Strategy

It is an oldest teaching method given by idealism philosophy. It is most important teaching method in our schools. It is one of the autocratic teaching strategies. The lecture is often considered as communication strategy.

Focus- It may be used to achieve the cognitive and affective objectives.

Structure-Lecture lays emphasis on the presentation of the content. Teacher is more active and students are passive participants but he uses question-answer techniques to keep them attentive in the class. Teacher controls and plans for all students activities.

Principles of Teaching-It employs the following principles

(a) The content is presented as whole.

(b) The main stress in on presentation.

(c) The students learn better through listening.

(d) The subject-content is correlated with other subjects.

(e) The new knowledge is linked with student 'previous knowledge.

Applications-The presentation can be made effective-but it should be used with great precautions. Teacher should make use of the teaching aids in the description and explaining concepts. Developing question should be asked to make the presentation purposeful and interesting.

Advantages- The following are the major advantages of lecture strategy

(1) The habit of concentration may be developed among the students.

(2) It is an economical teaching strategy. Large subject-content may be taught relatively in small duration.

(3) Teaching activities are dominated by the teacher and there is no place for student's abilities, interests and their learning.

(4) It is not based on the principles of psychology. The individual difference are not considered implementing teaching strategy.

(5) It cannot be used for achieving the psychomotor objectives and the highest order of effective objectives.

(6) Usually teacher deviates from the subject-content and teaching points therefore. student can not perform well in examination. .

(7) An effective teacher can use this strategy effectively, because teacher should have mastery over the content.

Suggestions-The following precautions should be observed to use this strategy effectively-

(1) The language of the lecture should be simple, easy and comprehensive.

(2) The developing questions should be asked to make the students attentive

in the class.

(3) The students remain inactive or passive participants, hence the teacher uses humour to release their tension and monotony of the class.

(4) The strategy should be used from secondary level to upward classes.

(5) The teachers should explore their previous knowledge and make the efforts to link with new one.

(6) The strategy should be supported by question- answer technique and appropriate teaching aids. maps, charts, diagrams, pictures etc.

Tutorials

Tutorials strategy is considered both autocratic and permissive type of teaching, It is generally considered to be one of the most valuable educational experiences. Lecture strategy is followed by tutorials because individualized type of teaching.

Focus- Tutorials aim to provide remedial help of the learner or to help individual difficulties of the learners. The cognitive and affective objectives may be achieved by the tutorials.

Considering the homogeneous type of difficulties of the learner forms structure- Tutorials classes. One teacher assigns the smaller homogeneous group. He has to give remedial help to the learners. Tutorial is also follow up programme.

Principles --- It is used upon the following teaching principles:

(1) Considers the individual difference.

(2) It establishes the rapport with learners.

(3) It provides educational guidance.

(4) It organizes remedial help to the learners.

Type of Tutorials- Tutorial covers a wide range of teaching activities. These may be classified under three heads:

(a) Supervision Tutorials -In this type of tutorial students teacher meanings are arranged regularly. A students reads an essay and defends it with arguments. This strategy can provide an opportunity to depend his understanding of subject for able student. It stresses on the mastery over the basic skills of scholarship.

(b) Group Tutorials-These tutorials are useful for an average students. These call satisfy the needs of less exceptional students. The teacher should have the background of social psychology and group dynamics so that he can deal with group tutorials effectively in solving their problems.

Practical Tutorials-These tutorials are commonly used for both group and individual basis to achieve psychomotor skills in laboratory, workshop and rehearsal. These tutorial are basically employed to achieve the psychomotor objectives.

Group tutorials are more useful in adult teaching. A tutorial strategy is more useful for achieving higher-order cognitive, affective and psychomotor objectives.

Advantages-The following are major advantages of the tutorials:

(1) I t is valuable teaching strategy from individual differeilce point of view.

(2) It provides an opportunity to organize remedial teaching.

(3) It can fulfil the need of entering behaviour of the learners.

(4) It provides full freedom to the learner to seek the clarification of their problems and can raise their level of performance.

Limitations- It has the following disadvantages

(1) One teacher cannot solve the difficulties related to difference point of

view.

(2) The teacher becomes basis and does not take interest in the problem of each student.

(3) Usually some students dominate the tutorials group and get equal opportunity to participate.

(4) Tutorial-group develops the feeling of jealous.

Suggestions- Tutorial may be improved by observing the following suggestions

(1) Tutorial groups should be formed of some background, abilities and entering behaviours

(2) Teacher should have very objective dealing with the students.

(3) Teacher should provide the remedial help in the subject of his own interest.

(4) The tutorial groups should be formed on the basis of students, difficulties in different subjects.

(5) Teacher should encourage every student to place his difficulty.

(6) Programmed Instruct'

Discussion

There is no comprehensive definition of 'group discussion' but it is considered as a democratic teaching strategy. The pupils are more active in it. Teacher's job is to supervise and to provide guidance to pupils activities, It is child-centered teaching strategy. It may be of two types: (1) By the teacher and (2) By the students.

(1) By the Teacher- This type of discussion is more autocratic in style.

(2) By the Students-In this situation, discussion is more permissive or democratic in style.

Objectives-The affective objectives and higher order cognitive objectives may be achieved.

Structure-The group discussion is organized in two forms-Formally and informally. In formal group discussion, Proper schedule is prepared and certain rules are observed.

The group discussion is organized on any educational problem of curriculum. Teacher acts as a leader of the group, but in the absence of a teacher, pupils have to select a students to act as leader of the group:' The leader of the group prepares a plan for discussion. In the group-discussion, due weighted is given to the answers and questions of the pupils.

Principles- The strategy is based upon the following principle of teaching

(1) Principle of active participation.

(2) Principle of freedom for work.

(3) Principle of group work and equal opportunities to ask questions and to answer them.

Advantages-The following are the main advantages of this strategy:

(1) It has the greater scope of criticism for incorrect approaches, ideas and concepts

(2) It develops the feeling of group work and group participation.

(3) It helps ill developing the creative ability and thinking among pupils.

(4) It develops the problem solving attitude and the tolerance to hear one's own criticism.

Suggestions-It may be improved and can be effectively employed by observing the following precautions:

(1) Every student should be provided an opportunity to participate in the discussion.

(2) Students should be encouraged and motivated to participate in the discussion.

(3) Irrelevant criticism should not be encouraged.

Brining Storming

It is completely permissive style of teaching strategy. It is based on an assumption that a student can learn better in a group rather than in individual study. 1t is a prob1em oriented strategy teaching.

Objectives-The higher order of cognitive and affective objectives can be achieved.

Structure-This strategy consists of a problem solving situation in which come to their mind. The group is encouraged to provide even unusually suggestions. They have to analyses and evaluate the workability of their own suggestions of the problem.

Osborn's Brain Storming Steps-He has suggested the following steps for this strategy of teaching:

(1) P1an all phases of the problem and think about the sub-problems which may emerge.

(2) Select sub-problems to be attached.

(3) Think about the data or differences which may help involving them.

(4) Select the probable sources of data and collect most relevant data.

(5) Decide the possible ideas through Free Wheeling with suspended Judgments hints to the solution.

(6) Select ideas most likely to lead to the solution.

(7) Consider the possible way to test these ideas.

(8) These ideas are tested in terms of relevance, adequacy and sufficiency.

(9) Imagine all possible contingencies and ways of meeting them.

(10) Take decision about the final solution of the problem.

Advantages-It has the following advantages'

(1) It has both psychological and educational basis of teaching.

(2) It is more creative strategy of teaching and encourages for the original ideas.

(3) It provides more ideas of good quality.

(4) It creates the situation for more independent thinking among learner.

Independent Study

Independent study, which more usually called' project work' has been defined by Baskin(1961) in his book. It helps in developing student's initiative, responsibility, and understanding for what they study. This strategy is more useful for a training programme.

Objectives-The affective and cognitive objectives are achieved by this teaching strategy.

Structure-Independent work or reading is organized in small groups, but such takes place in the absence of teacher and interview of certain regularly scheduled meetings. The programme is defined precisely in terms of objectives and criterion test. I t is a part of regular teaching and is organised for superior students. Teaching repeater is used in this type of situation.

Principle-I: is based upon the following leaning principles

(1) Freedom. of work and reading, (2) Sell'-study', (3) Principle of individual difference and (4) Principle of involvement in the task.

Advantages-The following are the main advantages of this teaching strategy:

(1) It encourages the student's participation.

(2) It develops independent ,or original thinking among students.

(3) It develops social and cognitive abilities.

(4) It is definitely superior teaching strategy for traditional strategies.

(5) It creates the situation for the learners to work according to their own

abilities.

(6) Teacher provides individual guidance to the students.

(2) SEMINAR

Teaching is. a continuum from conditioning to indoctrination. It is organised form memory level to reflective level. Our teaching is confined up to memory level even at college and university level. At the most teaching can be organised at but understanding level, instructional situations should be organized in such a way so that teaching may be done at reflective level. At the most teaching can be organised at but understanding level, instructional situations should he organized is such a way so that teaching may be done at reflective level. Higher objectives of cognitive and reflective domains are achieved by creating such conditions of learning. As the development of higher cognitive and affective abilities is essential at the higher stage of education. Several institutional techniques have been evolved with human interaction as underlying pedagogical principles, viz, a discussion, seminar, debate, panel discussion. buzz session, role-playing, brainstorming, etc. Description here is however con fined to the seminar technique.

Meaning and Definition of Seminar

A seminar as an instructional technique involves generating a situation for a group to have guided interaction among themselves on a theme which is generally presented to the group by one or more members. The person who presents the them should have studied the theme thoroughly before hand. This would mean selection of relevant material at its organization. The collected material is put in the form of paper which is circulated among the participants in advance or before the paper reading. It provided the structure of the theme, to facilitate its communication.

Thus, seminar is all instructional technique of higher learning which involves paper reading on a theme and followed by the group discussion to clarify the complex aspects of the theme.

Objectives of Seminar

The Seminar technique is employed to realize the higher objectives of cognitive and affective domains which have been enumerated as follows

(a) Cognitive Objective -This technique creates the learning situations so that the following higher cognitive objectives may be realized

(1) To develop the higher cognitive abilities: analysis, synthesis and evaluation as compared to the situations involving human interaction.

(2) To develop the ability of responding in .this manner would involve higher cognitive actions valuing, organizing and characterization of quick comprehension. of the situation, examination, of it against the knowledge he possesses and construction of his reactions to the situation.

(3) To develop the ability of keen observation experiences, feelings and to present them effectively.

(4) To develop the ability to seek clarification and defend the ideas of others effectively.

(b) Affective Objectives-The following higher aspect of affective domain are developed by employing the instructional technique:

(1) To develop the feeling of tolerance the opposite ideas of others.

(2) To develop the feelings of cooperation with other colleagues and respect of the ideas and feelings of others.

(3) To develop the emotional stability among the percipients of the seminar.

(4) To acquire the good manners of putting questions and answering the questions of others effectively.

The human interaction under this technique develops the good manners and skills among the participants.

Roles of Seminar

In organizing a seminar the following roles are performed

(1) Organizer or Instructor (2) President or Chairman or Convener of the seminar (3) Speakers of the day (4) Participants and (5) Observers.

(1) Role of the Organizer-It is the responsibility of an organizer to plan and prepare the whole programme of the seminar. He decides the topic or theme of the seminar and assigns the different aspects of theme to different persons who have to play the role of speakers. He decides the data, time and place. Generally he also suggests the name of convener of the seminar. He prepares total schedule of the seminar.

(2) Role of President-The participants proposes the name of president. In suggesting the name of chairman, it should be taken in consideration that the person must be well acquainted with the theme of seminar. He must know his rights and duties as chairman of a seminar. Virtually the conveners conduct the seminar's activities. He directs the whole programme. He encourages the participants to take part in discussion. He keeps. the discussion on the theme of seminar .

In certain situations he also teach higher Techniques of Teaching takes part in the discussion. He provides the opportunities to each participant. At the end he has to summarize the discussion and may present his viewpoint on the theme. He has to give thanks to the speakers, participants, guests and observers.

(3) Role of Speaker-The organizer assigns the topics to the speakers. They prepare the topics thought and cyclostyle copies of the papers are prepared and these are distributed among the participants before the commencement of the seminar, so that participants should also prepare themselves on the theme. It encourages the discussion to last long. The speakers should be ready to defend the questions the speakers should have the tolerance of ideas or criticism of others.

(4) Role of Participants-The participants of the seminar should be well acquainted with. the theme. They should appreciate the performances of the speakers. They should be able to seek clarification and put questions. They should place their own ideas regarding the theme on the basis of their experiences. They should address the president for seeking clarification. They should not put question directly to the speakers. There are 25 to 40 participants in the seminar.

(5) Role of Observers-Some guests and observers are also invited and allowed to observe' the activities of the seminar. Generally they are not permitted to participate in the discussion. They should be allowed at the end to discussion and present their- observations with the permission of the chairman.

Procedure of the Seminar

Seminar as an instructional technique involves creating a situation for a group to have guided interaction among themselves on a theme which is generally presented to the group by one or more members. The person who presents the theme should have studied the theme thoroughly before hand. This would mean selection of relevant material and its organization.. Generally, this organized material put in the form of a paper which is circulated among members in advance. The paper helps to structure the theme, facilitates its communication, and focuses the scope for discussion. After the theme is presented it is discussed by the group. During the discussion participants may (i) seek clarification of the theme presented. (ii) make observations in the light of their knowledge and experience regarding the theme, and (iii) raise issues relating to the theme for further analysis and evaluation.

A chairman who may be knowledgeable about the theme will guide proceedings of the seminar. The chairman's role would be to keep the discussion on track. Stimulate maximum participation and consolidate at appropriate stages the view-points expressed. Seminar as an instructional technique seeks to provide maximally for interaction among the members. This means that sufficient time should he allowed for the discussion session; if this necessitates cutting down the time for presentation, it could be done since the main purpose of the presentation is to initiate the discussion.

The interaction in a seminar can be likened to the field of forces in machines. Different viewpoints or options expressed will represent forces in varied directions. However, unlike physical forces which when acting in opposite directions. at times, result in zero, the different view-points or even opposite opinions will' not result in neutrality but will induce further thinking among participants. It is, this stimulation for further thinking that should be reckoned with significance as the net instructional value of the seminar. When there is an agreement of ideas among individual members, these may be considered as forces acting in tl1e same direction and thereby having a reinforcing affect on the individual's view of the theme. In either cases the individual is benefited as he is either led to further analysis and evaluation of his view points, or helped in validating and thus strengthening them.

Advantages of a Seminar

From the above description of the basic mechanism of inter-action in seminar, it may be said that the seminar as an instructional technique has the potential to develop several abilities in students

(1) Due to the process stimulation of thinking brought about through interaction. different higher cognitive abilities like, analytical and critical thinking synthesizing and evaluating the ideas will tend to be developed.

(2) Apart from these cognitive ability certain effect attributes like tolerance for others views openness to ideas cooperation with others, emotional stability and

respect for other's feelings will be inculcated among the participants during the course of such sessions.

(3) These effects attribute represent the norms of behaviour for the group in the seminar situations. Moreover, these norms are the same as these of a democratic society. Deliberate efforts to adhere would of necessity be made during the course of seminar discussions. The adherence to these group norms would gradually inculcate the affect attributes in the participants.

(4) Concomitant effect of seminar as instructional technique will be the development of better habits. While preparing for presentation and participating in the discussion learners will get induced to pursue independent study, engage in post-seminar discussions covering the theme discussed as well as related ones, develop critical outlook to any idea there- by leading the learner to self-initiated learning which will be more permanent in nature.

(5) It can be seen from the above, seminar has great instructional value as it makes the instruction learner-centered and provides for learning through enquiry which is based on a very natural characteristics of inquisitiveness in humans.

(6) This natural way of learning through seminar establishes an important place for this technique at all level of instruction. From the practice, however, one may notice that it is mainly confined to higher education.

Essentials for Seminar-A situation seems to have arise mainly from the presumptions that the technique demands maturity in terms of language, social and emotional make up and the facility to deal with abstractions. Since the students at lower levels of education do not possess the maturity of this extent, it is generally considered that seminar is less feasible to be adopted as an instructional technique at these levels. Such a demarcation of feasibility regarding the use of seminar stems from the rigid notion about the nature of theme to be discussed therein. It is generally 'considered that the seminar should have an abstract theme to be presented and discussed. Although there is nothing against the suitability of such themes for seminars confining only to cover there is more of historicity of the technique rather than its demands about the nature of the theme. In fact the value of seminar should be seen interims of the basic mechanism of the involvement of learners. Here the learners are expected to present to others their ideas or experiences who would react to them in the light of their own experiences. And, it is this interaction on the ideas or experiences, however. high or low, concrete or abstract they may be in nature, that should be aimed at through this technique. Seeing seminar in this perspective, it may be quite feasible to utilize this technique effectively even at lower levels of instruction. At these levels the theme for seminar could be even simple and concrete experiences which could be narrated to follow children who in turn could discuss them in the light of their own. Interaction on such themes also would involve behaviours like questioning, making observations, evaluating the themes by compariilg it with their own experiences.

Types of Seminar

The said mechanism is employed in conducting a seminar but seminars are organized at different levels. On the basis of levels or organization the seminars are of four types: (1) Mini-Seminar, (2) Main Seminar, (3) National seminar, and (4) international seminar.

(1) Mini Seminar-A seminar organized to discuss a topic in class is known as mini-seminar. The purpose of the mini-seminar is to train the students for organizing the seminar and play different roles. It is simulated situation for the students. In an institution such seminars should be organized before the main seminar.

(2) Main Seminar-Such seminars are organized at departmental level or institutional level on a major theme. All the students and staff members take part in such seminars These seminars are organized weekly or monthly in departments. Generally specific themes are selected for main seminar.

(3) National Seminar-A national seminar is organized by an association or organization at national level. The experts are invited on the theme of the seminar. The secretary of the seminar prepares the schedule theme, time dates. days .and venue. Generally NCERT organizes such seminar at national level, on educational theme.

Educational Technology, Population Education, Trends of Education, Distance Education, Non-formal education, Quality control of educational research in India.

(4) International Seminar **-** Generally such seminars are organized by UNESCO and other international organization. The topic or theme of seminar is very broad, e.g., students unrest or activisms, Innovations in teacher-education and Examination reforms. A nation can also organize such seminars on international theme.

Limitation of Seminar

A seminar technique has the following limitations:

(1) A seminar cannot be organized on all the content of a subject matter. Some topics arc highly structured. A theme of a seminar should be such on which discussion may he held.

(2) The technique cannot be used for all levels' of education. It can be used for higher level of education. The members of seminar should have social and emotional maturity. This it cannot be used for lower level of education.

(3) When a seminar is being organized, the persons who speak too much dominate the discussion of the seminar and do not provide opportunities to others

to take part in the discussion. It means that the discussion confines only few persons rather than whole group.

(4) During the discussion, groups are formed in two ideas; anti-ideas and favourable ideas on the theme. As a result they try to win over the other. The purpose of the seminar is not served. The chairman should discourage this type of activities.

(5) If the two groups already exist among the participants, they generally try to oppose even for the constructive or relevant ideas of the opposite group. The opposition is done for the sake of opposition. The instructional situations of such discussion are not conducive for learning.

TEAM TEACHING

The present system of education demands too. much from a teacher by curtailing his freedom. He has to teach same subject matter every year and he is forced to teach the same content to two or three sections of the same class. It is very boring to him and ceases his interest in the subject. Some times he is assigned to teach the subject in which he has no interest to teach but he is forced to do so. This may be an important reason that present structure of education has failed to cater the needs of the students. More-over the present day classroom are appropriate only for the average students.

In these circumstances, when teachers and students have to work under so many constraints. we feel an urge to use' Team-teaching'. The innovation of team-teaching is widely spreading to improve teaching-learning process in the classroom.

Origin of Team Teaching

The concept of 'Team- Teaching' has its origin from America during the mid 1950. It reached England in the 1960. J. freeman's team teaching in Britain gives an account of its growth in the country. It has occupied a place for itself in schools and colleges.

Harvard University is the first institution, which has initiated an internship plan, is 1955. The second milestone in team teaching is the project in Lexington

(1957 -64) which bas been influenced by the Harvard programme.

Francis Chase of the University of Chicago has developed the need of team teaching to use the best teachers more effectively.

J. Leyond Trump made valuable contribution for the success of team - teaching. Team teaching was not only confined to educational institutions but its application was extended to armed forces for teaching purpose during Second World War.

It is difficult to trace the origin of team teaching because so many individuals and organisations have been conducting studies in their own areas for the last two decades all over the world.

In India many educationists are aware of this system, but they have designed to implement it even though it will the best suit to our teaching learning' situation.

Definition of Team Teaching

Several persons have defined the term 'Team Teaching' because they have designed and conducted exponents to understand the nature of team teaching. Warwick has tried to define the term more comprehensively. His education is both descriptive and promotive in nature. It also evolves the theoretical basis.

Term-teaching is a form of organization in which individual teacher decides to pool resource, interests and expertise's in order to device and implement a scheme of work suitable for the needs of their pupils and the facilities of their schools.

Team teaching has been defined as:

"A type of instructional organization, involving teaching personnel and the students assigned to them, in which two or more teachers are given responsibility of working together, for all or significant part of the instruction of the same group of students."

Carlo-Oison has defined the term team-teaching:

"An instructional situation where two or more teachers possessing complementary teaching skills cooperatively plan and implement the instruction form single group of student using flexible scheduling and group techniques to meet the part of the instruction of the same group of student.

Another definition of term-teaching is:

"An arrangement whereby two or more teachers, with or without teacher aids cooperatively plan instruct individual one or more class groups in an appropriate instructional space and given length of time so as to take advantage of the special competencies of the members".

It may be inferred from the definitions of team-teaching that it has the following characteristics:

(1) It involves two or more teachers to teach a class.

(2) It is an instructional strategy rather than training strategy.

(3) A team or group teachers of the same subject work together to deal a significant content to same group of students jointly.

(4) It can be termèd as co-operative teaching, in which individual teacher plans to pool resources, interests and their expertise for teaching a content for the same group or class of students.

(5) Every individual teacher gets an appropriate instruction space and length or Lime so as to use of special competencies of teaching a content to a group of students.

(6) A group of teachers has shared reproducibility's of planning, organizing. leading. controlling and evaluating the teaching of the same class of students.

(7) In team-teaching the group teachers has to consider the needs of their pupils and they should teach jointly to satisfy their needs and remove the difficulties of their students.

Type of Team- Teaching-There are various ways to classify the team teaching but a better way is to classify it on the basis of its organization. Team-Teaching may be organized mainly in three types:

(a) A team of teachers from the same department.

(b) A team of teachers from inter-departments but from the same institutional.

(c) A team of teachers form inter-institution.

First type of team-teaching is organized in secondary schools and higher secondary where there are more than two teachers in the same department. This type of team-teaching can be organized at each level of education it there are more than two teachers of the same subject. A number of experiments have been designed and conducted in Britain and the USA to ascertain the effectiveness of this type of teaching in Science, English and Social studies.

Second type of team-teaching can be organized can be organized effectively in education of training departments. The experts of psychology, philosophy and statistics departments can be invited to teach B .Ed and M. Ed students along with department personal who are interested in teaching the course to their students. The approach can be best utilized to encourage and introduce the inter-discipline of teaching.

Third type of team-teaching can be organized at every level of education the experts of the. subject from other institutions can be organized at college level, if there are more than two colleges in the same locality. The cooperative-teaching can be organized in inter institutions but in the same discipline.

There may be other types of team-teaching. Warwick has mentioned that it can only he organized entirely based upon the needs or difficulties of the students not to teach a special content.

Team- Teaching Two Phases-Lead lecture and follow up group work. A lead lecture is one given at the beginning of lesson. The team of teachers try to present all information which they want to communicate in their lead lecture. The lead lecture is followed by group work which is immensely valuable for the lecture. The lead lecture is followed by group work which is immensely valuable for the students. The group work is helpful of the comprehension of the information, which has been presented, in lead lecture.

Objectives of Team-Teaching

The teaching strategies have been designed to achieve certain objectives. The team teaching has been evolved to realize the following objectives:

(1) To make the best use of expertise of teachers under team-teaching.

(2) To improve the quality to teaching. It involves two or more experts of the subject to teach same group simultaneously.

(3) To develop the feelings of co-operation or group work in teaching learning situation.

(4) To help the students, to satisfy the needs and difficulties relating to the special content.

(5) To develop the sense of shared responsibility in teaching and evaluation of students learning outcome.

(6) To minimize the scope of teaching wrong things to the students.

The team-teaching is directly conditioned by these objectives. Usually it is organized to achieve either of the objectives.

Principles of Team-Teaching

The team-teaching is based upon certain general principles which are helpful in organizing team-teaching. The principles provide a guideline for planning and organizing team-teaching. The following are the important principles of this team-teaching

(1) Principle of Size and Composition-The concept of fixed size class is becoming obsolete. The size of the group or class should vary according to the objective or purpose of team-teaching. For example, if the purpose of team - teaching is to the group should be small involving the students who have similar type of difficulties.

(2) Principle of Level of Instruction-It is basis of organizing this type of team teaching. The entering behaviour of the organizing team-teaching may suit to the level of the group.

(3) Principle of Duties Assigning to Teachers of the Team-The team reaching involves two types of tasks-lead lecture and group-work or follow-up work. Therefore, duties signed to teachers should be appropriate according to their competencies of teaching. Every teacher cannot lead the lecture with excellence therefore, this task must be generated' by employing appropriate according to their competencies of teaching. Every teacher cannot lead the lecture with excellence therefore, this task must be assigned a competent person.

(4) Principle of Learning Environment-Every subject even a topic of a subject requires its own learning situation or environment.' Therefore, learning environment must be generated by employing appropriate teaching aids and equipments, e.g., laboratory, workshop, field work, good library and lecture room etc.

(5) Principle of Time Factor-The team -teaching is well organized teaching task, therefore time schedule should be prepared by allowing to sub topics, lead lecture task and group-work or follow up task. In this type of teaching time arrangement should be fairly fluid time table.

(6) Principle of Supervision-The focus of team-teaching is to develop the mastery over subject-matter by employing the expertise of teachers. The supervised-study is essential for assimilating the knowledge of topic of concepts. The. nature and duration of the supervision of the students activities depend upon the .purpose of team teaching.

Procedure of Organizing Team-Teaching

The team-teaching serves several purposes of teaching and it has different norms or types. Therefore, it is difficult to provide a general procedure for organizing Learn teaching, but it involves the following steps Step I-Planning, Step 2-0rganizing and Step 3-Evaluating. The details of activities of these steps have been given in the following paragraphs.

Step 1-Pldnning of Team-Teaching- This first step involves the following activities:

(a) Formulating the objectives of team-teaching.

(b) Writing these objectives in behavioural terms.

(c) Identify the entering or initial behaviours of the learners of the group.

(d) Deciding the topic to be taught.

(e) Preparing a tentative schedule of teaching.

(f) Assigning duties to teachers, considering their interest and competencies

(i) Lead Teacher (ii) Follow-up work and (iii) Supervision.

(g) Fixing up the level of instruction.

(h) Selecting appropriate teaching aids and teaching equipments for generating learning environment.

(i) Deciding ways and means for evaluating the students performance Oral or written question for practical work, etc.

These activities are finalized by-the team of teachers who are taking part in the team teaching in planning of team-teaching, expertise of every teacher must be fully utilized. There should not be imposition of activities on them.

Step 2-0rganizing Team- Teaching- The organization of team-teaching is decided by considering the purpose of needs of. the learners of the group. The following are the general activities which are usually performed by team of teachers

(a) Determining; the level of instruction-Some questions are asked to explore the background of the learners.

(b) Selection of appropriate communication strategy by considering the level of language comprehension.

(c) Presentation of lead lecture by a competent teacher of team: other teachers listen the lecture and note down the elements of topic which are not easily understandable to the learners group or not appropriately presented.

(d) Follow-up work, the other teachers have to supplement the lead lecture by explaining the elements of the topic in a more simple way so that learners can understand easily.

(e) Providing motivation or reinforcement by teachers to the learners in both the situations-lead lecture and follow-up work.

(f) In Supervision of students activities which are assigned in lead lecture of group work or follow-up work. This stage is considered to be important for assimilation.

Every member of the team should be conscious about time schedule and about the duty assigned to him, He must he well prepared and ready for that.

Step 3 Evaluating Team-Teaching- The evaluation is an important aspect of any type of teaching and instruction. It is helpful to measure the performance of learners that determines about the objectives whether they can be achieved or not. It also provides the reinforcements to team of the teachers and the learners. Thus, it involves the following activities:

(a) Asking oral questions writing questions and practical work. The expert an unit or element should put a question. Each question should measure an particular objective of team-teaching.

(b) Taking decision about the level of performance and realization of the objectives.

(c) Diagnosing the difficulties of the learners and provide the remediation.

(d) Revising the planning and organizing phases of team-teaching on the basis of evaluation of the students.

Advantages of Team-Teaching

The team-teaching is a perspective and economical device, of teaching to cater the needs of the students. It is highly flexible. It has the following major advantages

(1) The team-teaching utilizes the competencies of the teachers. It has been devised to make best use of the expertise of the subject-matter.

(2) It creates the learning environment to the comprehension or mastery

over the subject among the learners.

(3) It provides an opportunity for free discussion in the classroom teaching. All the students of the group get an opportunity for free expression and discussion in the classroom.

(4) The learners and teachers develop the social relation in school environment. The learners and even teachers require practice in human relation in schools and colleges.

(5) It provides an opportunity to the teachers to develop the professional status and competency in teaching by observing teaching of content expert.

(6) It exposes the learners to be more specialist of the subject and they are benefited by the special knowledge of various teachers.

(7) It considers the needs and difficulties of the students. The specialists of subject content are involved in team spirit to work jointly in solving the teaching difficulties of the students and catering their needs of learning situation.

(8) It utilizes the teaching aids and equipments of teaching in an appropriate manner. The team of teachers makes the best use of multi-media advice. These are also helpful to reinforce the learners.

(9) It is an economical teaching device. Time and energy are saved by the team teaching. It maintains the discipline in the class and creates a conducive environment of learning.

(10) It is highly flexible method of teaching while traditional methods of teaching are rigid. It develops the creative aspect to learners.

(11) There is smooth sailing from primary to high level of teaching. It fosters mutual trust and cooperation among teachers and students.

(12) It enables the students and simultaneously to the other experts of the same area, It brings excellence of teaching in then.

The teachers can evaluate the teaching of one another and can give suggestions to improve it. Quality of instruction is definitely improved in team teaching organization.

Limitations of Team-teaching

It is not a perfect method of teaching. It has the following limitations

(1) It is very difficult to seek cooperation among teachers and enables them to work jointly in teaching-learning situation. They can never agree with the solution or an issue of teaching. They hesitate to work because no body wants to expose oneself.

(2) It is not feasible in practice to assign powers and responsibilities to the group of teachers. The responsibility of a group of teachers virtually the responsibility is of none.

(3) There is no mutual regard and respect among the teachers. Every teachers considers himself as an expert of the subject. Every teachers has own sty1e of teaching. They cannot work like football or hockey team.

(4) The teachers do not have lime to deviate from the routine method of teaching and they do not prefer any change in the system of education. Generally they are of the opinion that this can be used in Western countries not in Indian schools.

This type of attitude of teachers hampers in the progress and improvement of educational system.

Suggestions Regarding the Use of Team-Teaching

The team-teaching can be used effectively by incorporating the following suggestions

(1) The research studies has established for workability and effectiveness but its Success will depend upon the way it works in practice. The meaning and understanding of team-teaching should be given to the schoolteachers and favourable attitude should be developed among them towards team-teaching.

(2) The success of team-teaching rests upon the cooperation and devotion of the teachers. Only those teachers must be invited in this method who are willing to participate.

(3) The teachers should not be assigned the duties but they themselves should prefer the activities of teaching. They should be given full freedom to work at various stages of team-teaching.

(4) In teacher education departments and institutions, pupil-teachers should be trained for this type of teaching. The teacher-education must demonstrate in dealing with the causes so that they can carry the idea to practise their institutions.

Anderson, Warwick and other experts in the field of team-teaching consider hierarchical structure and composition as q very logical and attractive arrangement. The success of team-teaching plan largely depends upon a balanced team in which all the teachers feel their responsibility and will co-operate willingly in organising, teaching.

DEVELOPMENT OF EVALUATION TOOLS

Evaluation is ,an integral part of the process of teaching- learning. It is inseparably linked with teacher's responsibility. This is the end result of teaching. It is a comprehensive term. Sometimes it is confused with measurement which is more restricted. Measurement is concerned with the administration and scoring of tests of various kinds. But, these measurement data are collected for certain purposes such as for the purpose of guidance, for. the purpose of identifying students' difficulties, for the purpose of describing the suitability of some students for certain jobs, and so on. These purposes come under evaluation. Thus, measurement forms an important aspect of evaluation, a basic of evaluation. Thus, measurement and evaluation have means-and-end relationship. Measurement in itself has no purpose. The purpose is derived from evaluation. Evaluation, thus, is much wider a term as compared to measurement. The measurement helps us in evaluating the progress of the students. The essential purposes of measurement and evaluation are:

1. To facilitate student progress.
2. To assess student progress.
3. To understand the individual student.
4. To facilitate student self-understanding.
5. To evaluate instructional programs.
6. To assist in administrative judgments.
7. To contribute to knowledge of abilities and instruction.

Tools of Evaluation: Teachers use various kinds of devices for evaluating students performance. They may be classified as :

1. Observations
2. Interviews
3. Questionnaires, schedules and checklists.
4. Psychological tests.

The psychological tests are of various kinds such as :

(i) Tests of intelligence,

(ii) Tests of Attitudes,

(iii) Tests of Aptitudes,

(iv) Tests of Interests,

(v) Tests of Personality,

(vi) Tests of Creativity,

(vii) Tests of Achievement or performance.

Since all instructional designs are inevitably concerned with the assessment of terminal and auxiliary performance of the students, this section will deal with various aspects of performance tests wily. Student performance constitutes the nucleus of all instructional designs and strategies. In fact this was the First and. foremost part of instructional designs which came under the influence of educational technology. Pressey was the pioneer in this field who developed several innovations regarding test development and test scoring. Performance assessment, then, received n1ore attention from Skinner when it formed an integral part of programmed instruction.

PERFORMANCE ASSESSMENT

As described by Glaser (1962) performance assessment is concerned with measuring and cva1uating student's performance at the end of instruction or even at different times during the instruction, In the beginning or during instruction performance is assessed for knowing whether the students have acquired the requisite behaviors necessary for acquiring further or higher level knowledge. This is sometimes, knows as auxiliary performance, Assessment of this performance plays an important role in progrmmned instruction as well as in developing new instructional designs or models of teaching. This kind of assessment reveals whether the students have the requisite entering behaviours for learning something. This assessment provides the base from where the teacher has to take off Terminal performance on the other hand aims at knowing whether the instructional objectives have been achieved or not. This information may be used for diagnostic and guidance purposes too. Performance assessment is the fourth component of Glaser's Basic Model of Teaching which serves several purposes.

Students performance can be assessed in several ways. There may be interviews, oral tests and written tests. Observations and rating scales may be used for indicating. what and. how much the student has acquired. This section will be devoted lo a discussion of construction of objective type performance tests. The first part of discussion will be confined to norm-and criterion-reference tests.

Norm-Referenced and Criterion-Referenced Test: This is a very popular classification of performance tests. Two things may happen as a result of instructional processes. If the instructional strategy is very effective the standards of students attainment wili be high and the top position holders will really be very competent and capable persons. Now, if the instructional strategy is ineffective, the standards of students' attainment will be low. But, still some students will get top positions. In this case, however, top positions will not necessarily mean competent and able students. If the standards of attainments are very low, even the best student in the group may be quite ignorant knowing nothing in the field. Thus, positions in the group and standards of attainment are two different dimensions of students performance. Positions in the group or the class refer a norm-reference dimension. Attainments of standards refer to criterion-reference dimension of performance, criterion being external and expected standards. It may not be objectively definable external criterion or standard and may be just vaguely present in the mind of the instructor. It is a different matter. Important is that. the test scores arc interpreted in terms of some predetermined standard or criterion.

Criterion-related standards are absolute standards. They tell us where the student must reach after having studied a unit, what and how much they must acquire. Criterion-referenced test is a test which tells how much a student has achieved when judged against this standard. A test using criterion-referenced standards provides information about what a student can do and what he can not do, Hence, it is a test. which uses norms that are based on predetermined external criterion or some absolute standard. This external criterion describes the precise amount of end- of unit or end of course competence, which the student is expected to attain.

Norm-referenced tests use relative standards. They are based on comparative performance of the students within the group itself. These standards compare the, performance of one student with that of the other students in his own group. Norms prepared for this kind of test tell where each -student stands in comparison to other students. They provide information whether a student is superior to or inferior to any other student in the group. Tests' using these. standards may tell how many students are superior to or inferior to a particular student. But, they don't tell how competent he is with respect to some specified standard. He may be the best of all; but he may not have achieved even minimum of what is expected. A major shortcoming of norm-referenced test is that the students admitted -to next higher class on the basis of scores obtained on this test may not be competent enough to study courses of that class or grade. That is exactly what is ,happening in our country. Admissions to B.Ed. and some other courses, selections made for some jobs on the basis of entrance tests and interviews, etc. are creating such problems. The best of only the least competent persons are being selected with the result that the selected people are not able to cope with the courses or the responsibilities of the job. Admissions and selections should be made against some external standards defined in terms of some essential knowledge, skills, and attitudes. This only emphasizes that the scores on the test etc. should be interpreted in terms of some external criterion that prescribes some minimum essential cut off. In other words criterion related standards should be used for deciding whether a person getting a particular score should be 'admitted/ selected or not. All students must meet the standard of acceptability .expressed as an essential external criterion.

The foregoing philosophy makes a difference in the procedure adopted for constructing tests of performance. In case of norm referenced tests we include in the test items of high low and average difficulty so that the test yields a normal distribution of scores. The test is so devised that equal number of individuals gets high and low scores while the largest number get average scores. Judged against what the individuals should have learnt after having studied one or more units of a subject, all of them may be found very ignorant. Yet, this kind of a test will label at least 25 percent of them as the best ones. On the other hand even if the group consists of very brightest and competent persons, this kind of a test will label at least 25 percent of them as below average. In this kind of a test always certain very difficult, certain easy and larger number of average difficulty level items is kept.

In case of criterion-referenced test the difficulty levels of the items are linked. with the acceptable performance of the students. Each item is validated against this acceptable performance, the external criterion, and not the performance of the individuals in the group. These tests define very explicitly the terminal behaviours with reference to acceptable performance, which is considered necessary for further progress and learning, for doing a job efficiently. The external criterion against which the item of the criterion-referenced test is validated' consists of the nature of the content, instructional objectives and entering behaviours required for the next sequence of instruction. A few differential characteristics of criterion-referenced and norm- referenced tests (relative standard tests) are mentioned by De Cecco and Crawford (p.414) in tabular form. The characteristics of criterion- referenced tests are.

1. Difficulty in establishing norms or standards.

2. Allows all or any number of students to pass or fail.

3. Allows direct comparison of students from class to class or year to year with reference to a specifically defined level of performance.

4. Performance is judged in terms of how well or poorly students do in

terms of how they should do.

5. Requires intense scrutiny of every item.

Similarly, the characteristics of norm-referenced tests are

1. It is relatively easy to establish norms or standards.

2. Permits the least definition of instructional and testing objectives.

3. Generally requires a specified number classified in each grade or category.

4. Allows performance comparison based only on how high or low one group performed in relation to another.

5. Allows judgments only in terms of comparing one student or groups of students with another.

6. Allow inclusion of items which may not have been carefully examined and which may be hastily and un carefully written.

CONSTRUCTION OF EVALUATION TOOLS

In general construction of all kinds of evaluation tools with slight differences here and there involve the following activities:

1. Planning
2. Preparation
3. Try-out
4. Standardization.

A. Planning the Construction

At this stage various decisions are taken and certain activities are completed. But -before doing all that it is suggested by Stanley and Hopkins (p. 172) that certain principles should be taken into consideration. These principles are:

Principles of Planning.

1. Principle of adequate provision for evaluating all important outcomes of instruction
2. Principle of emphasis of the course (approximately)
3. Principle of purpose
4. Principle of conditions under which the test is to be administered.

The first principle is quite clear. It simply says that the test should be so designed that it measures the most important outcomes of instruction or objectives. The second principle says that if the test has to cover a large amount of material, it would be necessary to determine which part or aspect. of that should receive what weight age in terms of number of items. Proper sampling has to be done. This should respective importance of various components of the course. The third principle says that the purpose of the test should be made clear and kept in mind. It means clarifying whether test will employ relative, or absolute or criterion-related standards of achievement. The validity and reliability of the tests are linked with these purposes. Different methods of providing for reliability and validity are used depending upon these purposes. The fourth' principle requires that decisions should be taken regarding the number of items to the finally kept in the test, time to be allowed for completing the test, how frequently test will be administered, what will be the format of the test, what kinds of items will be included in the test, how the responses of the examinees will be recorded, and so on.

Steps of Planning; Planning of a performance test involves the following steps:

1. Identifying the learning outcomes.
2. Defining the outcomes in terms of specific behaviours

3. Outlining the subject-matter content.
4. Preparing a table of specifications.
5. Using the table of specifications.

IDENTIFYING LEARNING OUTCOMES

In constructing the objective type performance test the first order of business is to identify the instructional objectives which are intended to be measured. This is a difficult job. One useful guide" however, is the Taxonomy of Educational Objectives. Learning, objectives in other areas such as skills, attitudes and interests are measured,-by rating scales, checklists, anecdotal records, inventories and similar non-testing procedures. It is only cognitive domain objectives, i.e. knowledge, and intellectual abilities and skills, which can be measured through paper, pencil tests. These cognitive objectives of the Bloom's Taxonomy are divided into two major areas, (i) knowledge and (ii) intellectual abilities and skills. These are further divided into six areas as shown below.

KNOWLEDGE

A KNOWLEDGE (of what has been learned)

1 Knowledge of specifics

2 knowledge of terms

3 knowledge of specific facts.

a knowledge of ways and means of dealing with specifics

1 knowledge of conventions

2 knowledge of trends and sequences

3 knowledge of classifications and categories

4 knowledge of criteria

5 knowledge of methodology

b . knowledge of the universal and abstractions in a field

1 knowledge of principles and generalizations

2 knowledge of theories and structures.

Intellectual Abilities and skills

B COMPREHENSION (understanding the meaning)

1 Translation

2 Interpretation

3 Extrapolation

C APPLICATION

D ANALYSIS

1 Analysis of elements

2 Analysis of relationships

3 Analysis of organizational principles

E SYNTHESIS

1 Production of a unique communication

2 Production of a plan or proposed set of operations

3 Deviation of a set of abstract relations

F EVALUATION

1 Judgments in terms of internal evidence

2 Judgments in term's of external criteria

All these objectives are arranged in order of increasing complexity. Subdivisions within each area are also in order of increasing complexity. The whole structure of objectives is hierarchical in- nature. This Taxonomy is very useful in planning the performance test.

2. Defining the Objectives In Specific Terms

Having identified the learning objectives they are, then, defined in specific behavioural terms, which provide evidence that the outcomes have been achieved, For this purpose the objectives are written in sentences which use action verbs such as ':recognizes", "identifies", etc.

3. Outlining the Subject-Matter Content

Taxonomical learning objectives are general and may apply to any topic or area of the subject matter. A performance test is designed to measure those, objectives which cover students abilities and skills, their mental development, their reactions as well as the knowledge of the subject matter taught. It is, therefore, essential to identify how much and which aspects of the subject matter will be covered by the test. Only the major elements need to be listed.

4. Preparing A Table of Specifications

Having identified he learning outcomes and outlined the course content a table of specifications is prepared which relates outcomes to content and indicates the relative weight to be assigned to each of the areas of the subject matter. The table ensures that the test will measure a representative sample of the learning outcomes and the subject matter content. The following table roughly illustrates how it is done.

Table of Specification

Content / Outcomes	Area-1	Area-2	Area-3	Total No. of Items
Known terms	2	3	5	10
Knows procedures	4	-	2	6
Understands principles	3	2	2	7
Can apply principles	-	3	2	5
Can analyze facts	2	2	4	8
Total Number of Items	**11**	**10**	**15**	**36**

The figures in the cells indicate the number of items (weight age) to be given to each area and each outcome.

5. Using the Table of Specifications

While preparing the performance test items have to be constructed according to the table of specification. Thus, the table serves as a guide, a blue-print for constructing the test.

B. Preparing the test

Some of the most important points to be kept in mind while preparing the test as mentioned by Stanley (1964) are:

1. Have more items in the first draft of the test than decided to be kept in the final form.

2. Most of the items should have 50 percent difficulty levels.

3. After a gap of some time make a critical revision of the test.

4. The items should be arranged in ascending order of difficulty.

5. A regular sequence in the pattern of correct responses should be avoided.

6. The direction to the examiners should be as clear, complete and concise as possible.

There are a variety of item-types completion be true- false, constructing a performance test, matching and multiple-choice type etc. Of all these multiple-. choice type tend to provide the highest quality items. They provide a more adequate measure of learning outcomes than the other items. Again, they can measure a variety of outcomes ranging tram simple to complex. Hence, the following section is devoted to listing a few rules of constructing multiple-choice items.

Rules of Constructing Multiple-Choice Items: following are the important rules:

1. Present a single, clearly formulated problem in the stem of the item.
2. State the stem in simple, clear language.
3. A void repeating the same material over alternatives.
4. State the stem in positive form, unless not possible.
5. If using negative form of stem, underline the negative wording.
6. Make certain that the intended answer is correct or clearly the best.
7. Make all alternatives grammatically consistent with the stem and parallel in form.
8. Avoid verbal clues which might enable students to select the correct answer or to eliminate an incorrect alternative.

Similarly of wording in both the stem and the correct answer, stating the correct answer in textbook language or stereotyped phraseology, stating the correct answer in greater detail, including absolute terms (all, any, never, none, only, etc.) in the distracters, including two responses that are all inclusive and including two responses that have the same meaning should be avoided.

9. A void use of the alternatives "all of the above", and "none of the above".
10. Vary the position of the correct answer in a random manner.
11. Control the difficulty of the item by the problem in the stem or by

changing the alternative.

(For explanation and examples of these rules consult N.E., Gronlund Constructing Achievement Tests, Prentice-Hall, inc. Englewood Eliffs, N.J. 1968)

Having written out the items, they are arranged and assembled in the foml of a complete test. Then, again, the thus-completed test is reviewed and shortcomings found are removed. After this direction for the examinees are prepared.

The directions should contain information about (i) the purpose of the test, (ii) time for completing the test, (iii) ways of recording the answers, (separate answersheet or in the text booklet), (iv) instruction for not to guess, etc.

The test and the instruction, thus prepared, is then reproduced either in the form of photocopies or cyc1ostyled material or printed material.

C. Item-Analysis

For the purpose of item analysis the preliminary form of the test is administered to a representative sample of the population for which it is meant. It is, then, scored and all the test booklets are arranged in a pile according to the size of the scores serially, the topmost score being at the top.

Purpose of Item-Analysis: the purpose of item analysis is to find out how the items and the distracters of the items in the test are working. In other words the purpose is to find out which item is good and which is bad so that bad items, items which are ineffective may be eliminated and, finally, a test of good items may be constructed.

Bases of Item-Analysis : The item-analysis is done on the following bases:

1. Item-difficulty index
2. Item validity index
3. Effectiveness of the distracters index

These three statistical indices constitute the criteria on the basis of which an item is selected or rejected.

Procedure of Item-Analysis: there are a number of different item-analysis procedures that might be applied. Downie (1967) presents a detailed discussion of these. But, the most simple, popular and effective procedure is described below and is illustrated by taking an example of 47 test papers arranged serially from top to bottom according to the magnitude of the total scores. Following steps arc involved:

1. By taking approximately one third of the total from top and one-third from bottom two top and bottom groups are fanned. The middle group is set aside. Out of a group of 47 top 15 and another group of bottom 15 is formed. The middle 17 papers are set aside.

2. For each item number of students in top and bottom groups selecting each alternative is counted and recorded. The results for each item are presented itemwise on a sheet of paper as follows :

Item No. 1 Alternatives	A	B	C*	D	E
Top 15	1	1	+	4	3
Bottom 15	2	2	4	3	4

*=correct answer

Such kinds of tables are prepared for al the items. After this item-statistics (difficulty index and validity index) for all the items are calculated as follows:

(A) Item-Difficulty: This is calculated by applying the following formula:

$$\text{Difficulty Index} = \frac{\text{Number answering correctly}}{\text{Total number in both groups}} \times 100$$

In the previous, example 10 students (6 -+- 4) in both the groups answered the item correctly out of the total of 30 (total in both groups).

$$\text{So, DI} = \frac{10}{30} \times \frac{100}{1} = 33.3 \text{ or } 33\%$$

This is the simplest procedure based on the top-bottom groups. This provides a close approximation to the estimate that would be obtained with the total group. The foregoing item has a difficulty level of 33 percent which means that out or 100 only 33 students answer the item correctly. The difficulty index is interpreted in such a way that higher the index, easier is the item and lower the index difficult is the item.

Some people call this facility index instead of difficulty index. But they mean the same thing.

(B) Validity Index: Validity of an item means the extent to which the item measures the same thing which is measured by the whole test In a way it is an index of homogeneity of items. This is also known as discrimination index because it is calculated on the basis of discrimination an item makes between the top and the bottom groups. The two groups are formed in such a way that the top group is of high ability students and the bottom group consists of low ability students on the trait being measured by the whole test. So, if an item also measures the same trait it must also function in the way the whole test is functioning, i.e., larger number of students in the top group and lesser number in the bottom group must answer it correctly. If this is so, the item is said to be significantly correlated with the whole test. In other words if the item significantly discriminates between the two groups, it is said to be valid and that is its validity index. It is a kind of bi serial correlation between the item and the test. It is calculated as follows:

$$\text{Validity Index} = \frac{T - B}{N}$$ in which T = total number of students

Answering the item correctly in the top group and B = total number of students answering the item correctly in the bottom group, and N = number of . students in either of the group.

Taking the example of the foregoing item we find

$$V.I. = \frac{6-4}{15} = \frac{2}{15} = +0.133$$

16

Validity index is interpreted in the same way as correlation is interpreted. It is always between ±1.0. Higher the validity index greater is its relationship with the test.

Highest discrimination or validity index is obtained with items which have difficulty level of around 50 or 50. That is why the test-makers try to select items which have difficulty index of 50 or around 50.

(C) Effectiveness of Distracters : A good distracter is one which is selected by larger number of students in the bottom group as compared to that in the top group. I-knee, effectiveness of the distracter is determined by comparing the numbers selecting the distracter in the top and the bottom groups. In our example the distracter D is not at all effective, while A and Band E are effective.

The foregoing procedural steps of item-analysis can be modified to fit particular situations. In case of teacher-made tests, for example, these statistics may not be needed to be calculated. Just by inspecting the data items may be selected. A1so, it is not a hard and fast rule to form top-bottom groups by taking one- third of the total. Sometimes these groups may be defined as top 25 percent and bottom 25 percent if the total number is sufficiently large. Top 27% and bottom 27% are preferred when the total number is as large as 400. Important thing to remember is that larger the fraction of the groups, more useful information is obtained.

Selecting the Items: Having made this kind of analysis, there comes the most important responsibility of the test-maker; and that is to select the most suitable items for the final form of the test. Selecting or rejecting an item is a difficult job as there is no universally accepted criterion of lacking such a decision. But, generally. the decision is taken on. the basis of the three indices worked out as stated earlier.

Generally those items are selected which have the difficulty level between 30 and 80 and validity index of 0.25 and onwards But, this is not a rigid criterion. Depending upon the purpose and the situation these criteria may be shifted to either side. For example, if the test is meant for a small, class and its analysis is done, on a small group even the item having difficulty level of 20 to 80 and validity index of 0.20 and onwards may be selected if it is found that its distracters are working effectively, if it measures educationally significant outcome. Similarly if the test is mean', for selection purpose or it is criterion referenced test items with the difficulty levels of 50 and around have to be selected. The principle is that the purpose and the situation should determine the criteria of selecting the items.

Having selected the items in this way, they arc arranged again to prepare the final form of the test. This may be either cyclostyled or printed for use as may be considered necessary.

D. Standardization of the Test

The standardization of a test involves the development of uniform procedures for the administration and scoring of the test. Efforts, at this stage, are made to design procedures that minimize possible errors creeping into the scores and maximize the reliability and validity of the test scores. The test is administered on a large sample of population, and its reliabilities and validities are calculated. Generally, it is the following characteristics which are established.

1. Reliability
2. Validity
3. Norms

1. Reliability

A reliable test measures performance accurately and consistently. The concept refers to two aspects of the scores yielded by the test. These are (i) consistency (ii) stability. Consistency refers to the 'extent to which the scores obtained on two halves of the test are found to be similar. If these two sets of scores differ widely, the internal consistency of the test is said to be poor. Stability refers to the extent to which the scores obtained at two different times with a gap of few days are found similar. If they differ too much the test is said to have poor stability of scores. Thus, reliability is defined as the extent to which a test measures something accurately as ret1ected in the consistency and stability of its scores. There are several types of reliability depending upon the method' which is used for establishing it. Mainly there are following types of reliability:

1. Test-Retest Reliability
2. Split-Half Reliability
3. Equivalence Reliability or Parallel Form Reliability.

Test-Retest reliability is calculated by administering the test to the same group of individuals twice with a gap of few days and finding out the correlation between the two sets of scores so obtained. This coefficient of reliability is known as coefficient of stability of test scores.

Split-half reliability is calculated by obtaining two sets of scores on two halves of the test, 'one consisting of old items and the other consisting of even items and then correlating them. This coefficient is known as coefficient of internal consistency of the test. The coefficient, thus, obtained gives the reliability of. only the half of the test. Hence, the reliability coefficient for the whole test is estimated by applying the following formula known as the Spearman- Brown prophesy formula:

$$R = \frac{2r_{\frac{1}{2}\frac{1}{2}}}{1 + r_{\frac{1}{2}\frac{1}{2}}}$$

If the obtained reliability coefficient of the half test is .60, then by the Spearman-Brown formula the reliability (R) of the whole test will be

$$\frac{2x\,.60}{1+.60} \quad \frac{1.20}{1.60} = .75$$

It may be seen that the increase in the length of the test increases the reliability coefficient of the test.

One great advantage of split-half method of reliability is that the test is administered only once which saves a lot of time and provides greater convenience. But, probably the simplest means of estimating the reliability of test scores from a single administration is by using Kuder-Richardson formula-21 which runs as

$$R\ (KR\text{-}2l) = \frac{M(K - M)}{Ks^2} \quad \text{in which}$$

k = Number of items in the test

M = Mean of the test scores

S = Standard deviation of the test scores.

Kuder-Richardson formula. provides a conservative estimate of reliability. In other words it provides a smaller correlation coefficients than other methods. It is also indicative of internal consistency of test scores. It is not appropriate with speeded test like the split- half method.

In case of parallel form method of reliability two forms of the test are prepared. These forms are made similar as far as possible with regard to the item statistics, estimated means and variability of scores judged by observation or computed experimentally. The scores obtained on these two forms administer to the same group simultaneously are correlated which yields a coefficient known as coefficient of equivalence. In a way split-half method also yields a coefficient of equivalence between two halves of the test. An extension of this method is coefficient of equivalence and stability. This is calculated by finding out a correlation between the two forms of the same test given at two different points of time with a gap of few days in- between.

Factors Affecting Reliability: There are several factors which affect a test's reliability adversely. Some of them are as follows.

1. Poorly constructed Items: If the items of the test have very low or very high difficulty levels, i.e., if most of the items cluster at the extremes the reliability of the test is decreased. Similarly, if the items have low discrimination indices, the reliability will be adversely affected.

2. Length of the Test: The length of the test also affects its reliability. A short test of very few items cannot be very reliable. Increasing the length of the test increases its reliability also. The application of Spearman-Brown. formula has clearly demonstrated this fact. But, a very lengthy test, too, may affect reliability adversely by way of causing fatigue, monotony and disinterest in the students.

3. Inadequate Scoring Methods: These also lower down reliability. If the scoring is subjective as is the case with the essay type examinations it affects reliability adversely. Similarly, giving differential weights to some items also reduces reliability.

4. Inadequate Time: If sufficient time is not given to the students to complete the test, this also reduces tests reliability.

Relation with Validity: It is also important to note how reliability is related to validity. A reliable test need not be essentially valid. A hundred percent reliable. test may be invalid or may suffer from poor validity. For being reliable a test need not be valid. But the contrary is not possible. A test cannot be valid unless it is reliable. For validity, reliability is an essential condition. If a test docs not measure something reliably, how can it be valid. If a test fails to measure something with consistency, it cannot purport to measure anything at all.

Thus, when a test is standardized all these facts are taken into account while establishing its reliability.

A standardized test has a proved validity, Hence, standardization of the test involves calculation of its validity also, Validity of a test means the extent to which a test measures what it purports to measure. If it is a test of performance, then its validity would mean the extent to which it measures the objectives or the outcomes of learning. Hence, validity is calculated by correlating the scores of the test with the scores on the criterion (i.e. the scores on some other measure of performance)

Types of Validity: French and Michael (1966), and a committee designated by American Psychological Association, the American Educational Research Association and the National Council on Measurement in Education (A.PA. 1966) have described three types of validity which is a standard and widely adopted classification system. These three types are:

1. Content validity
2. Criterion-related validity
3. Construct validity

Some writers mention concurrent validity, predictive validity and factorial validity also. But. these can be considered as sub- classifications of criterion-related validity only.

Content Validity : Content validity means to what extent the test measures performance objectives identified and stated for the purpose of constructing the test. It is specially important in achievement testing or. in constructing a perfol1nance test. The purpose of this kind of validity is to know how well the test measures the subject matter content and learning outcomes It; is, concerned with the, sampling of, a specified universe of. Content. All that is that cannot be measured in a single test, Hence, the test items sample the most critical aspects. But, these should be representative of the whole that has been taught., If not so, the content validity, can not be high or even satisfactory. Thus the content validity of a test tells us whether the items of the test cover sufficiently well: the appropriate content. Every subject has a definite structure of knowledge consisting 'of certain facts, concepts, major understandings, principles, generalizations, etc. A high content validity test samples all of these in a very judicious manner. If any of these area is' not well represented, the validity of the test can not be considered to be high or satisfactory.

Content validity is not determined -statistically. Hence, it has no statistical index. It is determined by inspection of the test items and by relating them to an outline of the subject matter, or by checking them against the table of specifications. Just by inspection the test-maker of the test-user tries to find out the extent to which the content areas of a subject and taxonomic performance behaviors are reflected in the items. If the items are found to be a good match to the content areas and performance objectives the validity of the test maybe estimated to be high.

Criterion-Related Validity: This kind of validity is a sort of relationship of the test with some external criterion. The criterion may be some future performance or phenomenon or some current phenomenon. If the test is related to some future performance .or phenomenon, this is known as predictive validity. Predictive validity is a kind of criterion validity. But, when the test is related to the criterion currently available, it is known as concurrent validity

Criterion Validity becomes important when the performance of an individual or a group of individuals on some criterion is to be predict; d on the basis of the test under construction. For example, if the test under construction is meant for predicting success of the students in the final examination, the test-maker should establish predictive validity of the test for examination marks or result. Similarly, a test for vocational selection must have high predictive validity for that vocation. In case of selection test predictive validity is a must. Predictive validity is established by correlating the test scores with the indices of success or performance on the criterion (examination marks or indices of vocational success) which is made available in near future.

Concurrent validity is obtained by correlating the test scores with the indices of success or performance on the criterion which are made available currently- at the same time when the test is being constructed. The purpose served by this kind of validity is to a have substitute for the test under construction or just to establish that the test under construction measures the same trait which is measured by another test'; already constructed and validated. For example, correlating a test of intelligence under construction with the already available test of vocabulary will yield concurrent validity of the intelligence test, which will tell whether the intelligence test has any relationship with student's acquisition of vocabulary.

Both predictive and concurrent validities are forms of criterion validity with the difference that in case of concurrent validity the criterion is made available at the same time when the test is being constructed while in case of predictive validity the criterion is made available at any time in future. Both of these are expressed in terms of statistical indices which are obtained by finding out the correlation between the test scores and the scores on the criterion.

Construct Validity: Sometimes, the test under construction intends to measure some trait which is just a hypothetical entity or quality and not a concrete phenomenon, which can not be observed directly. For example, intelligence, aptitude, attitude, interest, etc. are such entities. They can only be indirectly inferred from experimental data or evidence, but can not be explicitly defined. Hence, when a test constructor constructs such a test (intelligence or attitude test), it becomes necessary for him to collect evidence to show that the test constructed by him really measures intelligence or interest or attitude and so on. This evidence must enable him to say with some confidence that the test measures that trait. Establishing this fact means establishing construct validity. Thus, construct validity means the extent to which a test measures. the same trait which it was intended to measure.

It is difficult to establish construct validity of any test as valid criteria are, generally, not available. Constructs are hypothetical qualities which can only be Inferred from certain behaviors. For example, intelligence can only be inferred from students success in the examination (school marks), teachers ratings of students, intelligent behavior, other tests claiming to measure intelligence. But, these criteria are not found. to be sufficiently valid. Hence establishing construct validity of a test against less valid criteria creates a problem, And this is a problem ad infinitum.

3. Norms

All test constructors develop norms for the tests they construct. Norms are derived or transformed scores. The raw scores obtained by a large representative sample on the test are converted into standard scores which are the units of a scale which is universally. understood bi all in the same way. There are two scales which are used for preparing norms. They are (i) percentile norms and (ii) standard scores. Standard scores have a variety of transformations such as sigma (a) scores, t-scores, T scores, and stanines. They are calculated statistically with the help-of the mean and standard deviation. Percentile norms are very popular. Norms help in the interpretation of scores. They render the scores obtained by any person or group of persons meaningful.

Characteristics of Standardized Tests

The standardized tests have the following characteristics:

1. The standardized - tests follow the guidelines and technical recommendations made by American Educational Research Association and National Council on Measurements Used in Education (1955). Hence. These tests are carefully developed tools. Their items are selected after a thorough scrutiny. Experienced experts prepare the items. They are subjected to a vigorous analysis and try-out. These test are item-analyzed on a larger and more representative sample. Systematic studies are made for establishing their reliability, validity and useability. Obviously they are of better quality and have wider applicability. They are more reliable and valid in general.

2. Standardized tests have carefully prepared manual, which describes the instructions of their administration and other details. The instructions are well standardized. They give specific information to the examinees as well as to the test users with the result that the scores obtained on the test can be interpreted uniformly in the same way everywhere and by every one.

3. The standardized tests have standardized procedures of recording the examinees responses and scoring them. This minimizes the variations in the scores and errors creeping in the results.

4. The standardized tests have various kinds of norms which are, generally, established on large samples and for various groups of population. They provide valuable information and great help in interpreting the scores obtained by any single individual or any other group of individuals.

5. The scope of applicability and use of standardized test is, generally, very wide, both in terms of purposes and populations. They can be used for purposes of survey, selection, guidance, diagnostic assessment in the classroom, assessment of school programs and instruction, general assessment of student abilities and

achievement and for providing a criterion of standardization of other tests being newly developed. They can be used at national and, in some cases, even at international level.

Comparison With Teacher-Made Tests: Although standardized tests ate similar to teacher-made or classroom tests in several respects, there are differences, too, between them. They are similar in following respects as described by DeCecco and Crawford (p.454).

1. Both are means of performance assessment.
2. Both use the same types of test items.'
3. Both require validity, reliability, objectivity and efficiency

The differences between, them, according to the same authors are:

1. The classroom tests may have more content validity because it is constructed with special reference to classroom objectives and subject matter taught in the class. Standardized tests are constructed for common and broad objectives and subject matter. They may, for that reason. miss certain immediate classroom objectives and subject matter. Hence, their content validity for classroom use may be lower than that of the teacher-made test.

2. The quality of the items of standardized test is superior as compared to that of the teacher made test. The reason is that specialists construct standardized tests.

3. The standardized tests have higher degree of reliability and validity.

4. The procedures of test administration and test scoring of standardized tests are carefully described and more adequately standardized as compared to those of the teacher made tests.

5. The standardized tests have norms which help in interpreting obtained scores on them very meaningfully. Classroom tests, generally, do not have norms.

6. All standardized tests have published manuals which is nova case with teacher-made tests.

Meaning of Norm-Referencing

Raw scores are expressed n terms of different units, such as the number of traits taken with. in specified period to reach a criterion, the number of correct responses, the number of wrong responses, total time taken in assembling objects and so on. All types of raw scores are meaningless. There are two reference points that are applied in interpreting the test scores.

(a) Norm-referencing and (b) Criterion referencing. The first way is to interpret an examinee's test score with the standard scores of a specific group (boys or girls) of examines on the test. This process of interpreting the raw scores is known as 'norm-referencing. Norm is the average performance on a particular test made by a standardization sample. By the standardization sample means a sample which is true representative of the population and takes the test for the express purpose of providing data for comparison and subsequent interpretation of the test scores. In order to interpret the raw scores are transformed into what is called 'derived scores'. There are two purposes for such transformation of scores.

First, the. derived scores provide the basis for direct comparison of the examinees' own performances on different tests, because they are expressed in the same units for different tests.

Second, the derived scores denote the examines relative position in the standardization sample and therefore, his performance may be evaluated in relation to other examines.

Meaning of Criterion-Referencing

The second way of interpreting a test scores is to evolve an external standard or criterion and compare the examinees' test scores with it. This process is called as "criterion-referencing'. In a criterion referenced test there is established performance criterion. If an examinee passes some predetermined number of items (the criterion) or answers them correctly. It is said that he is capable of the total performance demanded by the test. The test items are objective centred or behaviour centered.

"The criterion-referenced test may be defined as one in which the test performance is linked or related to same behaviour measures or referents".

-Glaser (1963)

"A major criterion for referencing a test is the training, which results an increase in the skill or proficiency".

-Cox and Vargas (1966)

The following are the important features of criterion-referenced test.

(1) The test is usually based upon a set of behaviour referents, which it intends to measure.

(2) The test represents the samples of actual behaviour or performance. (3) the performance on a criterion-referenced test can be explained in terms of predetermined cut-off scores.

There is no clear distinction between norm-referenced test and criterion referenced test. There is the similarities between the two types of tests, the content, type of items, purpose, duration, scoring etc., are similar in both the types of test. Generally norm-referenced test is known as achievement test and criterion-referenced test is the objective-centered test and it is based on predetermined cut-off-score where as a norm-referenced test is always based upon the perfon1 1ances of a nonnative group or standardization sample.

The criterion-referenced tests are used to determine which of certain specified objectives of instruction of particular pupil has attained. Norm referenced tests arc used to determine how much over all knowledge of same subject a particular pupil has achieved criterion referenced are best to assist in categorical pass- fail decision with respect to separate specific terms or competence. The norm-referenced test is useful in measuring a students general level of knowledge or understanding of a subject.

DISTANCE EDUCATION

Holmberg (1981) has defined distance education as : the various forms of study at all levels which arc not under the continuous immediate supervision of tutors present with their students in lecture rooms or no the same premises, but which, nevertheless, benefit from the planning, guidance and tuition of a tutu, in organization. It should be noted that distance learning is seen, by the Council for Educational Technology (CET) 'and the Scottish Council for Educational Technology (SCET) as one type of open learning; and that open learning systems are defined as "those which offer students measure of flexibility and authority, to study the programmes of their choice when and where they wish, and at a pace to suit their circumstance" (David Butts). While talking about distance learning potential in the Third World countries, I should like to focus on the following generalizations which have acquired as somewhat genuine credibility.

(l) Distance learning, including the use of broadcasting, is a manifestation of Educational Technology.

(2) The best use that Educational Technology can be put to make is to the

average teacher a better one by helping him rather is to than by attempting to replace him.

(3) Distance learning is making of a positive contribution to the quality of instruction.

With these modest assumption in view, I would like to call upon those in power as also those who put them in power to prepare themselves for comprehending and putting to an effective use the 'new information order'. The UNESCO) Secretary-General Amadou Mahtar M. bow strikes the right note when he says that the new information order envisages a multiplication of source of information and an increase and diversification in the expression and dissemination of points of view. Such an order calls for an intimate and dynamic sharing of communications technology at the global level.

Educational Technology is useful a learner so far as it increases the range of available alternatives in a strategy of learning. Media can prove effective not just because they involve more than one senses but because they add to the possibilities of a learner going for grouping, image-fixing organising categorizing and associating. Aligel Paiene Scotish council for Educational Technology has drawn attention to what he calls, Technology, whereby as many different media as possible are evoked as being essential to a particular learning package for no better reason than that exists.

It is here that Educational Technology has to playa vital role, the main thrust of educational technology so conceived, is to provide a meaningful linkage between the process of learning, the media component of learning and the product of learning. This could be done by injecting the spirit of system approach designing, executing and evaluating teaching learning situations.

Objectives of Distance Education

The following are the man objectives of distance education

(1) To advance and disseminate learning and knowledge by a diversity of means.

(2) To provide a second opportunity to study to those who missed such an opportunity earlier.

(3) To have a chance to those who could not go to the conventional system and they would no like to study.

(4) There is shortage of scientific and technical manpower in some countries and the traditional system is unable to cope with the demand. The media of distance education and open universities are established with a view to meet such demands.

(5) To improve the quality and standard of education. There is a need to make educational relevant to the needs of the country and to provide life long education for working people and house wives.

(6) Another, objective of distance-education and open school is to reduce the pressure of the secondary education students.

(7) The Indira Gandhi National Open University (IGNOU) has the following objectives:

(a) To provide opportunities for higher education to a large population.

(b) T 0 promote the educational standard.

(c) To encourage the system of distance-education.

(d) To coordinate and determine the standards of education of the country.

(8) It facilitates the provision of our constitution i.e. equalization of education opportunities.

Distance Education: Growth

There does not seem to be total unanimity regarding the concept of distance education. It is in a practical sense an open system which takes out the barriers on the various sections of population and offers them opportunities of education. As a concept, distance education has recent origin. It has emerged as a result of rapidly changing national and international situation marked by new human needs and aspirations. Change has become watchword of successful living and education has been recognised as the tool for bringing this change in the desired manner. The growing wealth of experience, increasing funds of knowledge and continuous explosions of information, has changed the concept of education itself. The continuous and growing research, development of new frontiers of knowledge and application of new technologies and doctrines have smashed the water-tight and closely designed compartment disciplines of past and has given birth to interdisciplinary approach. This clearly indicates that the traditional model of education system is not sufficient to open the educational opportunities to everyone who wants education-children and adults, men and women, urban as well as rural and tribal population. This demands. a new viewpoint to look towards education. Education can not be a one-time exposure to learning. I t is a continuous process to be more precise, it is a life long learning. The 1972 Charter of UNESCO has given a concept of 'learning to be which emphasizes that 'dimensions of living experience must be restored in education by redistributing teaching in space and time. It stress that life long education in the full sense of the term, means business and industrial firms also will have extensive educational functions. It further stresses that access to different types of education and professional employment should not depend only on each individual's knowledge, capacity and aptitude; should not be consequence of ranking. In this sense, the concept of life long education is a revolutionary ideas of this century which would include accessibility, institutional openness, need based learning, competency based education, cooperative education and credits for prior learning. This, demands complete openness of education system.

Open University As Distance Education

The term distance education covers various forms of study at all levels which are not covered in lecture rooms or on the same premises but which nevelihcless, benefit from the planning, guidance and tuition or a tutorial organization. The concept of education as a learning instrumentality is, however. reinterpreted in distance education. In distance education, learning takes place, that is the external reality is internationalist through the mediation of teacher but through the message and message that the puss out, In distance education, the learning process is mediated by the books, materials and electronic messages the manage from the teachers, in that sense distance education is conceptually a new form of education. It is a method of imparting knowledge, skills and attitudes which is rationalized by the application of division of labour and organizational principles as well as by the extensive use of technical. media, especially for the purpose of producing high quality teaching materials which makes impossible to strict great number of students at the place wherever the live. It is an industrialised form of teaching and learning. Distance education is quite innovative, flexible, and less expensive. The learner is to make progress according to this own capacity. Nothing is imposed on him from outside and he achieves everything. That is why the system is an effective instrument of social and psychological upliftment of passes. It can be rightly termed as democratic because millions of aspirants can fulfil their ambitions and unfulfilled dreams by undertaking' a course in this system. Distance education is emerging to prominence in every part of the world. The outlook of society towards education and educational technology has totally changed. We have witnessed a radical change in the system of education with changing aspirations of people. The concept of distance education helps every educated, person to have further education with or without formally enrolling himself in an educational institution. It enables a worker to acquire knowledge, ability and skill in order to be better worker and improve his chance of earning more. The Commission Education (1964-66) has rightly pointed out that "good correspondence courses in thoughtfully identified fields of service will create demand for themselves and can help participation by the people in introducing better methods of production. Further it helps to refresh the knowledge of the educated persons and enables him to keep pace with the new knowledge in the field of his interest. Not only this there is continued incongruence between the reality of lifelong learning and institutional and system response. Distance education learning is also useful to those who desire to enrich their lives by studying subjects of cultural and aesthetic value like art appreciation, literary criticism, etc. Thus, the system not only helps to uplift economic standards of society but to enrich its cultural, intellectual and aesthetic standards of people.

Components of Distance Education

The conventional education has restricted itself to a privileged class of society. Traditional education is based on the personal communication and distance education is based on industrialised and technological communication. The fundamental aspects of distance education throwing light on the nature of distance education can be enumerated as

(1) The absence of a discriminatory entrance requirement.

(2) A result driven concept of quality.

(3) A success based concept of programme and service design.

(4) A multiple strategy and matching model approach to programme delivery.

(5) A developmental concept of equality.

(6) It is the most flexible educational system which is not limited by time

and place restrictions.

(7) It can be used at any level from primary to higher stage.

(8) Under this system leaner can progress at his own speed.

(9) It can supplement the studies of regular students along with being a separate system.

Learning System

Distance education is a fairly new term. It denotes the forms of study which are not led by teachers present in the classroom but are supported by tutors and an organization at a distance from students. This implies for the students, interaction with the course material, with tutors and counsellors. The study is an individual activity, and the students basically work on their own. These non-contiguous activities may be supplemented by on campus tutorials; lectures, laboratory work, counselling sessions and other face to face interaction with the tutors and other fellow students.

The term distance learning system is used here to indicate projects that attempt to develop the full potential of distance learning model, without relying on traditional educational structures. The major features of the system are

(1) Great flexibility in teaching methods and students groups covered as compared to conventional education.

(2) Production in bulk of. learning materials (such as text, kits and broadcast etc.), and system search for and use of existing infrastructure and facilities in higher education (libraries, broadcasting organisation, space, printers and publishers). .

(3) Lower recurrent unit cost per student than the conventional classroom teaching and lower capital cost per student.

Organizational Structure

The organizational structure for distance learning by and large is common and is shown as developed by Miller and Rice (1967). Two major operational systems are distinguished in distance learning institution

(a) Course sub-system, and

(b) Student sub-system

(a) Course Sub-System

It is concerned with design, production, distribution and reception of the teaching materials used by the institution.

The course sub-system is largely influenced by availability or suitability of a particular media, or media chosen by the organizers of distance learning organizations. Various alternatives are available taking into account the target learning group, nature of course and application in real life situation. From this point of view various media can be classified into following categories

(1) Printed Material-This is largely (direct reference to the self-learning guide) useful for providing basic understanding and self instructions. It is self instructional material available in the form of books, booklets, instruction kits, guidance instructions, self instruction manuals, reference book and do it yourself kits etc.

(2) Audio Material-it is a verbal instruction material available in various forms. Pre-recorded lectures can be reproduced by this medium. It has limited utility but very good ready reference. Telephone, telephone conferences Cyclops. A .T.R. recorded radio programmes are the various media available in this category.

(3) Video Materials-The visual attributes have greater impact on learners. It has a great accessibility and wider coverage. It involves no human interaction. Educational television broadcasts, films, relay tapes, slides, prestel aid opted systems, lights and sound programmes are some of the media available in this category. Retention capacity, ability to display real life situations make the media more effective and useful.

(4) Interaction Sessions-These are the oldest and most popular conventional media of learning and teaching. It involves human interactions to varied extent lectures, small group discussions, seminars, sýmposia, workshops, conferences, tutorials, self-help groups are some of the most popular techniques under this category, Supported by a mix of audio and video it can create a great impact on the learners. It helps to develop higher cognitive abilities and effect attributes as well as basic understanding of the subject matter. Apart from these methods, laboratory and field work, assignments, experimental kits, practical experience based equipments, tools, and kits are other media of instructions.

(b) Students Su b-System

This sub-system decides how to admit students, allocating them to various courses, local centres, tutors and counsellors, collection of fees and ensuring that they receive teaching material, administering assessment and examination processes, issue of certificate to successful candidates and maintenance of records. This sub-system essentially is administrative one involving management and control of students through the institution.

Factors influencing the Learning System

The students sub-system is mostly influenced by certain factors which the organizers have to consider in order to gain proper response from the students. Opening of opportunity for education to new target population, deprived previously because of geographical isolation, lack of formal academic requirements, caste, creed and religious bias, employment condition or socio economic cultural barriers. Another factor influencing the system is the identification of-particular target groups with their key characteristics (need, age, time available for study, local facilities, etc.) to enable appropriate courses, learning methods -and delivery systems to be delivered for them.

Selecting strategies of Distance Education

Distance education postulates a design for instructions that is comprehensive in coverage, permanent in nature, multilevel in offerings, multi-media in approach .and need based in focus. From this point of view, a decision on distance learning has to be taken after careful screening. One has to decide whether existing educational system is meeting the important educational needs of a specific discipline and of the population, if not whether in further such needs will be met by expanding existing provision. The strategy of formal education is unquickening in this regard. Various parameters indicating limitations of formal education system offer more liberty and autonomy to the learner, in the entry process. It seeks to quicken the very intellectual self of the learner. Distance education perceived this is a self renewing exercise for the learner taking place every moment he encounters his life, and emerging with his inadequacies on the one hand and in built strength on the other, Looking to this background, to basic issues pertaining to adopting. an appropriate strategy has to be considered.

First issue will be whether potential students are capable or motivated to learn independently. The criteria relating to target group might include .large numbers distribution over a large area, heterogeneous compositional (age, occupation, etc.), inability the use the conventional provision (reason being employment, distance, cost, age, inadequate formal education, etc.).

Second issue regarding the courses will be standardization of learning material, providing communication facilities. This might include:

(a) Lack of well qualified teachers in sufficient numbers.

(b) Indeciduate funds for expansion of conventional provision and recurring cost of teachers salary.

(c) Urgent need for training and retraining courses in specific areas (Particularly for working adults).

(d) Difficulties faced in modifying the conventional provisions to cater the needs of specific groups.

An Appropriate Model of Technology

Distance education systems of future are expected to cater the needs and aspirations of various categories of learners with varying attitudes, aptitudes and interests on a reasonable cost with appropriate' time adjustment strategies. They should be in a position to produce quality and excellence in our human resource development programmes.

Careful planning and effective management strategies are required to design a workab1c technology for distance education system for the future.

Development and use of the appropriate technology is the most important problem relating to development of distance education system. Technology for this purpose is defined as the "process of transforming inputs into outputs".

The concept of technology is that of a social as well as mechanical process. All transformations of inputs into outputs occur in a social context and not in vacuum. Hence, any decision taken or plans proposal for the introduction of new technology to the educational process must be undertaken with the social context of technology clearly in mind. In fact, what is really needed today arc not more machine. Technologies, like computers, satellite communication, video discs, and dilemmatic systems of various kinds but the technologies which increase not only the physical power of human being but his mental power and capacity. Technologies are created by human beings even those applied to the transformation of person and as such must be required in their use by a basic humanism, i.e. what is most appropriate and beneficial to the person. To do otherwise is to dehumanize the persons.

The new information technologies bring four elements together, store information in vast amounts, process the information to logical procedures, display such information in multiple format and send such information to multiple receivers. Because of these abilities of new technologies, one can conclude that this technology can perfectly stimulate human thinking. There is however. a vita] difference between what new technologies do when they process, store, send and display information and what human minds do when they think. If these differences are not recognised, they might lead to a tragedy rather than triumph. The reason for this being that the mind thinks with ideas and not with data. And the development of the thought process of a persons is a universal- goals of education. Our goal in distance education must be to use new technologies to assist in a human based learning process.

The introduction of new technology into an existing distance education system should not be undertaken as a result without due attention to the fact that this will not only change the distance education system but affect as well, the larger ecological system of which distance education is a component.

Planning for the introduction of anew technology in distance education, therefore, should not be restricted to the distance education or technology itself. It is the entire ecological system which should be though of in bringing out the changes. In the words of Gunvant B. Shah, "Let us not look upon the distance education as a mere innovation. Let us try to look upon it as a pragmatic approach of extending education to the millions of people for whom the word 'school' does not remain a distance education at a massive level is not too distance a dream. Even if it is a dream that deserves to be real.

Student Support Services

INSANT-IB is now well placed in the geostationary orbit at a height of 36,000 kilometers above the equator. The space bird is supposed to perform its assigned job well over the next seven years of so. If fully utilized, the INSANT-IB programme can prove to be of immense value for educating the millions of place even before they could he made to read and write.

Viewed in this frame of reference of the potential of distance education is considerable for a developing country is like India where, even after massive expansion of the conventional formal system there is still, for every school or college student, another young person in the age group of 15-35, who does not receive formal education. 'television and Radio are costly no doubt, but the unit costs of such media are relatively low.

(1) India has used the system of correspondence education successfully in many fields. Summer School-cum-Correspondence Course leading the B.Ed. degree was started in the year 1966 at the four Regional Colleges of Education of National Council of Educational Research and Training. It was approved by the concerned affiliating universities with certain minor modifications. The courses are being offered for the last seventeen years and the main object of introducing them was to clear back-log of untrained teachers.

The majority of correspondence institutions in India began in the seventies. Most of them were established as constituents of universities, State Board Education, or the private sector. The duration of courses varies from three months to three years, with an average on one year. The enrolment varies ranging from. 25 to 6303, and declines over a period. The language of instruction is mainly English followed by Hindi and regional languages. The pass percentage of students in correspondence courses ranges from as low as 4% to as high as 100% with the average being 40%.

(2) A working group was appointed by the Reserve Bank of India in December 1967 to study the training facilities of commercial banks. The report of the working group recommended that a national institute be set-up. The recommendations made in the report were accepted by Government of India, Reserve Bank of India and the Banking Industry in May 1968. As regards the training component of the banking system, National Institute of Bank Management (NIBM) has used programmed instruction strategy to a great extent. The institute has so far published programmed learning texts on topic like 'Cheques' 'Preparation Vouchers', 'Safe Deposit Valult', and 'Traveller's Cheques', etc.

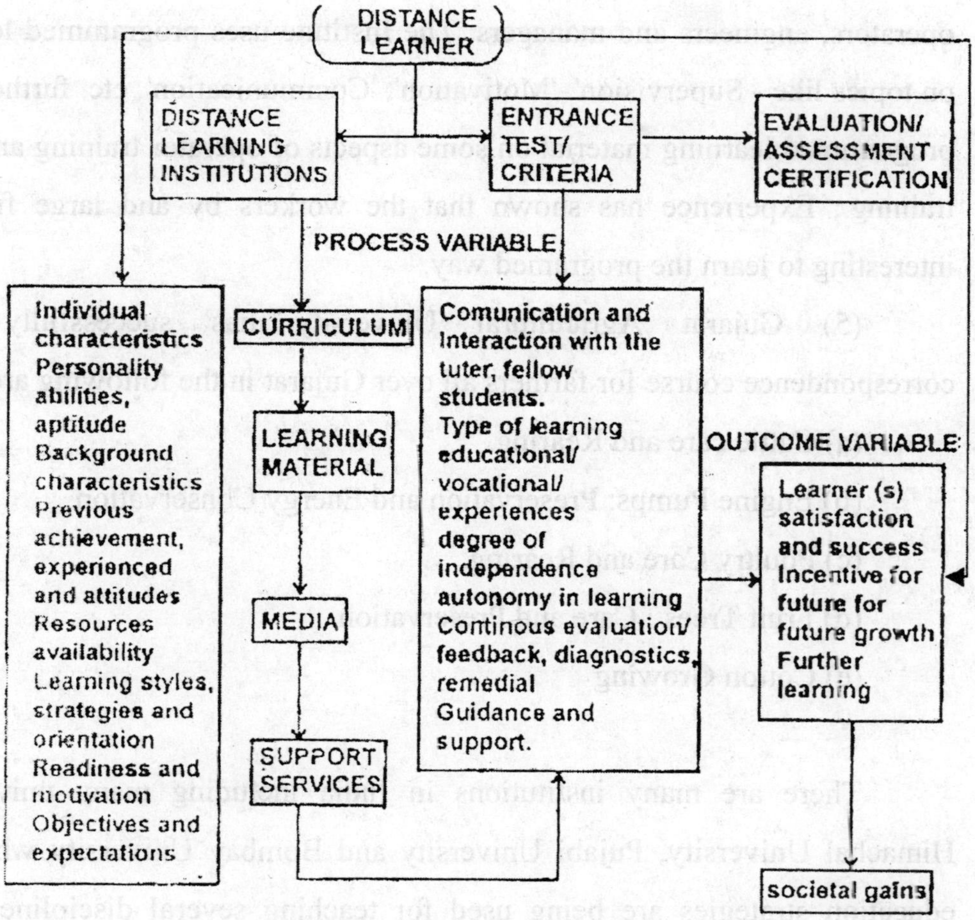

(3) Life Insurance Corporation of India has also adopted the programed learning strategy for the training of new agents. They have prepared and got published programmed learning texts on topics like introducing Life Insurance. 'Plans of Life Insurance' and 'Easy Steps in Selling'. Beginning in 1975, these booklets have since gone through more than four editions in English with a tota.1 number of more than a hundred thousand copies supplied to the new agents for the purpose of self-instruction. Furthermore, the booklets have been translated into ten other Indian languages, viz., Hindi, 1samesc, Bengali, Oriya, Tamil, Telgu, Malayalam, Kannada, Gujrati and Marathi,

(4) Rashtriya Chemicals and Fertilizer (RCF) Limited is getting assignments from other countries or commissioning and stablising fertilizer plants" The Trairling Institute of RCF is responsible for training technicians

operators, engineers and managers. The Institute uses programmed learning texts on topics like - Supervision', 'Motivation', 'Communication', etc. furthermore it has programmed learning material on some aspects of operator training and technician training.; Experience has shown that the workers by and large find it quite" interesting to learn the programed way.

(5) Gujarat Agricultural University has successfully conducted correspondence course for farmers all over Gujarat in the following areas

(a) Cattle care and Rearing.

(b) Engine Pumps: Preservation and Energy Conservation.

(c) Poultry Care and Rearing.

(d) Fruit Trees : Care and Preservation.

(e) Cotton Growing

There are many institutions in India including many universities like Himachal University, Pujabi University and Bombay University where distance education strategies are being used for teaching several disciplines leading to university degree at graduate and post-graduate levels. It is not the intention to provide a consequences of distance education programme in our country, but it appears to me that a sample of cases referred to here would suffice to impress upon us the fact that distance-education is emerging as viable alternative in our contexts. Therefore, let me conclude by sharing with certain facts based on research.

The basic feature of distance education is that the education should be impart to where people arc rather than expecting them to come where education is. Such reversal of the trend would be required in order to educate the masses in the Third World Countries where a large number of people live below poverty line and where population continues to expand. If the global population where to settle in Australia alone the population density would be equal to that of Bangladesh to day. The situation in many Third World Countries is in no way different than that of Bangladesh. In such a situation, education has to playa wider role and therefore, it can no longer remain confined to a classroom or a campus. We must appreciate the trend toward .'distance'. Let us hope that distances would result in bringing the disadvantages million nearer to what we- call education.

Support to Instruction

As a support to instruction the teacher or the student as a word processor for writing letters or instructions regarding the courses and materials can use the computer.

To sum up a computer can do much more than a distance tutor can do for his/her students.

In all these cases we are thinking of a distance learner with a personal" computer at home or a terminal at the study centre near his/her home. He/she interacts with the computer software and benefits from this limited interaction. If his/her computers linked with other computers through telephone lines, the opportunity for his/her interaction becomes wider.

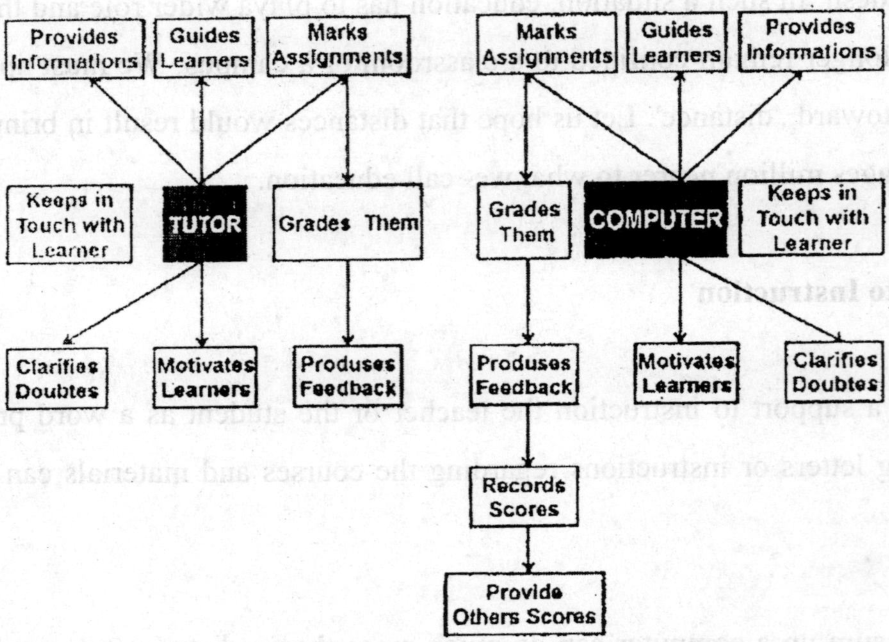

Figure -Comparison between the Tutor and the Computer.

One of the recent development using the computer net work is computer conferencing. This has great potential as it brings the distance learners in different parts of country closer to each other, thus breaking their isolation. This is the highest form of interactional opportunity a distance learner can get. Computer conferencing, therefore, is becoming popular with distance education institutions. The use of video text and video disc is also being experimented within several distance.

Teaching Qualities of the Computer

While observing groups of students working with the computer, you would notice that students enthusiastically participate in the learning programme. The computer's novelty, the challenge involved in the programme, the wonderful display of tasks-all help in creating and sustaining their motivation. Learning with the computer is level dull and monotonous. Some illustrations given below would reveal a few more qualities.

The progrmnme called CODEBREAKER is a programme which keeps asking questions and the students supply the answers. In pedagogic terms this question-answer sequence provides an opportunity for useful interaction which is essential for successful learning.

The programme called YELLOW RIVER KINGDOM is a problem solving activity. The computer displays a vast kingdom with a lot of resources. Can one imagine creating such a difficult situation in the classroom without a computer? The computer is capable of simulating such complicated situations for the purpose of teaching learning. It can be simulate dangerous situations such as a burning forest of division of atom.

A programme called VARIETEXT is a part of the text with blanks for the students to fill in. For each blank four alternatives appear on after another and the student has computer to display the correct words. This instant feed hack is a part of the programme and no other technological instrument can be faster than the computer in providing such instant feedback.

These pedagogic qualities of the computer can be summed up as follows. That the computer:

-Motivates the learners

- Interacts with the learners

- Stimulate; situations which are difficult aid dangerous, and

- Provides instant feedback

Such a powerful instrument has several uses in the field of distance education where technological media are a basic necessity. There is hardly any distance education institution in the world which does not make use of media such a radio and T.V. Regular, though in a small scale. Radio broadcasts and TV telecasts are a part of distance education courses in India too.

In this technological atmosphere, the use of computers cannot be a far-fetched or duration idea. We have successful examples in countries like Britian, Canada, the Netherlands and Germany where computers are used on a large scale by the distance education institutions.

Some of the major advantages of using computers in distance education are given as under:

- Computer being flexibility and individuality to the study process.
- Computer reduces the insolation of distance learners.
- Computer-based study materials are cost-effective when produced on a large scale.
- Computer stimulates students to experiment, design and create solutions to the problems.

Framework an Instructional Strategy in Distance Education

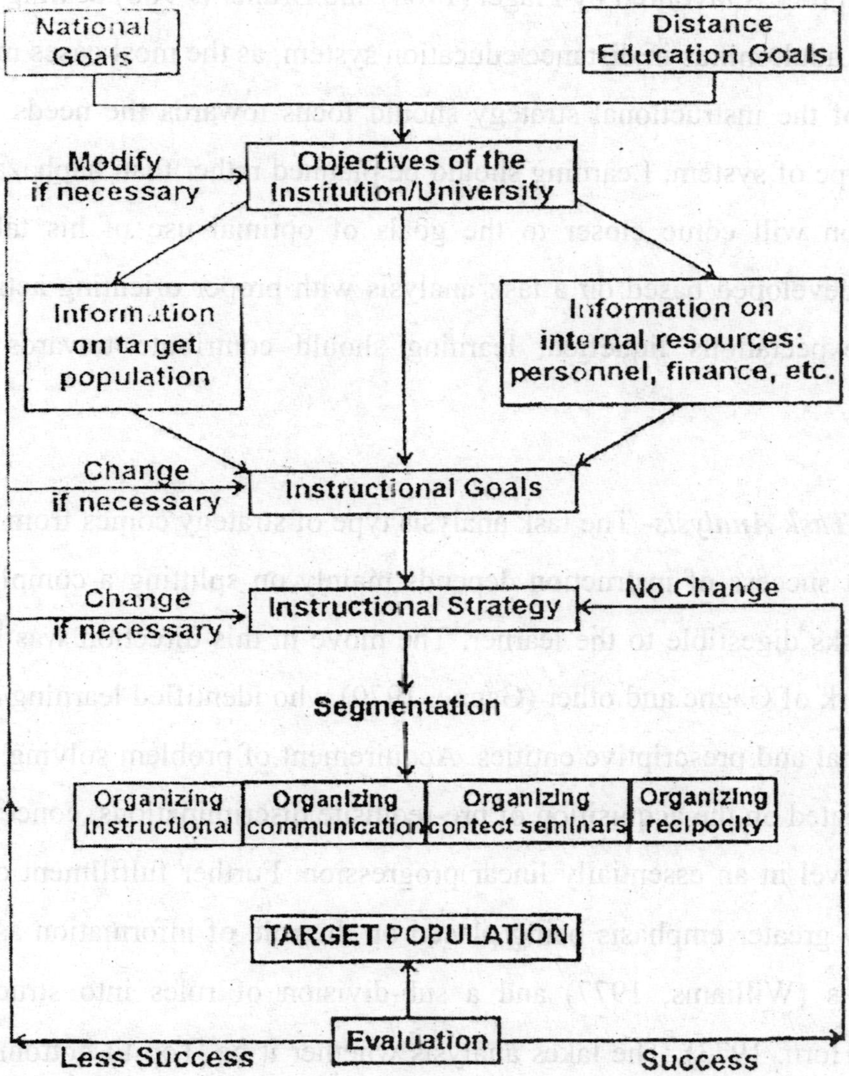

Attending to the needs of all and creating and maintaining the conditions. under which academic learning can occur is increasingly difficult in complicated and remote environment of distance education systems. We have to accommodate a more academically heterogeneous population of students manifesting variety of learning needs.

It is true that there are epistemological and other differences on how instruction must be carried out. Hacker (1984) points out that interpalization of new facts concepts, principles and models are more frequently achieved by direct instruction methods as suggested by Gagne (1970) rather than by cognitive restricting process favoured by Piaget (1964) and Bruner (J 966) dealing with able, nature and adult minds in distance education system, as the most cases may be, the attention of the instructional strategy should focus towards the needs for a task analysis type of system. Learning should be planned rather than haphazard so that each person will come closer to the goals of optimal use of his talents. The materials developed based on a task analysis with proper orienting activities and learning expectations liquefied, learning should contribute towards optimum learning.

(a) Task Analysis- The task analysis type of strategy comes from the strong be1ief that success of instruction depends mainly on splitting a complex task to simpler tasks digestible to the learner. The move in this direction was stimulated by the. work of Gagne and other (Gagne, 1970) who identified learning out comes as sequential and prescriptive entities. Acquirement of problem solving behaviour was predicated on the acquisition of pre-requisite discriminations, concept or rules at lower level in an essentially linear progression. Further fulfillment of Gagne's model saw greater emphasis being placed on the role of information as an entity for analysis (Williams, 1977) and a sub-division of rules into structures and progress (Horn, 1973). The takes analysis whether it be 'Top to bottom Analysis' or 'Front-end Analysis' the instructional designer goes through all steps that are necessary for the development of actual materials. These include a decision making process for over coming performance deficiencies, description of mastery performance criteria, break down of jobs into simpler task and steps. The outcome of such a task analysis mapping in an instructional system is an increased probability more efficient learning to take place.

(b) Orienting the Learner-Several orienting activities have emerged during the .past few decades. Gagne (1985) provides orientation to instruction by informing learners of lesson expectations. Advances organizers (Ausubol 1968) are another of lesson orientation. Which help to activate the cognitive structure of individual learners.

The importance or orienting activating is related to both cognitive theory building and instructional pedagogy (Hannafin & Hughes 1986). From a theory, building perspective, the effect of adjunct strategies designed to improve encoding must be better understood. Models for better understanding the effect of orienting information can be evolved to clarify relationship amount new information within existing cognitive net works. Orienting activities can also aid retrieval by influencing schemata and as a result of supplying relevant retrieval by influencing schemata and as a result of supplying relevant retrieval cues.

(i) Questions-The use of questions prior to the textual information activate the learners mental processes which focus on relevant information. This can be partially attributed to an increase in attention. This can be partially attributed to. an increase in attention drawn to the criterion elements of the question. Where pre-questions are specific, intended, but did not incidental learning is generally improved (Hannafn and Hughes, 1986). Learners tend to focus effort intensively on information related to orienting questions. Learners will try to identify meaningful relationship and transfer learning when not limited by very specific orienting questions (Clark and Voogel, 1985). Integrative questions require greater effort and processing during encoding, and can help to promote learning of both low and high level lesson content (Glover, Plake & Zimmer, 1983). Learners may also view orienting questions as focusing mechanism for lesson information but the clarifying function of pre-questions may indirectly improve motivation, for lesson participation.

(ii) Advance Organizers-Ausuble's idea of advanced organizers comes from his view that learning and retention of unfamiliar but meaningful verbal material could be facilitated by advance introduction of sub-suming concepts.

Advance organizers act as submerses of information whereby input can be collected into a more meaningful and inclusive schema (Ausubel, 1960). In fact, proponents suggest that advance organizers provide a vehicle though which new information can be subsumed meaningfully within individual cognitive. structures. Several advance organizers have been studied. Advance organizers in the form of programme titles, abstracts subordinate generalizations, and conceptual questions are embedded effectively in many televised instructions. (Nugent, Tipton and Brooks, 1980). Ausubel advocates that the organizers appropriately relevant and inclusive introductions that are maximally clear are to be introduced in advance of the learning material itself and are' also presented at a higher level of abstraction, generality and inclusiveness; and since substantive content of a given organizer of series of organizers is selected on the basis of their appropriateness for explaining, intergradations interrelating, the material they precede, this strategy increases the organizational strength of the cognitive structure. The principal function of the organizer is to bridge the gap between what the learner already knows and what he needs to know before he can successfully learn the task at hand (AusubeI, 1968).

(c) Performance Expectations- The expected learning outcomes must clearly be clarified in any instructional processes. According to Gagne (1985) stating performance expectations in advance of instruction serves several functions, First learners made aware of either the general or specific nature, of both the general and specific nature of forthcoming instruction. Informing of expectations is believed to activate the learners mental set (Gagne, 1975, p. 94) set is usually activated through instructions which direct the learner to attend selectively to certain attributes of the instruction. Performance expectations can also function to focus attention to specific information considered central to the task. Statements of a non-explicit integrative nature, on the other hand, are more akin to general statements of performance expectations described by Gagne: "To guide attention without over-prescribing specific information or detail. Several authors have reinforced the necessity to include statements of expectations when producing instructional materials.

Transmission of Materials

The delivery system forms on of the most important aspect in instructional strategy meant for distance education. This can be done through printed notes, Radio/Television lectures, video tapes and electronic messages. Though in a country like India with its vastness and remoteness and the complications in communication one may think more towards print outs which can easily be transmitted to the learners. Not doubt it is the most important and easiest mode of communication. Through radio programmes are getting more less interesting one important area of interest in this regard is television. With the government able to cover almost 70% population with its T.V. net works television lectures becomes the most important component in any distance education system. Moreover, these lectures arc becoming popular too. Once the T.V. lectures are prepared video taping is only a technicians job. These video cassettes could easily be sent to different centres for their worth while use.

Technological advances in communications make physical distance less of a barrier. Developments over the last decade allow people to communicate across great distances at rapid, speeds; masses of information can be reproduced and;; distributed simultaneously through out the world; knowledge- resources can be shared and interactions enriched by people who may never reach face-to-face. These technological advances also enable people to respond and pose questions directly to others around the country and conduct personalized interactions about-topics-of mutual interest.

Evaluation Strategy in Distance Education

Preparing an framework for an instructional strategy for distance education will have to be done at three levels (i) National level, (ii) University level, and (iii) Instructional level. The national goals together with the distance education goals should form the official overlying objectives while the university or the institution concerned will develop the piratical overlying objectives. Based on these the instructional designers formulate the operative goals. These objectives should decide the parameters within an instructional manager can work on.

Any instructional strategy developed should be based on the structure 6fthe distance education system. The efficient realisation of the instructional strategy calls for the following instructions:

- Segmentation (formation of target groups)
- Organizing instructional materials (Development, printing etc.)
- Organizing communication (advertising, personal communication etc.)
- Organizing contact seminars, and
- Organizing reciprocity (fees, finance etc.)

The instruments must effectively be combined to form the overall nature of the instructional strategy. The academic aspects in the instructional strategy involve the following steps:

(1) Needs Assessment

(2) Preparation of instructional materials

(a) Task analysis

(b) Orienting the learner

(i) Questions

(ii) Advance Organizers

(c) Performance Expectations

(3) Transmission of materials, and

(4) Performance assessment..

The author's main focus in this paper is some of the essential considerations for instructional material development as this will be the most important factors in an educational system where personal interaction is minimized.

The coordination between task arrangements in the academic programme and the management systems represent the key ingredients in the teaching learning process in the distance learning system. If a mismatch between the two should occur, success of the programme is less probable.

Needs Assessment

Needs assessment is concerned with determining goals and identifying discrepancies between goals and status. It is the process of determining the gap in the results between 'what is' and 'what should be'. This gap in results is more than just academic with gaps in resources, the means to the end etc. The first refers to things, or the outcomes of activities which contribute to individual, group or societal' self sufficiency', while the latter refers to activities which may lead to that end. The first may result in changed organizational goals, while the second many simply call for doing more or less without necessarily influencing the goals, either positively or negatively (Hung, 1986). In education and-training they form the basis of instructional design an curriculum development and in organizational management the human specification plan.

Counseling in Distance Education

Miss Bragdon has mentioned the following situations where counselling is required

(a) When a pupil requires not only reliable information's but also an interesting interpretation of those information's which can solve his personal difficulties.

(b) When a pupil needs intelligent listener who has more experience than the pupil, to whom he can recite his difficulties and through which he can seek suggestions for his working plan.

(c) When the counsellor has an assess to those facilities which can help in resolving the pupil's problems but the pupil does not enjoy such an access to these facilities.

(d) When the pupil has some problem but he is unaware of that problem and his development, he is to be made aware of that problem.

(e) When the pupil is aware of the problem and difficulties created by the problem but he feels difficult to define it and to understand it, i.e., when the pupil is familiar with the presence of the problem and its nature but he in unable to face the problem due to this temporary tension and distraction.

(f) When the pupil suffers the main mal-adjustment problem or some handicap which is temporary and which needs careful long due diagnosis by an expert.

STEPS IN COUNSELLING PROCEDURE

Williamson and Darley have mentioned the following six steps of counselling procedure-

Educational, Vocational Guidance and Counselling

(i) Analysis-It is the procedure in which facts are collected so that the pupil may be studied.

(ii) Synthesis - In this step, the collected information is organized.

(iii) Diagnosis - In this step, the reasons responsible for the problem are sorted out.

(iv) Prognosis - The statement regarding the use of diagnosis is known as prognosis.

(v) Counselling- The steps taken by the counsellor and the client for adjustment constitute this step.

(vi) Follow-up -- This step includes the evaluation of effectiveness of counselling services or efforts to help the pupil in solving his new problem.

Rogers has also summarized various steps as follows

(i) A person comes for help and he has taken a tentative step.

(ii) The help-situation is often defined. The client is familiarized with the idea that the counsellor does not possess the answers. The client himself is to search out the answers. Counselling has its own timing if he desires so.

(iii) The counsellors encourages independent expression. This independent expression is in the context of some problem. This prevents anxiety and guilty consciousness. The counsellor does not try to convince the client that he is at fault or he is correct. The counsellors accept the client as he is. He encourages independent expression only.

(iv) The counsellor approves negative feelings. He identifies them and makes them more distinct. The counsellor should react to the client's feelings.

(v) The tentative positive expression should occur after a person's negative expression.

(vi) The counsellor identifies positive feelings and approves them.

(vii) Self-understanding and insight occur.

(viii) Clarification of possible decisions and possible direction to the tasks.

(ix) Initiation of important positive

(x) Further, more development understanding.

(xi) The developed feeling of independence and increasing need of assistance.

These activities, not necessarily, should occur in this sequence. These steps are client-centred.

NOTES

NOTES

NOTES

NOTES

NOTES